# TRIBAL ASSETS

# TRIBAL ASSETS

## The Rebirth
## of Native America

**ROBERT H. WHITE**

A Donald Hutter Book

Henry Holt and Company / New York

Library of Congress Cataloging-in-Publication Data
White, Robert H. (Robert Hooper), 1955–
Tribal assets: the rebirth of native America / Robert H. White. — 1st ed.
p.  cm.
ISBN 0-8050-0846-2 (alk. paper)
1. Indians of North America—Politics and government.  2. Indians
of North America—Government relations.  3. Self-determination,
National.  I. Title.
E98.T77W48   1990
323.1'197—dc20                          90–4378
                                          CIP

Henry Holt books are available at special discounts
for bulk purchases for sales promotions, premiums,
fund-raising, or educational use. Special editions
or book excerpts can also be created to specification.
For details contact:
Special Sales Director, Henry Holt and Company, Inc.,
115 West 18th Street, New York, New York 10011.

First Edition

Designed by Katy Riegel

Printed in the United States of America
Recognizing the importance of preserving
the written word, Henry Holt and Company, Inc.,
by policy, prints all of its first editions
on acid-free paper. ∞
1  3  5  7  9  10  8  6  4  2

FOR MY PARENTS,
*Bobby and Ellen,*

FOR MY WIFE,
*Kaatje,*

AND FOR MY DAUGHTER,
*Katie*

# Contents

# A Note about Usage

*In this book, the terms* Native American, Indian, *and* American Indian *all apply to indigenous peoples within the political boundaries of the United States.* Native American *enjoys a current political and academic vogue, but Indians on the reservations I visited rarely used the term. More often they referred to their own tribal affiliations ("I'm a Choctaw." "I'm a Passamaquoddy."), and most referred to Native people in general as "Indians." Maybe they feel that a misnomer applied to their ancestors more than five hundred years ago by an Italian adventurer is the least of their concerns.*

# TRIBAL
# ASSETS

# Introduction

In the midsummer of 1857, Henry David Thoreau took a ferry halfway across the Penobscot River to Indian Island, a three-hundred-acre community of Penobscot Indians north of Bangor, Maine. There Thoreau hoped to "obtain an Indian" to guide him on an excursion along the rivers and lakes of the Maine woods. At that time there were some 360 Penobscot Indians left in the world. Thoreau had concluded from his brief, earlier encounters with Penobscots that poverty, smallpox, and helplessness would soon extinguish the tribe.

But if Thoreau had hoped to obtain a suitably tragic specimen of a vanishing race, he must have been disappointed. Joseph Polis, the Penobscot who agreed to guide him, lived in a white two-story house Thoreau described to be "as good as an average one on a New England village street." The Polis household was surrounded by a garden, an orchard, and a farm of corn and beans. Polis owned a fifty-acre plantation in nearby Old Town and hired white laborers because, in his words, "they keep steady, and know how." Polis was worth some $6,000, all told—a small fortune in those days.

In the tradition of Joseph Polis, the Penobscots continue to defy the odds against Indian survival through profitable Native enterprise. Today, there are close to two thousand Penobscots on the tribal rolls, and they are too busy to take tourists on camping trips. Since 1980, when the tribe won a large cash settlement in a lawsuit against the state, the Penobscot Nation has grown from its little river island to more than a hundred thousand acres of Maine land. The tribe has also built an audiocassette manufacturing plant, which has virtually solved the tribe's long-standing unemployment problem, while grossing some $11 million a year.

This book is about four Native American communities that are breaking the mold that has encased this country's indigenous peoples since the Europeans arrived. They are: the Passamaquoddy Indians in Maine, the Mississippi Band of Choctaw Indians, the Ak-Chin Indian Community in Arizona, and the Warm Springs Confederation of Indians in Oregon. Like the Penobscot Nation, they represent the vanguard of a new phenomenon in Indian Country.

According to one observer, the American Indian was, until recently, "someone to whom something was done." Inhabitants of North America for at least twenty-five thousand years, the Indians are thought to have numbered as many as twelve million when the Europeans first began to settle the East Coast. Native Americans were at first far superior to their new neighbors in numbers and resources. In agreements with early colonial governments, Indian communities were treated as what they were—sovereign political entities. From before the American Revolution through the War of 1812, the outcome of military collisions between European powers on American soil depended on Indian alliances. In the course of that era, however, the foundations of Indian sovereignty were undermined. The majority of the Native population was erased, more often by disease than battle. As their land-based subsistence economy shrank in the face of European immigration, Indians were forced into a marketplace for which they had no experience or competitive advantage.

From the birth of the American republic, efforts by the United States government to transform Native Americans to commercial life have gone awry. Much of the failure can be attributed to greed or malevolence, as the resources that might allow Indians to compete fairly with whites are continually being stripped away. But at base, the problem has been structural—the solutions of one people imposed on the problems of another. The lands reserved for Indians in treaties with federal and state governments became their prisons, and their resulting destitution inaugurated an era of utter dependency. In the opinion of a Senate committee in 1880, "If [the Indians] are compelled to accept a prison as a home, they will naturally prefer to compel the keepers to feed and clothe them."

Between the Civil War and the early years of this century, the Native population shrank to its nadir of two hundred thousand. Many Americans believed that Indians would survive only if they became "more white." The Indians' apparently helpless position gave the dominant culture every opportunity to impose its ways upon them, and the tactics of assimilation assumed an Orwellian countenance. Indian children were rounded up by federal officials and delivered to boarding schools far from their homes and families, where faculties composed primarily of Christian zealots made every attempt to beat their cultures out of them and the work ethic into them.

In 1887, the government increased its efforts to assimilate Indians into white society by forcing them into farming. Under the Dawes Severalty Act, most Indian reservations were splintered into tiny allotments, one for each Indian household. President Theodore Roosevelt called it a "mighty, pulverizing engine to break up the tribal mass." The policy succeeded, in its darkest sense. With no experience or capital, most would-be Indian farmers went bankrupt or sold their holdings. White Americans absorbed two-thirds of the remaining Native land base. The resulting checkerboard of Indian and non-Indian properties continues to saddle reservations with tangled jurisdictions and land titles.

In the early part of this century, a growing number of non-Indian Americans began to realize that efforts to remake Natives in their image had failed. American officials finally bowed before the persistence of Native Americans *as* Native Americans in the 1930s, when FDR introduced an "Indian New Deal." The Indian Reorganization Act of 1934 consolidated Indian holdings dispersed under the Dawes Act fifty years earlier, allowed Indians to establish their own governing structures, and made other provisions for Indian self-determination.

This first stab at making it possible for Indians to chart their own course was a clumsy one. The federal government's idea of "Indian self-government" turned out in most cases to be a constitutional democracy ill-suited to the traditional society upon which it was imposed. Nevertheless, the Indian Reorganization Act proved to be a turning point. For the first time in hundreds of years, Indians were empowered, albeit imperfectly, to take their affairs into their own hands.

For a while after World War II it looked as if the gains of the prewar era would be lost. A number of attempts to abolish the reservation system, withdraw federal recognition and support of tribes, and pull Indians into mainstream society were made with a series of congressional moves under the rubric of "termination." By the 1960s, these policies had been successfully thwarted by united Indian dissent or had collapsed of their own misconception. Since then, American Indians have made substantial political gains. From all indications they are also well past any danger of extinction, either physical or political. The number of Native Americans in the United States (including American Indians, Eskimos, and Aleuts) is now approaching two million, or .5 percent of this country's population. The federal government now recognizes some five hundred extant and distinct Native American communities.

Despite these hopeful developments, one dark legacy has remained—the vast and enduring poverty of Native America. A heartbreaking number of Native Americans still fit the stereotypical adjectives—underemployed, undereducated, impoverished. The official unemployment rates for Native Americans have varied between 35 and 60 percent during the mid-1980s, depending on which agency was counting. In 1989 the Bureau of Indian Affairs estimated unemployment on the Rosebud Reservation in South Dakota at 90 percent.

Four hundred thousand Native Americans—one out of four—live below the poverty line. That ugly ratio rises to 40 percent on and around reservations, where almost half of the Native population resides and where one person out of seven lives on less than $2,500 a year.

The wages of long-term poverty are Indian Country's social problems. The infant mortality rate among South Dakota Indians in 1986 ran 50 percent higher than in Bulgaria. Indian life expectancy—the lowest in the nation. (Among the Confederated Tribes of Warm Springs, Oregon—one of the most prosperous Native American communities—the average life expectancy barely exceeds forty years.) Indian suicide rates—the highest in the nation. Educational levels—the lowest in the nation. Continuing problems with alcohol abuse reached new heights in the 1980s: recent studies estimate that one in four children on the Pine Ridge Reservation in South Dakota is born with the mental and physical defects of fetal alcohol syndrome.

The majority of Native Americans live off reservations, mostly in the cities of the West and Midwest. Life for urban

Indians is not much better than for those on reservations: a quarter of them are unemployed and impoverished.

Without the means to establish economic sovereignty, most Native Americans remain America's internal exiles, living within confines established by their conquerors hundreds of years ago. The tragedy is that Indian destitution is entirely unnecessary. Many Native communities hold the raw materials of true self-determination in their hands. Reservation land has always constituted a major chunk of the United States, and through litigation and legislation over the last fifty years, Native Americans have reassumed a larger (though still paltry) fragment of their ancient domain. Native American property within United States boundaries is greater than the land mass of New England, plus New Jersey and Maryland. At sixteen million acres, the Navajo Nation alone—which sprawls over sections of Arizona, Colorado, Utah, and New Mexico—is larger than ten of the fifty states.

Among these Indian lands are some of the country's most valuable resources. More than half of America's uranium, a third of its low-sulphur coal reserves, and almost a sixth of its natural gas lie under Native American soil. Indians control as much commercial forest as some of America's largest paper companies. Cash from legal settlements and the lease of mineral rights increase the Native endowment by another $2 billion. Even tribes with few physical resources have the financial advantages of local, state, and federal tax exemptions.

In the last two decades, several tribes have recognized the extraordinary value of these assets, not only in terms of their material worth but in terms of what they mean for the quality of Native life. After centuries of decline as the objects of subjugation and neglect, these tribes have established and sustained profitable tribal economies—internally generated, not federally imposed—as a strategy for addressing long-standing social problems and establishing authentic independence. Employing every strategy from congressional lobbying to leveraged buy-outs, each community, in its own way, has learned to play white society's games, but by different rules and according to different scorecards. These communities are beginning to enter the mainstream economy so long denied them to mount a quiet economic revolution, which has the potential for reestablishing a Native American independence based on economic sovereignty.

This is a book about Native American accountants, engineers, government officials, and chief executive officers; a book about auto-parts factories and sewing plants, hydroelectric generators and four-star resorts; about agribusiness and cement factories. Finally, and most importantly, it is a book about how business development within these tribes has made a profound difference in the lives of their inhabitants. Along any indicator of Native American societal health, from employment to freedom from substance abuse to the preservation of indigenous culture, these communities are ascending.

Most news out of Indian Country has been about what's gone wrong, but there is more than enough room for a book about what's gone right—as long as the reader keeps in mind that such success stories are still few and far between. Less than 10 percent of America's Native communities have gained any control over their economic fate, and within that fraction are many tenuous improvements. It would be wrong—and dangerous—to infer from four triumphs that the problems of Indian Country are suddenly and miraculously behind it.

Nevertheless, we can now recognize magnificent development opportunities that are unique to Indian Country. Because tribal businesses are ultimately accountable to local tribal governments (and because their tribal employees are also in effect their owners), these enterprises provide powerful leverage for human development.

These are unprecedented accomplishments, not only among American Indians, but in America. Communities bound by blood and mythology and by long, long suffering are securing the means to solve their own problems in their own ways. No outside law or benefaction could ever be enacted or bestowed with the intimate knowledge these tribes bring to themselves. Their optimism is palpable, infectious, and beautifully at odds with a surrounding society that has much to learn from them, if only we can learn to pay attention.

MAINE

CANADA

*St. Croix River*

*Penobscot River*

INDIAN
TOWNSHIP ■

Calais •

INDIAN ISLAND ■
(PENOBSCOT)

• Old Town

PLEASANT
POINT ■
(PASSAMAQUODDY)

• Eastport

Bangor •

Columbia Falls •

• Augusta

Thomaston •

Portland •

*ATLANTIC OCEAN*

# 1

# The Passamaquoddies: 1987

Blue-jeaned Passamaquoddy Indians stood in earnest conversations with gray-suited bankers, while federal officials laughed at the soft-spoken jests of Finnish businessmen. The crowd inside the brand-new factory was surely the most assorted one ever assembled in Eastport, Maine. In one corner, the state's attorney general paid his compliments to a West German engineer for her work on this fifty-thousand-square-foot slab of concrete and sky-blue corrugated steel.

The occasion, on a cold afternoon in late November, was the opening of Passamaquoddy Homes Incorporated—PHI, a high-tech housing manufacturer. The $5-million enterprise was a joint venture between the Passamaquoddy tribe of northern Maine, and Makroscan, a company based in Finland. The Passamaquoddies were a community of barely 2,700 people, with a tiny reservation next to Eastport, America's most eastern city, and another in the Maine woods fifty miles inland. Yet the tribe had the financial leverage to meet its Finnish partner as an equal.

In 1980, after a ten-year legal battle all the way to the White House, the Passamaquoddies had won a $40-million land-claim settlement. Through a series of shrewd subsequent business investments, the tribe had already doubled its money. By the mid-1980s "Passamaquoddy" was well on its way to becoming a Wall Street commonplace, even if few Americans outside of Maine had ever heard the name.

The Passamaquoddies were certainly known in Maine, where they already owned a gargantuan cement factory, the state's third largest commercial wild-blueberry farm, two radio stations, a supermarket, a mall, and a forestry operation. The tribe's 120,000-acre domain placed them among Maine's largest landowners. In sum, they controlled the state's third largest private portfolio.

As far as the Passamaquoddies were concerned, these remarkable and rapid financial conquests were dress rehearsals. PHI was opening night: this business would at last deliver good jobs near the reservation for tribal members. If successful, PHI would be a glowing exception in the hardbitten, Down East economy of Washington County. For the Passamaquoddies, who had struggled for generations as Maine's poorest and most despised minority, it would be a miracle.

At a table full of orangeade and cookies (as a matter of policy, alcohol is never served at official Passamaquoddy functions), I met PHI's president, Larry Horwitz. Larry's business degree and his suburban St. Louis upbringing made him seem an unlikely manager for a tribal enterprise. But Larry had broadened his background considerably in the 1960s as a volunteer for Jesse Jackson's Operation Breadbasket. On this day, though he was suited up like the bankers, he preserved the old activism in a walrus mustache and an unrestrained bush of black hair. "PHI happened because the Finns read about the Passamaquoddies in *Forbes*," he told me. Makroscan approached the tribe, which thought a housing business made sense, given the tribe's timber resources, its labor pool, and a growing need for housing in Maine. The Passamaquoddies would provide the factory, the equipment financing, the labor force, and some working capital. Makroscan would provide technical expertise, marketing, equipment, and overall management. The tribe invested $750,000 of their own equity and $800,000 in a federal Urban Action Development Grant. From a local bank, they borrowed another $1.4 million for the building and $2.5 million for equipment and working capital.

According to Larry, Makroscan's "panelized" building system represented the next wave of construction technology. Instead of building from scratch on site, the Scandinavian approach called for assembling discrete pieces in an automated factory process and then assembling them afterward. Maine's market seemed ripe for this innovative approach. Larry told me that although this was the official opening, PHI had been operating for several months and already had to its credit commercial buildings, luxury homes, affordable townhouses, and a hotel in Brunswick, Maine, called Captain Daniel's Inn.

As we talked, the inaugural crowd gradually converged on PHI's manufacturing equipment. Melvin Francis, tribal governor of Pleasant Point, the Passamaquoddy reservation adjacent to Eastport, cut a ceremonial ribbon with Jim Tierney, Maine's attorney general. Then Melvin pushed a red button, and a huge band saw sliced through a piece of a ready-made wall, which was lifted onto a conveyor belt by mechanical arms and turned over onto a table. The mostly Passamaquoddy work crew, clad in blue hard hats with Day-Glo orange ear protectors and armed with nail guns, shot together the components of a particle board and two-by-four panel in seconds, to general applause.

The day's master of ceremonies was a plump sixtyish man with steel-rimmed glasses and a high forehead, named Joseph Nicholas but called "Cozy" by his Passamaquoddy compatriots. There was little about Cozy that distinguished

his Indian heritage, although his accent held something beyond a Mainer's half-British drawl. With his short, carefully
swept-up hair, he looked a lot like a small-town barber. (He
had, in fact, cut hair in Bangor for five years.) But in the
1960s, Cozy had resurrected Ceremonial Day, an annual
Passamaquoddy celebration of Native traditions credited
with salvaging a large portion of Passamaquoddy culture.
Sporting a blue blazer, gray flannels, and a bolo tie, Cozy
mounted an impromptu podium of semiconstructed PHI
siding, adjusted the microphone with a practiced twist, and
bellowed genially.

"After years of seeing other people's business signs
around here saying 'Passamaquoddy This' and 'Passamaquoddy That,' we now have Passamaquoddy Homes Incorporated, and it belongs to *us*. Non-Indians are beginning to
respect Passamaquoddy money. Soon they will respect us as
a *people*."

Cozy was followed by Wayne Newell, a representative
from Indian Township, the inland Passamaquoddy reservation. Wayne also wore a blazer and a string tie. He was in his
early forties and wore his heavy black hair over his ears and
parted in the middle. Wayne, like Cozy, spoke English as a
second language, but his post-graduate education augmented his accent with an almost patrician resonance. "This
is a great victory for the Passamaquoddies," he said in a deep
and gentle voice. "Bobby Newell [the tribal governor of Indian Township] told me to say to the young ones that this is
the beginning of a new life. But that no matter where we go,
we must remember we are Passamaquoddies and never forget the richness of our heritage."

Carl Shaw, director of public affairs for the federal Bureau
of Indian Affairs, spoke next. He was a sincere, suited man
of Native descent, with deep-set eyes and a tendency to
extend his final consonants in the manner of a Baptist
preacher. "Time and time again-nuh," he said, "I use the

Passamaquoddies as the best example of economic development in the country." Shaw went on to say that his boss, Secretary of Indian Affairs Ross Swimmer, believed the federal bureaucracy should get out of the way and let tribes develop their own economies. "You have a chance to succeed-uh," Shaw said, "and you also have the chance to fail."

The Finnish president of Makroscan was a man named Ilkka Riissanen, whose sandy hair was cut in straight bangs. He addressed the crowd in perfect school-book English with something like a Yorkshire accent. "We read in Europe about the problems of manufacturing in the U.S.," he said. "It may be true. It may not be true. But if it is a question of people, this country, this county, this tribe has the people, and it's going to be a success."

Tom Tureen, who doubles as the tribe's attorney and investment banker, was tugged up on stage by the tribal delegates like an old friend. Tom is short, and Cozy vamped for him, yanking the mike down practically to the floor to make sure Tom could reach it. When the guffaws of insiders died down, Tom reminded his audience that the purpose of the Passamaquoddy land claim was to return the tribe to the position of importance it had occupied two hundred years ago—and would have occupied all along if old treaties had been honored. "The way we hope to get there," said Tom, "is to create a local economy for the Passamaquoddy people—to create opportunities, to create jobs—and that's exactly what PHI is doing. I've already seen PHI's erection crews at work, and I'll tell you, these guys are developing a reputation for carpentry like the Mohawks in New York have for high steel."

Cozy closed the speech-making by reminding the guests of a supper buffet at the Pleasant Point community center. "For you pilgrims," he said, smirking at the gray suits, "we're celebrating Thanksgiving early."

A number of tribal members had disappeared into the factory restrooms, and now they emerged—fringed, beaded, and deerskinned in tribal dress. A young Passamaquoddy girl pounded a simple rhythm on a large hide drum, while Wayne Newell rattled a cow horn filled with pebbles and sang loud songs of celebration in his long-voweled Native tongue. Led by the Pleasant Point governor, Melvin Francis, the dancers performed intricate high steps in circles before the cheering Passamaquoddies and the riveted visitors. After several passes, the dancers joined hands to form a winding snake, which gathered segments of the audience as it grew and grew. Within minutes, everybody in the room was dancing: the lithe Native experts and the clumsy, self-conscious bankers and bureaucrats. Hundreds of stamping feet sent sawdust from the shop floor up to the fluorescent ceiling lights. The snake's shadow rode the building's aquamarine cinder-block walls.

I was pulled into the line next to a tribal member named George Stevens, who is the public works director at Indian Township. A quarter of a century ago, George stopped a white man from developing a parcel of Passamaquoddy land—the first of a thousand steps toward the tribe's land-claim settlement. I asked George if back then he thought he'd see a day like this. He said nothing for a moment. I thought the din had drowned out my question. Then he answered, "No. I thought we were on the way out."

I had taken my first trip to Passamaquoddy Country several weeks earlier. On a blindingly sunny afternoon near Halloween, I drove to Indian Township, a thirty-seven-square-mile spread of woods and lakes twenty miles south of the Canadian border. Leaving the coast to the bus loads of autumn tourists, I drove inland from Portland on the Maine Turnpike to Bangor and broke east on Route 9, a roller coaster of frost heaves and hairpin curves nicknamed the "Airline" by locals, who avoid it whenever they can. I dodged logging trucks all the way to the border town of Calais, and took a left on old Route 1.

After twenty miles I passed through the town of Princeton, which boasts one fine old church, a video store, Joe's Pizzeria and Restaurant, a corner store labeled "Live Bait," and a post office hidden inside the Hungry Tiger Take-Out. At the west end of Princeton, Route 1 enters the Indian Township Reservation over a small bridge spanning a thin neck of water connecting Lewey's Lake to the west and the Grand Falls Flowage (a twig off the west branch of the St. Croix River) to the east.

On my left was the "Strip," a straight line of small houses packed closely together between the highway and the lake. On the right was the Tribal Administration Building, a big, graceful pile of blond shingles decorated with ceramic mosaics derived from traditional Native American designs. The building's red roof had several long overhangs, giving the structure a tentlike appearance. I walked through its glass doors and found a reception desk on my left, which faced a large television set blaring game shows. Several women, one carrying a baby, surrounded the desk, smoking and schmoozing in Passamaquoddy.

I asked for directions to the tribal governor's office, and the receptionist answered in English with a heavy Maine accent. "You go right up the stayuhs," she said. The lobby was a little like that of a Unitarian church. Alongside framed black-and-white prints of tribal members from previous generations, the walls carried several alcohol awareness posters and a notice about aerobics classes. I walked up a broad winding staircase and took a seat on a reception couch in the lofted, skylit second-floor landing.

Tribal officials from both Pleasant Point and Indian Township had convened a joint council meeting in the office of Indian Township's governor, Bobby Newell. The office door was ajar, and through it the office appeared smoky and packed, mostly with men, some sitting on the floor with their backs against the wall. An hour went by, and the door opened wide as the group surged out in a blur of jeans and leather jackets.

I was ushered into Bobby's office, which had handmade bows and arrows on the wall; a round fireplace, like those in ski lodges; and brown wall-to-wall carpeting. There were venetian blinds on the expansive windows, and a wobbly oak-veneer table. The Doors played softly on a boom box in the corner.

Bobby stood behind his desk in a leather jacket and a bold-striped shirt, eyeing me all the way to my seat. He had the face of a Hollywood supercop, crowned with glossy waves of black hair and fronted with thick eyebrows and a sparse mustache. His expression, in repose, was fierce. I couldn't help thinking that he knew he looked forbidding and was entertained by the effect he had on strangers. "I take it you left your horns outside," he said softly, unsmiling. When he caught my bewildered expression, he pointed to my bald pate and broke into a warm chuckle.

Bobby grew up in Indian Township in the 1950s, when the Passamaquoddies were wards of the state and victims of misguided charity. The backs of his hands were dotted with the hairline scars of a nun's ruler. The nun taught in the Indian Township school, and she was quick to punish tardy responses to her rapid-fire questions. "How the hell was I supposed to know what she was saying?" said Bobby. "I didn't speak English. I was really prejudiced against whites for a long time after that." Bobby kept working on his education anyway, and was only a few credits shy of a master's degree in community economic development.

As we talked, a crowd of people waiting to see Bobby grew in the corridor outside the office, and he had to speak louder and louder to be heard over their rising hubbub. "*Costaqs!*" he finally growled. I asked him what that meant. "It means 'shut up,' but don't think it'll make any difference," he sighed. He was right. The crowd began to invade the office. A very young lieutenant with the Indian Township police force came in to tell Bobby about a brand-new recruit who'd been slapping speeding tickets on practically every car passing through the reservation. "I'm worried he's going to get hurt or shoot somebody," said the lieutenant, "if you don't lean on him a little."

Several stacks of paper arrived for Bobby's signature. Then the phone rang, and Bobby answered it. "Yeah . . . yup . . . well, you's always saying you needed a job, so we got you one." The caller was a young tribal member at the tail end of a two-year prison sentence; he had written an angry letter to the tribal newspaper saying that if he couldn't find work when he was released he might end up back in jail. Bobby had found him a clerical job in the Township administration, and the boy had called to thank him.

Bobby kneaded his eyes with the heels of his hands. "I'm here every day from seven A.M. on, talking to all these people who need help," he said. "When I'm not here, I'm on a plane." Bobby is a seasoned Passamaquoddy leader, having served as governor of Pleasant Point in the 1970s. But this was his first term as governor under the tribe's post-settlement federal status, and the job had complicated itself exponentially. Indian Township's budget, for instance, had ballooned from $1,700 to $2 million in eight years. A third of the Township's budget is federally funded, and to maintain contact with those money sources, Bobby travels to Chicago, where Housing and Urban Development's Indian programs are headquartered; to Washington, D.C., for talks with the Bureau of Indian Affairs; and to Nashville, Tennessee, to the Indian Health Service.

The money is essential, but Bobby sees the tribe's own

public expenditures as subsidies to the feds. "We pay for a lot
of things that are really federal responsibilities," he told me.
"We pay for our own employees. This building was built
with tribal money: six hundred and fifty thousand dollars—
no federal loans, no grants." The tribe adds two dollars of its
own money to every federal dollar coming into the Township, and according to Bobby that only brings his government's services up to an acceptable level. "And you wonder
why tribes without resources are starving," said Bobby. "At
least now we can afford to stop fighting for every little
scrap."


"To really understand how far these people have come, you'd
have to know what their lives were like back when the idea of
a major land-claim victory was something they didn't even
dream about." Tom Tureen, the Passamaquoddies' lawyer,
financial adviser, and old friend, counseled the long view in
our initial conversations about his clients' more recent and
newsworthy achievements.

Tom was twenty-five years old in 1969 and fresh out of law
school when he moved from Washington, D.C., to Washington County, Maine. On behalf of the first client of his career,
the Passamaquoddy Indian tribe, he took on the state and
federal governments in one of the longest, most hard-
fought, and most significant legal cases of this generation.
When it was over, Tom was thirty-seven.

"To go back as far as you need to go, you've got to predate
my involvement by years and years," he told me. "Go talk to
John Stevens. He's the father of the Passamaquoddy land
claim."

I visited Indian Township again, just before Christmas.
The first winter storm was out in force. I parked outside the
tribal offices, walked across the lot to a neat clapboard
house, and knocked. The door was opened by a short, bear-

ish man with a face of umber clay and a strong fleshy nose under large eyes set at a sad, downward angle. I had grown so used to the mixed-blood appearance of many Passamaquoddies that I embarrassed myself with a double take at the sight of John Stevens's unmistakably Native countenance. (I later confessed my reaction to one of John's Passamaquoddy friends, who said, "Yeah, John's a real nickel Indian, all right.")

Along with a short, neat haircut, John sported blue jeans, crepe-soled leather boots, and a T-shirt proclaiming "Bellies Are Back in Style in Maine." Governor of Indian Township on and off for some two decades, John had narrowly lost the last election to Bobby Newell and had recently taken a job as the maintenance coordinator for Maine's three Indian schools.

John led me through the kitchen, where his fair-skinned, sandy-haired stepson did homework at the table, and into a parlor filled with unmatched furniture. Folding himself into a worn Barcalounger, John answered my first question with a three-hour story of Passamaquoddy ascent. His great head lolled back and forth in time with his memory, and he spoke in a mesmerizing accent—sluggish Down East vowels clipped short by a Passamaquoddy edge.

John Stevens was born in 1933 and grew up as the Passamaquoddies were sinking to the bottom of their collective history. Their subjection was so complete that for the five years before John's birth the tribe was under the jurisdiction of Maine's forestry department, like some endangered species.

"They owned us," said John. "All of our resources were controlled by someone else." All Passamaquoddies knew that Indian Township was supposed to be 23,000 acres of unalienable land, but the state had leased much of that acreage to paper companies, which proceeded to timber them clean. In the 1930s, when the paper companies went on a property-buying binge, the state was so eager to off-load Indian land that the legislature proposed a plan to splinter the tribe and allocate a handful of Passamaquoddies to every town in Maine. During World War II the federal government joined the party, commandeering a large chunk of Indian Township as an internment camp for German prisoners of war. Afterward, that land was broken into lots and sold to nearby white residents.

John's father was an educated man who spoke up loudly and often against these indignities. That made him a nuisance to the state and controversial even with Passamaquoddies, who were fearful of official reprisals. When John was three years old, his father went to prison. "He was accused of killing a man," said John. "He always claimed he didn't, but the state done a good snow job. I was labeled as a son of a murderer, and it made my life miserable."

John's father served ten years, and his wife and nine children sometimes went very hungry. John went to work in the woods when he was five, cutting trees for four dollars a week to augment the family's three-dollar stipends from the state's welfare department. "We'd chase deers out on the ice and kill them with clubs," said John. "It was an awful thing to do, a terrible thing, but when you're starving and there are nine people depending on you, you can't afford to think about cruelty."

Still, there were things about John's childhood that he missed in middle age. "Back in those days there was only about three hundred people here at the Township. We had nothing to do in the wintertime but go around from house to house, talking to everybody. I used to know them all by first name." The community was cooperative as well as close-knit. When John's brother George brought his bride back to town, they had no place to live, so George started to build a shack. He'd been working for only an hour or two when his neighbors Charlie LaCoote, Noel Gabriel, and Sammy

Tomah came by to help. The group had the newlyweds under a roof in a week.

John enlisted in the armed services when he was eighteen. "We always were brought up to be loyal to the country," he said. "Anyway, if you didn't serve in the army you weren't a man. George and I went down to look for a place to sign up, and we happened to walk into the Marine office. We both enlisted, but because George had a family he ended up joining the National Guard in Bangor. I ended up in Korea.

"The day we landed over there, all these Korean kids crawled all over us. They were starving, somebody said, and I realized then I'd seen the same thing here growing up. I'd seen my mother's friends die in childbirth because they were malnourished. I'd thought it was just the way things were. But in Korea I really found out how bad off my own people were. When I realized that, I couldn't eat. I had a three-day ration, and I just gave it away to those kids. I thought, 'What the hell am I doing in Korea? These people haven't done anything to me. I should be home fighting the system in Maine.' I made up my mind before I even came back here that I was going to do something for my own people, whether it was legal or not."

John came home and ran for governor of Indian Township in 1954, when he was twenty-one years old. At the time, tribal members were denied even a secret ballot. The candidates faced each other across a table, and a state official handed each voter a slip of paper. To cast a ballot, the voter had to walk up and drop a piece of paper in front of a candidate. "Elections ended up in a brawl every time," said John, "because everyone knew who everybody else voted for. Anyway, I won. I had thirteen votes and old George Dana [the incumbent governor] had twelve."

John's problems began with the realization that his victory was meaningless. The real governor of Indian Township—and its despot—was Hiram Hall, a retired fish inspector who had been appointed as the state's Indian agent. With total control over Indian resources and entitlements, and little or no interference from his superiors, Hiram Hall dictated the lives, and occasionally the deaths, of his wards. John told me there were Passamaquoddies who actually starved and froze when Hall withheld food and firewood to punish some transgression. I had read, but had not believed, that once when a pregnant Indian Township woman leaned against Hall's car to tell him her mind, he floored the accelerator, dragging her fifty feet along a paved road, after which she lost her child. John told me it was true.

His father was still alive during John's first term. The two of them took the Passamaquoddy horror show on the road, talking to senior citizens' groups, the League of Women Voters, any group of Maine citizens who would listen. Maine responded to its constituents' growing awareness in its own blundering way. In 1957, the state erected twenty-seven houses on the Strip. "The only thing that we had anything to do with those houses was choosing the color—brown or green," said John. "They were all two or three rooms, when people like my family had eight or nine kids. They were all dumped in about twenty feet apart, like barracks. The next-door neighbor looked right in your bedroom.

"I was so annoyed over that I went before the legislature, and finally one person listened, the speaker of the house, John Reed from Presque Isle; he happened to end up as the next governor of Maine. He said, 'What do you want, John?' I said, 'My freedom, damn it, my freedom!' He said, 'What are you talking about? Everybody *has* their freedom.' I said, 'Not on the reservation. We don't even vote for you people.' " American Indians had been granted full United States citizenship in 1924, but Maine was able to prevent its Indian residents from voting in state congressional-district elections until 1967 by claiming that only taxpayers could register. Indians living on trust land had no taxes to pay, so they couldn't vote.

Changes were few and hard to come by, and the tribe remained demoralized. At Peter Dana Point, a small Passamaquoddy settlement on Lewey's Lake next to the Township's school and church, the people were still harvesting ice for their drinking water in the winter and dueling with rats in their living rooms in the summer. In the mid-1960s, everybody in town shared a single pay phone.

The Passamaquoddies next-door neighbors were no help. The barber in Princeton refused to cut Passamaquoddy hair. When state authorities ordered him to cease discriminating or cease doing business, he closed up shop. (His shop is now a beauty parlor owned by a tribal member.) One day, deep in the winter of 1964, one neighbor finally went too far.

"I was driving back from work," said John. "I was working for Georgia Pacific, then. George was out on the side of the road, and he waved me over and said, 'Come down and take a look at this.' " The two went down to the lake and found a white man named William Plaisted felling trees on the Passamaquoddy shoreline. Plaisted had owned a group of tourist cabins on the reservation long enough to be tolerated as part of the local landscape. But this was different; he was working way out of his property bounds.

"There he was," said John, "chopping away. I said 'Geez, what are you doing?' "

"Clearing off my land," said Plaisted.

"That's not *your* land," said John.

"Yeah it is," said Plaisted. "I won it in a poker game." Plaisted told them the game had been played with Ken Savage, the owner of a nearby car dealership who had anted up with a parcel of Strip land. The Savage lot was one of many Passamaquoddy properties that had been leased by the state under 999-year contracts to finance Route 1's way through the reservation.

"Well, how far down does this land go?" asked John.

"Oh, about three houses down the other side of George's," said Plaisted. This was a hefty chunk of the remaining Passamaquoddy territory. By this time governmental and private land frauds had left the Passamaquoddies with but 17,000 of their original 23,000-acre Indian Township Reservation. Plaisted's expansion would squeeze the tribe almost up to the Princeton bridge.

"Oh no," said John, "you ain't goin' to get that."

Ignoring him, Plaisted began staking out his new acquisition until he got to the third house down from George's. The shack was occupied by two elderly Passamaquoddy women. Plaisted planted a stake in their backyard. One of the ladies ran out, lugging a rusty shotgun and screaming, "You get off my goddam property."

"*That* got his attention," said John, grinning and rolling his eyes. "He pulled that stake right up and said, 'Guess I better go across the road there.' I said, 'Ya, you better stay over there, too.' "

John convinced the tribal council to take the matter to the top, and a small contingent drove to Augusta the next day to see the governor. They might as well have stayed home. The governor let them cool their heels in his waiting room for half a day before telling them it was a local affair and out of his hands.

"That night we had an all-tribal meeting," said John. "We didn't have our own meeting place, so we met in the parish hall and planned out what we'd do." Plaisted had already started to bulldoze a driveway into his new back forty. The Passamaquoddies decided they would block the entrance to keep him from doing further damage. "I told them I didn't want any rough stuff," John said. "If we hurt somebody it was going to set us back another twenty years.

"The next day, a whole bunch of us got out there, and pretty soon a state cop I knew, Bob Desjordain, came by. Bob and I were pretty friendly, and he said he thought we were doing the right thing. But a couple of hours later he come down and said, 'John, I'm sorry. I just got my orders from the state: Arrest everybody that is on the property.' I said, 'You ain't going to take anybody, Bob. You go convey that message to your boss. You are going to have a fight on your hands you gonna touch us.' "

The standoff continued until noon, when the protesters grew hungry. "I left George and three other guys and four women in charge down there and took the rest up the Point to feed them. I got the last carload up there, and my sister-in-law was on the phone. She said, 'They just arrested George and the boys, and they already took the women away to Calais.' It turned out they dropped the guys in Woodland [eleven miles east of Indian Township] and made them walk home. But the women they locked up in the Calais jail, and I guess they were raising hell down there. I had to go bail them out—seventy-five dollars apiece.

"Then I tried to find a lawyer. We spent two or three days looking around Calais, but those local lawyers were all in it with the people we were having problems with. Said they were too busy to take our case. I know damn well they weren't *that* busy. Then a guy from Pleasant Point said, 'There's this young lawyer moved into Eastport; he's so smart he makes the judge look like an asshole.' I said, 'That must be the one we want.' "

The lawyer's name was Don Gellers, an overpressurized fireplug from Brooklyn who rode the first wave of disaffected urbanites migrating to Washington County in the 1960s to "get back to the land." Gellers was abrasive, uncompromising, and prone to megalomania. According to one acquaintance, he was the kind of guy who sued the fuel-oil company if the truck didn't come on time. But the Passamaquoddies could have cared less about Gellers's manners. "In the beginning, Don was like the Second Coming of Christ," said John.

Certainly the way Gellers handled his first tribal court case won him years' worth of Passamaquoddy loyalty. First, he established that the judge assigned to the case had helped Plaisted draw up his new land deeds, forcing the judge to disqualify himself. When the case finally came to trial, Gellers pulled out the Passamaquoddies' trump card.

"A few weeks before all of this," said John, "an old Indian Township governor had died, and his wife came to me and said he'd left all these old papers. The old lady didn't know what they were; she couldn't read or write. She told me I oughta come down and see them. I said, 'Ah, they're probably junk.' She said, 'Well, I'm going to throw them out, then.' I said, 'Okay, I'll come see.'

"She took me out to one of them old cars with a trunk with a lot of leather straps on it. When she opened it up, the first thing that hit me was that envelope. It was sort of weaved out of straw, and it had a funny kind of string on it. I untied that, and there was another envelope, made of some kind of cloth. It had a big red ribbon around it, so I untied the ribbon and I opened it up. There was this thick folded document, with a great big blue seal."

The document was the original treaty, established between the Passamaquoddies and the Commonwealth of Massachusetts in 1794 when Maine was still a part of Massachusetts. "It was all handwritten, in old writing," said John. "You could hardly make out what they were saying. Every time I turned it, it would rip. I told my wife, 'I'll get this to a museum somewhere that will tell me how to preserve it.'"

John took the treaty to the University of Maine, where it is displayed today. The university curators made John a laminated copy, which he took to Don Gellers. The treaty reserved in perpetuity for the Passamaquoddies Pleasant Point, some islands in the St. Croix River, and Indian Township—all 23,000 acres of it. This was the evidence Gellers introduced in court. "The judge took a look," said John, "and he threw the case out. He told Plaisted, 'You can't prove that you own the land, so there's no proof these women were breaking the law.'"

Gellers then decided that Maine itself had broken the law by not honoring the treaty of 1794, and began to explore various legal stratagems that would allow the Passamaquoddies to sue for return of Indian Township's missing 6,000 acres and other treaty promises broken after Maine split off from Massachusetts in the 1800s.

Gellers also went after Hiram Hall, on behalf of Hall's "trustees." These were Passamaquoddies whose money Hall had expropriated after unilaterally declaring them incompetent to manage their own affairs. The Calais judge summoned Hall to answer these charges. "Ya," said John Stevens. "Somebody come by one afternoon and served ol' Hiram a court order. It must've given him a heart attack. No kidding: he died right there in his office chair before that day was done."

In the meantime, the liberalization of the 1960s seemed to be softening even the Maine establishment. "Ken Curtis got into office as governor," said John. "He was helpful, once he was educated a little, so we started dreaming of what we might get him to do." The state's Department of Indian Affairs was created in 1965. Maine's Indians were no longer orphans wandering from one uninterested bureaucrat to another, but the sole purpose of an office dedicated to their needs. In Ed Hinckley, a veteran of Indian affairs appointed as the new department's commissioner, they also found a friend.

Hinckley was there to deliver. But he was used to federally sized Indian allocations, and because as wards of the State of Maine the Passamaquoddies were not recognized by the federal government as falling under its jurisdiction, they didn't qualify for many programs offered to Indians generally. During his tumultuous four-year stint, Hinckley continually broke his budgets trying to deliver a reasonable level of services to his constituents.

The governor was willing to live with Hinckley's deficits, but the legislature wasn't. Whipsawed between the two, Ed finally resigned in 1969, but not before he had pulled Indian schools out of the Catholic church and into state jurisdiction, or before the reservations received sanitation and better housing.

Just as the state began to feed the tribe some scraps of legitimacy, things began to fall apart for Don Gellers and for the Passamaquoddy land claim. Gellers had bought a crumbling Eastport mansion he couldn't afford to maintain. The house became a home for every hippie and runaway who ended up in Eastport, and Gellers gradually devolved from father figure to drug dealer. "He even tried to get *me* going," said John. "I said, 'I have too many problems to be pooped up on drugs and alcohol.' Then he started getting into heavier stuff, you know, and his mind was slowly going the other way."

A few days after he finally filed the Passamaquoddies' lawsuit in Massachusetts court, Gellers was raided by two carloads of state and local police, who conducted a room-to-room search that yielded three marijuana cigarettes. Much has been made of this timely coincidence, but the hindsight consensus is that Gellers's downfall was no martyrdom.

Gellers represented himself in court, and for his efforts earned the state's first prison sentence for drug possession. "I tried to warn him," said John Stevens. "When he got convicted, he convicted himself, because he wouldn't take advice from anybody. He represented himself and he goofed."

Gellers continued to represent the Passamaquoddies as he worked on his own appeal, but the tribe eventually dismissed him. "The day we let him go was the hardest day of my life," said John. "No matter what people say, Don Gellers gave us hope and tried to salvage what little dignity the Passamaquoddy tribe had left. He begged me not to fire him. I said, 'I'm sorry, but I want to see this resolution come about before I die. I'll always be your friend; if you need me, you call me.' "

Gellers never called. When it looked as if prison was a sure thing, he jumped bail and fled to Israel. "I didn't know what to do," said John. "We had no lawyer for the next year or so, and everything was at a standstill."

One day, a despondent John Stevens was in Washington, D.C., when a friend reminded him that Tom Tureen, a law student who had spent a summer working with Gellers for the Passamaquoddies, was still in town and about to receive his law degree. "Tom was just the opposite of Gellers. Very straight. The tribe already had great respect for him. 'That's the one we oughta get,' I thought. So I called him. I said, 'We would like to hire you as our lawyer.' And he said, 'John, I was waiting for you to ask me.' Oh God, my heart just grew. From then on, my mind was a little bit easier."

The Princeton-educated Tureen was considerably more polished than Don Gellers, but Tom's suit-and-tied five-foot-six-inch frame concealed a political and intellectual power-house. As the next dozen years wore on—and as the Maine land claims went from local to national news—newspapers around the country printed pictures of Passamaquoddy leaders in company with this smiling, unaging imp in a careless haircut, toting an outsized cigar.

Having relieved his Passamaquoddy clients with his personal self-containment, Tom proposed a scheme that made Don Gellers look like a legal conservative. Just before Christmas in 1971, at the meeting of the Joint Tribal Council, Tom suggested, almost casually—"for talking purposes," he said—that the Passamaquoddies forgo their 6,000-acre complaint and sue instead for the return of their entire aboriginal territory . . . more than a million acres.

"What?" said John Stevens.

"Yep," said Tom.

"Oh God," said John. "The tribe will go bananas."

For another hour, as his living room darkened and John faded to a silhouette against the backdrop of snow in early twilight, John told how Tom Tureen's preposterous ambition proved to be a stroke of genius. I knew Tom, from our brief acquaintance, to be an energetic, single-minded, impatient, sometimes acerbic man. John Stevens had suggested that these traits were essential to his achievement. I made the long, dark drive back to Portland with a growing wonder about this ardent, incongruous ally of the Passamaquoddies.

In an office that seemed worlds away from John Stevens's living room, Tom picked up the story of the land claims from the beginning of his involvement with the tribe. On the top floor of a restored warehouse in Portland's historic district, the room was sunlit and spacious, adorned with tokens of his clients and his work on their behalf. A photograph of him shaking hands with Jimmy Carter over a draft of the 1976 White House proposal shared the walls with original Oliphant and MacNelly cartoons about the land claims and copies of the House and Senate bills that settled it once and for all. Above the law book–stuffed shelves behind Tureen's desk were a Penobscot war club and two Passamaquoddy baskets.

These days, Tom looks more like an investment banker than a legal activist. His hair is cut more carefully and more often now and harbors some gray lights, which, along with an emerging belly, have allowed him finally to grow into his omnipresent cigar.

As an undergraduate, Tom had spent his first two years grooming himself to be Princeton's campus poet. But during his sophomore summer he spent two months in South Dakota, working at a government boarding school with Sioux Indian children. The children were kept at the school year-round because the government considered their home life inadequate. In an ill-conceived attempt to create a "healthy atmosphere," the government had turned itself into a children's jailer.

Tom's mind, already focused on the grand scheme of things, took a big picture of the situation. He discerned the underlying source of his students' deprivation in the warped structure of relations between the Indians and the United States. He was convinced that this institutionalized paternalism, in which Indians were seen—and in many cases had come to see themselves—as dependent on the government for everything, including parenthood, was the root of such indignities as that grisly summer school.

Abandoning *belles lettres,* Tureen set his sights on a legal education as the best means of attacking the underlying problems of Indian Country.

In the summer of 1967, after his first year at George Washington University Law School, Tom accepted an assignment from the Law Students' Civil Rights Research Council to help Don Gellers prepare the Passamaquoddies' land claim. "It was the most bizarre summer I ever spent," said Tom of his first Eastport sojourn. "There were forty days of unbroken fog, and the apple blossoms came out on the Fourth of July." But he was comfortable with his clients from the start. "Considering how much they'd been kicked around, the Indians were remarkably open. I don't remember going through a period of testing before they accepted me." In August, he returned to law school with powerful memories of the Passamaquoddy friends he'd made and a long hope that they would prevail.

After John hired him in 1970, the newly minted lawyer and his bride, Susan, moved up to Perry, next door to Eastport and the Pleasant Point Reservation. Although Tom's lifestyle was far less flamboyant than Don Gellers's, his legal strategies were even more far-out. Gellers had based his Passamaquoddy case on Maine's failure to live up to its treaty obligations. Tom decided to call the treaty itself into question. Hunting further back in legal history, Tom came across a federal law passed in 1790 called the Indian Nonintercourse Act. The law provided that no transaction involving

Indian land would be valid unless it was achieved by means of a federal treaty approved by Congress. The Passama-quoddy treaty had been drawn up four years after the Non-intercourse Act and had never been approved by Congress.

"If the law meant what it said," said Tom, "then the 1794 transaction and later treaties which wiped out Passama-quoddy holdings weren't valid. We asked the federal author-ities about this, and they said, 'Oh no, that stuff only applies to other Indians, not Maine Indians.' And we said, 'Wait a minute. The statute says no land owned by *any* Indians can be sold without these congressional okays.' And they said, 'Well, it's just the way we've always done it.' And we said, 'How do you know that's what the law means?' And they said, 'We know that's what it means because that's the way we've always done it.'

"And we didn't think that was right, so we did some research. We found out that the Nonintercourse Act, by and large, had been applied uniformly in the West, where the federal government dealt with the Indians before the states were created. In the original colonies, where the state and federal governments had been created simultaneously, the states were very powerful and much less willing to acknowl-edge federal authority. Tribes in these states were often left to their own devices, and more often than not lost their land in one-sided state treaties. As the years passed, those treaties became the unquestioned law of the land. But in fact, all the land that was taken from the Indians by Massachusetts origi-nally had been taken illegally. It dawned on us that we could sue for wrongful possession and damages going back two centuries."

The magnitude of the undertaking never phased Tom, apparently. He simply never thought he would lose. ("There is nothing remotely resembling a Hamlet in him," Jim Mer-ritt, one of his Princeton roommates, once said. "He just never seemed to have a moment of self-doubt.") Perhaps

Tom's penchant for long shots was a means of testing his self-assurance. Perhaps only a challenge as large and hopelessly unbalanced as the Maine land claims could accommodate his range of skills as litigator, polemicist, media expert, and street fighter. As one of his colleagues would later declare, "Tom Tureen could talk a hungry dog off a meat wagon."

"It was a long shot, no question," conceded Tom. "It came under the heading of a 'neat theory.' This would be the first time Indians had gone into court demanding land in a claim of right, not a claim of conscience. The Passamaquoddies were saying, 'Under *your* laws, this is what we're entitled to.' I'm a very practical person, and my question was what to do with that neat theory. We knew we were bringing a very, very large case, one that would press the limits of the judicial system. We just couldn't trust the outcome to the judicial process. That's not saying there's anything bad about the judicial process; it's just plain old reality that governments don't commit suicide. If the consequences of a court decision meant giving back a huge chunk of Maine real estate to fifteen hundred Indians—after one hundred and eighty years of private ownership—however much the law required it, it wasn't going to happen. In our judgment, the case was worth something only in settlement." His clients weren't looking for retribution. They were looking for justice, and for something they could call their own.

In Old Town, the Penobscot Indians—who in 1796 had traded some five million acres for groceries, ammunition, and a cramped reservation on an island in the river north of Bangor—got wind of the Passamaquoddies' legal actions. Their leaders asked Tom to file suit for them as well.

Together the suits amounted to a staggering 12.5 million acres of land, almost two-thirds of the State of Maine, plus damages amounting to $25 billion.

Tom set about building himself a powerful and talented legal team. In addition to securing the services of a brilliant young attorney named Barry Margolin, Tom went to the august Washington law firm of Hogan & Hartson for *pro bono* counsel. He also attached himself to the Native American Rights Fund, a public-interest law firm in Boulder, Colorado, which picked up the salaries for Tom, Barry Margolin, and a couple of additional lawyers who completed the Passamaquoddies' platoon of legal guerrillas. They were the first lawyers to undertake an Indian land claim without taking a cut of the ultimate award, and they were all working for about a third of what they would have earned in private practice.

The lawyers worked in a Calais office above an outlet for the local Hathaway shirt factory. In the winter, they stored their typewriters in the bathroom, which was the only part of the office they could afford to heat at night. There were some compensations, however, including a full federal library and access to a bush pilot, who flew them around to various courtrooms and clients along the New England seaboard. The pilot complained about Tom's hours (frequently 5:00 A.M. to midnight), so Tom took lessons from him as they flew, got his own pilot's license, and eventually bought the plane from the pilot.

"In 1972 we asked the federal government to bring action on behalf of the tribe," said Tom. "Now, why did we ask the old villain to champion our cause? Well, we certainly didn't want to trust it to Maine state courts. And if we had brought the action ourselves, there would have been some real questions as to whether a federal court had the jurisdiction to hear such a case. But if we could convince the feds to bring the action, there would have been *no* question, because the federal government can sue in federal court any time it wants. Also, the deepest pocket around to pay for a settlement was the federal government, and we thought the earlier we got it involved the better."

The Interior Department, the federal office in charge of

federal obligations to Indians, saw it a little differently. Interior officials tried to kill the case by stalling until the time limit for such suits expired. So Tom's team filed suit to *force* them to sue. In a hearing before a U.S. district court in Portland, Interior lawyers said they would decline to press the suit, citing a nineteenth-century Maine court ruling that the Passamaquoddy tribe was extinct. They argued this point in front of several dozen Passamaquoddy observers. The judge, Edward T. Gignoux, one of the most respected federal judges in the country, smiled—and ordered Interior to take the case.

In 1975, the federal court ruled that the Nonintercourse Act did indeed apply to the Passamaquoddies, and ordered the Justice Department to proceed on their behalf. The same ruling established the Passamaquoddies as a federally recognized tribe, eligible for all federal Indian services and protections. "We had dealt with the hardest theoretical issue in the whole claim," said Tom. "It was so theoretical that nobody who might be adversely affected paid much attention. The state officials treated the court's decision as something of a joke."

By then, John Stevens was in the odd position of working for the enemy, because he had taken Ed Hinckley's old job as the state's commissioner of Indian affairs. He had a chance to observe official attitudes at close range, beginning with those of Governor James Longley. "Longley was one way smart, the other way stupid," said John. "He was a good administrator, but a lousy lawyer. One day he asked me what I thought about the suit. I said, 'Governor, I am going to give you some quiet advice. Our case is tied to Maine real estate, and sooner or later it's going to tie up the state's resources.' He didn't believe me."

In 1976, the Maine bond market collapsed. According to

Tom, the Boston law firm of Ropes and Gray, which rendered opinions on New England bond issues, said, "Hey, wait a minute. If the Nonintercourse Act applies up there, and a municipality borrows money using property taxes as its collateral, and if that property may actually belong to the Indians, there's no way to ensure payment of those bonds." A million-dollar issue came along; Ropes and Gray refused to render a decision on it. The issue sank. The next day, a statewide $27-million bond issue sank as well.

"*That* got their attention," said Tom. "Longley was a real demagogue, and let me tell you, it got hot." The collapse of the Maine bond market—which left bridges, roads, schools, and a major shopping center in preconstruction limbo— finally woke up the state's non-Indian population, and things got nasty. Old animosities surfaced, and anti-Indianism became fashionable. Indian children were hounded by their schoolmates. Longley and his attorney general, Joseph Brennan (who would succeed Longley as governor in 1979), asked Congress to retroactively repeal the Nonintercourse Act. Their campaigning fed public fears with harrowing visions of homeowners put out in the cold, even though the Indians had stated repeatedly that they would take no such actions. Tom Tureen started carrying a gun.

When asked if he ever got frightened or discouraged, Tom answered, "Nope." I took this as the kind of response that had led one of his Passamaquoddy clients to say, "If we hadn't had somebody with balls like Tom, we would've been totally screwed."

Tom also had a chameleon's ability to color himself as either a radical legal activist or a detached, cosmopolitan dealmaker, as the situation decreed. He was as at home with his Native American clients as he was with state and national power brokers. When Longley badgered the Maine congressional delegation into introducing legislation that would have

repealed the Nonintercourse Act and locked the Passamaquoddies out of court, Tureen called up Archibald Cox. Cox
didn't know Tureen from Adam and, fresh from his job as
Watergate special prosecutor, was being courted by every
worthy cause in America. Tom reached him at his Harvard
Law School office early one morning before the secretaries
arrived to screen his calls.

"It turned out he'd been following our case all along,"
said Tom. "He said, 'I'm very busy, but I hope never too busy
to listen.' I said, 'Great, we'll see you this afternoon,' and
Barry Margolin and I flew down to Boston. 'I'll do it on two
conditions,' he told us. 'One: I don't get paid.' (We had no
trouble obliging him on *that* one.) 'Two: you help me get
around a possible conflict of interest, because my wife's a
Maine property owner.' I showed him that his wife's property was outside the disputed area—and that my own property was inside—so he signed on."

Tureen also managed to get his case into the national
news. From MacNeil/Lehrer to *People* magazine, they
trooped to Calais. "We learned some very important lessons
about the media," said Tom. "Since the state had forsaken
us, we had to make the people on a national level see this as
an important issue, so that Congress would view it as one
deserving federal attention." Eventually, this combination of
strategies worked. President Carter intervened with a White
House task force. In 1977, the task force proposed that since
the federal government had created the problem by failing to
enforce the Nonintercourse Act nearly two hundred years
earlier, it should bear cost of settlement.

Then came the hardest part: the Passamaquoddies, the
Penobscots, the state of Maine, and the federal government
had to agree on the final terms of the settlement. The Passamaquoddy negotiators included John Stevens, Bobby
Newell, Bobby's sister Molly Jeanette Neptune, George Stevens, and Cliv Dore, who was then Pleasant Point's governor.

There were concessions to be made on all sides, and it was very hard for all tribal members to agree to any of them. According to one member of the negotiating team, "We did such a fine job of convincing our own people we could win two-thirds of Maine that when it came down to the realities of the settlement process, they thought we were truly getting gypped."

"In theory, the tribes were entitled to billions of dollars and twelve point five million acres of land," said Tom. "On the other hand if we had gone to the Court of Claims, where all previous Indian claims had been adjudicated, the tribes would have gotten something like three hundred thousand dollars. How do you take responsibility for making a compromise, when any one of your constituents can say 'I could have gotten more'?"

John Stevens believes that if the process had run over into the Reagan administration, the tribes would still be at it. As it was, they finally reached a point where they were working together—Pleasant Point with Indian Township, and the two of them with the Penobscot Nation. Congress concurred, signing the settlement into law in October 1980.

The Passamaquoddies and the Penobscots split $80.6 million (a portion of which was to create a 300,000-acre land base for the tribes) plus full federal recognition and benefits. An additional $900,000 land fund was awarded to a small band of Maliseet Indians in the northern part of the state. In return, the Indians agreed to certain state demands like income tax from which other federally recognized tribes are exempt. It was the largest settlement of its kind in United States history.

A delegation of Maine Indians went to the White House for the signing ceremony. When they arrived, there was some confusion with the Secret Service. John's brother, George Stevens, had to be revetted before he was admitted, but once everybody was inside, a joyous bedlam prevailed.

"Everybody wanted to get into the act," said one of the delegates. "I didn't get close enough to President Carter to shake his hand."

For John Stevens, it was nothing but sweet revenge. "Oh God, I'm telling you. What a time, what a time," he recalled, rolling his head up to one side and grinning from ear to ear. "To rub it into them Maine politicians was a real pleasure. That Longley, when he shook my hand, he squeezed it so hard he nearly broke it off. 'John, I should have taken your advice,' he said. I said, 'Ya, *somebody* should have.'"

After the settlement went through, the Passamaquoddy leaders had to decide what to do with their new wealth. The tribe could have divided the money into chunks of cash and handed it over to each tribal member—about $20,000 per person. Proceeds from the land-claim settlements of other tribes had often been distributed in this per-capita fashion to unprepared tribal members, who had ended their resulting spending sprees no better off than before.

As John Stevens saw it, "We couldn't spend this wealth all on ourselves. It's for the people who came before us and who suffered for this victory. It's also for those who are not yet born. I don't want people to live the way we had to live. We want to open avenues for our children and grand-children. We want to give them an opportunity to make a decent living."

The settlement was divided into rough thirds. With one-third the Passamaquoddies bought land: the tribe now owns close to two hundred square miles of Maine. Half of their new property adjoins the original reservations, held in trust by the federal government and protected from ever being alienated again. The other half is an investment: timber hold-ings in the western part of the state.

The second third was put into low-risk securities, from which tribal members are now paid a modest dividend—

anywhere from four hundred to eight hundred dollars a year.

Because half the tribe was chronically unemployed, and because job prospects in Washington County were the worst in the state, the final third was committed to economic development. The tribe hired Tom Tureen, who, after the settlement, had gone into private practice with Barry Margolin, to create an economic development plan. Not that Tom had any formal training in financial matters. But then he'd had no practical legal experience when he took on the land claims. There was little about any new venture to intimidate him, and the Passamaquoddies trusted his instincts.

Tom envisioned a tripartite set of economic goals for his clients. Their most urgent requirement was a self-sustaining local economy, so that every tribal member would have an opportunity for a meaningful job. At the same time, they needed to ensure that their current and future holdings would retain their value in real terms, so that inflation did not rob them of what they had recovered in the settlement. Finally, they hoped to use their wealth to attain a position of influence and respect beyond the reservations, so that neither they nor their children would ever have to suffer the indignities of the past.

The strategy for achieving all three goals evolved during the first few years after the settlement and had its origins in a blueberry farm. "It was the third largest blueberry farm in the state," said Tom, "which made it the third largest wild-blueberry farm in the world, because the industry is centered here in Maine." The tribe came upon the 3,000-acre patch while shopping for land. Tom thought the tribe could buy the land and simultaneously invest in its first business. Some tribal leaders disagreed. They were worried about whether they could succeed in a white man's business. But in the end the tribe bought the Northeastern Blueberry Company (NEBCO, for short) and paid $2.2 million of settlement money for it.

They closed on July 28, 1981, "and started harvesting the next week," said Tom. The farm's previous owners stayed on briefly as consultants, but soon the tribe hired the former governor from Pleasant Point, Francis "Bibby" Nicholas, to run the business. It was a great first season. The Passamaquoddies harvested $600,000 worth of berries they hadn't paid to raise. They did well the next year too, and even better the following one. By then they had recouped two-thirds of their initial investment.

With NEBCO's success grew the Passamaquoddies' confidence. Maine's non-Indians, who had largely opposed the land-claim settlement and who had been consoling themselves with the thought that the Indians were sure to blow it, began to change their minds.

The NEBCO experience taught the Passamaquoddies some important lessons. Tribal officials learned they could run a business as well as anyone else. Tribal members saw how ownership could change non-Indian attitudes. The Passamaquoddies also discovered the benefits—and potential profits—of buying out an existing business. Never one to think small, Tom started looking for a larger acquisition— one that would give the tribe even greater visibility. "It was then I started realizing that even with all the cash the Passamaquoddies had, it really wasn't all *that* much," said Tom. If the tribe had to pay cash for everything it bought it would be greatly constrained in its growth; his clients would have to play the game the way other people played. Tom saw the future of the Passamaquoddies, and the future was leveraged buy-outs.

"No tribe had raised funds through commercial sources on anything like the level we had in mind," said Tom. Some of the reasons for this were purely logistical. For one thing, tribes are sovereign entities, like other governments, and contracts with them cannot be enforced without an effective waiver of their inherent immunity. But according to Tom the most important reason was that Indians were simply not viewed as sophisticated players; nor did they think of themselves as capable of competing in the business arena.

Tom went looking for a deal that would break the Passamaquoddies out of this cycle, one that could be accomplished primarily with borrowed funds. As with the land claims, he sought out powerful allies, starting with Kenneth Curtis, Maine's former governor and one of the very few state officials who had been sympathetic to the Passamaquoddies. Tom told Ken the story of the blueberry farm, mentioned his clients were looking for something larger, and asked him if he had any ideas.

Curtis had a close friend and political ally named Chuck Cianchette, who with his brother, Bud, owned Cianbro, Maine's largest construction company. Cianbro had just bought Dragon Cement, New England's only cement factory, from Martin Marietta. The plant was located in Thomaston, Maine, some 125 miles south of the Passamaquoddy reservations. The deal had been risky for the Cianchettes, who had never operated a manufacturing plant before, but it was also irresistible. Martin Marietta had invested $75 million in the plant and then operated it for years at a $3-million annual loss. The conglomerate was willing to unload it at the fire-sale price of $8 million. Still, Cianbro had tied up most of its credit in the process, and Curtis imagined his old friend might be interested in lightening his load. He arranged a meeting between Chuck Cianchette, Tom Tureen, and John Stevens.

Tom and John arrived with an audacious plan. The tribe would buy Dragon's physical assets from Cianbro for about what Cianbro had paid Martin Marietta for them, then lease the plant back to Cianbro. The tribe would get a guaranteed minimum lease payment, which would cover interest expense on the $6 million it planned to borrow, while providing a 5 percent return on the $2 million in cash it was willing to invest. The tribe would also get a royalty on cement production, which could boost its profits by as much as 50 percent if the business did well. As a fail safe, Cianbro agreed to buy the plant back at the end of ten years for $8 million if the tribe asked them to.

Bud Cianchette liked the idea, and he liked Tom and John. Which left only a $6-million financial hurdle. For this, the Passamaquoddies went to Fleet Bank in Providence, Rhode Island. Fleet had lent Cianbro the money for the original Dragon purchase but was nervous about dealing with an Indian tribe, until the BIA agreed to guarantee almost half the loan.

"In terms of today's Wall Street megadeals, it wasn't much," said Tom. Fleet was really only lending the tribe $3 million, and the loan payments were more than covered by the Cianbro lease, the proceeds of which were assigned to the bank. Nevertheless, a milestone had been reached. Three million dollars was being lent on the strength of the assets acquired by an American Indian tribe. This was leverage, the kind that could permit virtually limitless growth if future deals could be done with an even higher percentage of debt.

There were risks. Cianbro wasn't General Motors, and cement was a notoriously fickle business. But Cianbro had owned Dragon for only two months, and already it had managed to prune Martin Marietta's formerly unionized payroll to a lean work force, compensated on an incentive basis. The Cianchettes' plans for further cost cutting made sense, and the Passamaquoddies had hired the Cambridge, Massachusetts, consulting firm of Arthur D. Little for a second opinion. The tribe's final decision was based on the consultant's report, and their gut feeling that the Cianchettes could be believed. The tribe stood to see a handsome return on its investment, and because it had used its acquisition as collateral, it had only its down payment to lose. "We were persuaded if a third of what they expected to happen happened, it would be fine," Tom said.

The deal closed. Dragon's new board consisted of John Stevens, Ralph Dana (the Passamaquoddy governor from Pleasant Point, who also owned his own trucking company), and Bud Cianchette. From the beginning Dragon outstripped all projections. Maine's economy started coming around, the cement business boomed along with construction, and everything started to cook. Dragon was also paying the tribe in goodwill. The tribe received environmental kudos for cleaning up after Martin Marietta. As Thomaston's largest employer, the rejuvenated Dragon saved about one hundred jobs among the local non-Indian population, not to mention 40 percent of the town's tax bill. Best of all, the tribe was able to take out cash earnings after all expenses—close to $1 million in 1985 alone.

Dragon was doing so well that the tribe began to think it would be very nice to own the whole thing. "Bud Cianchette came in to see me one day with an idea for modifying the structure of the original deal," said Tom. "I said, 'How about having the tribe buy you out instead, Bud? You'd still run the place, but you'd be a tribal employee.' "

Bud Cianchette was very much a self-made man and a bit shocked at Tom's suggestion. "The last time I worked for anybody was for Uncle Sam in World War Two," he replied. But Tom had figured out a way for the tribe to borrow money more cheaply—and in the process render Cianbro's Dragon income tax–free. Bud was persuaded.

"We'd taken a very close look at the 1982 Indian Tribal Government Status Act," said Tom, "which said Indians could borrow tax-exempt as long as the loan was for an 'essential governmental purpose.' We were wondering how we would ever persuade the IRS that a cement plant was an 'essential governmental purpose,' when the government itself helped us out by defining any activity for which a tribe could get federal funding as an 'essential purpose.' Well, the BIA had already given us a three-million-dollar loan guarantee for the initial Dragon deal, so we fit."

Under the terms of the new proposal, the tribe would buy out the remaining term of Cianbro's lease and simultaneously acquire Cianbro's concrete business for $17.5 million. Cianbro would take out a tax-exempt note for $10.5 million, and the tribe was to borrow $7 million to buy out Cianbro. The whole thing was too exotic for Fleet's blood, so Tom went to Casco Bank, the biggest bank in Maine, for $13 million: $7 million to pay Cianbro and $6 million to pay off the original Fleet loan. But the deal was too rich for Casco's blood, so they referred it to their owner, Bank of Boston. "We wound up working with Ralph Fifield, a senior vice-president," said Tom. "He was just wonderful."

A phone call to Ralph Fifield confirmed that the feeling was mutual. "Tom was a gem to work with," he said. "Very knowledgeable, very businesslike. I liked the tribal leadership; John Stevens and Ralph Dana were outstanding guys. The whole cast of people involved were really first-class." Bank of Boston officers had only two concerns. One: the cement plant had not operated profitably under Martin Marietta, and there was no guarantee that the Passamaquoddies would do any better. Two: if by some small chance the plant went bust, the bank would be forced to foreclose on a still-poor and newly popular regional Indian tribe.

"But ultimately the deal made good business sense," said Fifield. "There were good asset values, and although the Passamaquoddies had no vast business experience themselves, they kept the original management team in place to run it for them. It appeared to be a very businesslike affair going in, and fortunately it proved to be."

The Bank of Boston put up a letter of credit, which allowed the tribe to issue a $13-million bond, known as a "lower floater," at remarkably low interest rates. "Our initial rate was under five percent," said Tom, "when prime was about ten." Cianbro wound up lending another $10 million in subordinate notes. The tribe had outgrown the need for its $3-million BIA loan guarantee, so they returned it. The bureau was so stunned it gave the tribe a half-million-dollar grant toward Dragon's purchase.

The assets passed from Cianchette to the tribe in a friendly atmosphere. According to Joe Koch, a Dragon vice-president, "Tom and the tribe were so forthright, and their relationship with Cianbro was so good, that during the last day of the closing, Bud Cianchette was adding things like trucks to their side of the balance sheet." The Passamaquoddies now owned the factory, the cement business itself, and a dozen redi-mix concrete factories scattered around the state: a $25.5-million stake, all told, and they still had paid no more than their original $2-million investment.

The leveraged buy-out, lease-back, buy-back history of Dragon is preserved in a Harvard Business School case study, served up year after year to aspiring entrepreneurs as an example of the way things ought to be done. On paper it has all the intentional precision of a Swiss watch, but at the time, Tom was learning investment banking on the fly. He made extensive use of college chums who had ended up in that world. In the summer of 1983, when they were getting down to the real intricacies, a financier who had graduated from Princeton a couple of years before Tom was spending a long summer vacation in Maine and began showing up at Tom's office.

Daniel Zilkha was an Egyptian, raised in France, who resided in the United States on an Italian passport. Born to a long line of bankers who had been doing business in the Middle East for several generations, Daniel had emigrated to Paris with his parents after World War II, and to America on his own a decade later. After Princeton and Harvard Business School, Daniel cofounded Soditic S.A. in 1971. A Geneva-based investment bank, Soditic had by 1978 become one of the major financial institutions in Switzerland. Daniel had married an American and was living in New York.

When forced to choose between moving to Switzerland to manage Soditic's explosive growth or leaving the bank, he cashed in his Soditic chips and founded *Art and Auction Magazine*.

Within four years the magazine was a full-color glossy with loads of advertising, a circulation of seventeen thousand, and high critical acclaim. But after the magazine had made it, the actual publishing of it began to bore Daniel. Which is why he was spending more time in Maine than New York, and how he fell in with Tom Tureen and the Passamaquoddies.

Tom had come to the conclusion that the Indians needed an investment bank dedicated to the management of their own affairs, and after the Dragon deal, he and Daniel decided to go into business together. On November 1, 1983, the two partners founded Tribal Assets Management, called "TAM" in company parlance.

When I met Daniel Zilkha at TAM headquarters, I found him as composed as Tom was frenetic. The phone rang, and Daniel chatted with the caller for five minutes, sometimes in French and sometimes in English. He lit a pipe and exhaled several cubic yards of smoke. "We started off thinking that we would be dealing only with New England tribes," he told me. "But the Dragon deal drove us into a national market. Now we represent tribes all over the country."

In 1985 TAM helped a Wisconsin band of Chippewa Indians secure $23.7 million to buy Simpson Electric, a manufacturer of electronic test equipment. The deal was done with *no* tribal cash down and involved no recourse to assets other than those acquired in the deal. In 1986, they arranged a $29-million junk-bond-supported leveraged buy-out of the Carolina Mirror Corporation (the largest mirror company in the United States) by the eastern band of Cherokees. TAM also configured a partnership between the Penobscot Indians and SHAPE Inc., a Maine electronics firm. The result was Olamon Industries, a factory on the Penobscot's Indian

Island Reservation, which manufactures high-quality tape cassettes and enough jobs to have slashed that tribe's unemployment rate from 50 percent to under 10 percent.

"Indians have been shut off from these avenues of economic development for years," said Daniel. "Our job is to give tribes access to capital and credit markets. Our approach has been to develop a variety of financing techniques, solve legal problems, create credibility, and provide opportunities to get our clients into the mainstream economy."

Both Tom and Daniel were quick to point out that their work is not charity. TAM bills its clients standard investment banking fees (except for the Passamaquoddies, who pay in accordance with returns on investments). "We won the land-claim suit because we were right," said Tom, "not because people felt sorry for Indians. People do business with us now because it makes financial sense."

Tom sees Tribal Assets' efforts on behalf of its Native American clients as more important than the big splash of the Maine land-claims settlement. "The land claims were a one-time deal," said Tom, "and they applied only to the Maine tribes." They also set Indians apart from their neighbors and made them lots of enemies. Tom expected that non-Indian jobs generated by Passamaquoddy business would transform any lingering tensions into gratitude. Furthermore, the precedents TAM was working to establish could be applied over and over again with tribes around the country.


I once followed Tom through a day in his professional life. We left Portland at 7:00 A.M. in his Beechcraft Bonanza, and on that crystal clear February morning made it down the Maine and Massachusetts coastlines to Boston's Logan Airport in less than an hour. We stopped first at the chic offices of a renowned money manager, who was hoping to supervise a portion of a western tribe's assets. A delegation from the tribe had flown in, and Tom was acting as mediator. The Indians were jet-lagged and city-shocked. The gray-flanneled Bostonians couldn't help staring at their ranch outfits. But Tom flitted between both groups until they forgot their mutual shyness.

The afternoon was spent at the Bank of Boston, where Tom was renegotiating a Passamaquoddy loan to reflect a recent drop in interest rates. Tom was barely seated, punctuating his argument with rapid gesticulations and jabbing the pinhead buttons of a high-tech calculator watch. On the flight back to Portland, he casually placed the plane's control stick in my rigid hands and radioed his office for messages.

Tom's Passamaquoddy clients deeply appreciate his tireless efforts on their behalf, and everyone I talked to praised his judgment and professionalism. At times, however, his intensity bewilders and amuses them. "I've known Tom for years," said one tribal admirer, "but I can hardly quiet him down enough to get him to talk about the Tom inside. There was one time. We'd flown somewhere for the day, and the weather went bad, so the plane couldn't fly home. We got stuck on a Greyhound for hours. And we had some real, wonderful conversation. That's when we became friends."


I returned to Eastport and Passamaquoddy Homes Incorporated several weeks after the gala opening. Without celebrants to fill it, the factory seemed almost deserted. Paul Weston, PHI's plant manager, a full-bearded white engineer in his early forties, clapped a blue hard hat on my head and took me onto the plant floor to explain why PHI's parallelized building system was a novel approach to construction.

"It takes eighteen hundred man hours to make a regular stick-built house," shouted Paul over the Uzi chatter of nail guns and the shriek of big saws. "The Finns average about six hundred hours, and they actually put the house together in three days. That's the system we're emulating." Like everyone at PHI, Paul insisted that the process was not "prefab." "Prefab is just building the way you would at a job-site but doing it indoors," he said. "It's the same old hammer, nails, and plywood." Not so at PHI, where pieces of buildings were constructed like widgets on an assembly line. At the front of the equipment stream, Paul stopped to point out the heart of Makroscan's technology—a pair of ominous, missile-shaped chemical tanks. The secret ingredients in each tank combined to produce a heavy foam that quick dried into the core of a PHI wall. As we watched, a rectangular frame of two-by-fours crept down the line into a sixty-ton press. The foam was pumped into it, like batter into a cake mold, and left to set for an hour. When all the panels of a building were baked, they would be loaded onto a truck in the order they would be assembled at the site, like a picture puzzle.

Of PHI's sixty employees, forty were Passamaquoddy Indians. In addition to the twenty Eastport factory workers were another dozen in Portland and twenty to thirty putting up the buildings in the field. According to PHI workers throwing the prebuilt parts up into a building was a sight to behold. A young, buoyant tribal member named Stan Harnois told me about the time he worked on the crew that erected the PHI exhibit for a construction trade show inside a Boston convention center. "We built a whole condo," said Stan. "Jeez, it had everything—concrete work, bay windows. We built it Monday and Tuesday, showed it Wednesday, and tore it down Thursday. Them other developers all had their little table displays, but the first thing you seen when you walked in was our two-story building. Jeez, it just blew everybody away. Some of them come up and donated plants to put around it. It looked really nice."

I asked Stan if it made a difference to him that the company he worked for was owned by his tribe. "Sure. I love it here. People ask me, 'You still working for PHI?' I tell 'em 'I *am* PHI.' I lost my company hat for a while and I was real upset, 'cause the company meant so much to me—and 'cause I'd earned it."

Stan's brother, Bill Harnois, worked upstairs in PHI's offices as Paul Weston's planning assistant. He had been a lab
technician at the tribal health clinic, "but the pay wasn't that
great," he said, "and my supervisor wasn't that smart. So I
quit. It took me seven months to get a seventy-cent raise
there. Here, it only took me three months to get a dollar
raise." I asked Bill if he noticed a big difference on the reservations since the land-claims settlement. "Not really," he
answered. "I don't think it's any better or any worse. If
they'd split up the money—now *that* would make a difference. I could have a new car, a house. The only difference
now is that we've got a lot of reporters coming 'round asking
us if it's any different."

Were his white neighbors a little more friendly than they
used to be?

"Aw, it's not a big deal anymore. Seven, eight years ago
there used to be a lot of trouble. The bridge [between Princeton and Indian Township] was like the DMZ. Used to be
fights on it all the time. I mean, it all goes back to when we
were so poor we used to steal people's blankets and stuff.
That's how a lot of prejudice started, and that's all over. Now
we got boys from Princeton coming over to the Township to
party, dating Indian girls. You know, it's all all right."

Stan Harnois felt differently. "I don't want to complain
about racism, but there are outsiders who would like nothing more than to be able to say, 'Look, we gave 'em eighty
million dollars and it's gone right out the window.' This place
is a direct reflection on the tribe. That's why I'm putting in
one hundred and ten percent, doing my damnest to make
sure things work out."

Between the Passamaquoddies' determination, the cali-
ber of their advisers, and their extraordinary track record,
PHI's success seemed a foregone conclusion. But I would
return to Maine in 1988 to be reminded that in the marketplace there is no such thing.

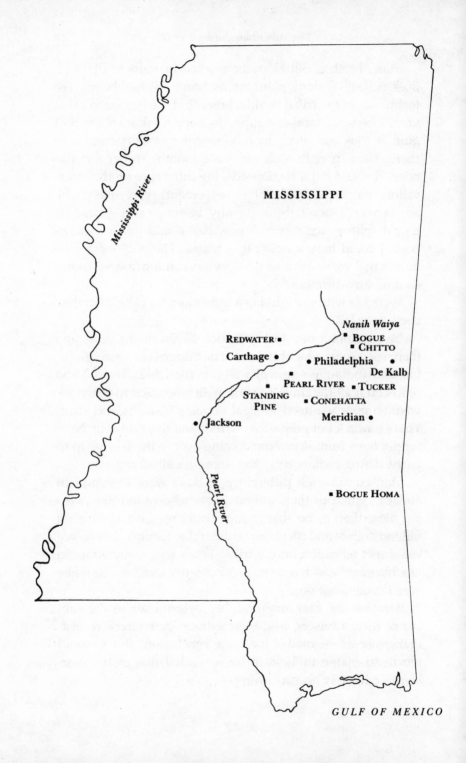

MISSISSIPPI

*Mississippi River*

*Nanih Waiya*

REDWATER ■
■ BOGUE
■ CHITTO

Carthage ●
● Philadelphia
● De Kalb

■
■ PEARL RIVER
■ TUCKER

STANDING
PINE
● CONEHATTA

● Jackson
Meridian ●

*Pearl River*

■ BOGUE HOMA

GULF OF MEXICO

# 2

## The Mississippi Band of Choctaw Indians

Although he is not yet forty, Beasley Denson is old enough to have spent his Mississippi childhood sharecropping. "Our family worked the land of a white preacher in a town called Missionary," he told me. "When we needed seed or fertilizer, the preacher would buy it up front. After the harvest, we'd pay him back before splitting the farm profit with him." One day, when Beasley was still a child, the preacher presented the Densons with a bill that included items Beasley's parents had never received. Beasley's father was so angry he actually raised his voice. He and the preacher nearly came to blows.

"That night the preacher got together with his white friends, and they came out to our place to teach my father a lesson." All night long, the white men circled the house looking for Beasley's father, while mother and children cowered inside, but Mr. Denson never showed up in Missionary again. Weeks after the incident, family friends came and took Mrs. Denson and her children to a place far away, where Beasley's father was waiting for them.

Beasley Denson is a Choctaw Indian, descended from a small band of Choctaws who remained on their Mississippi homeland while the rest of the tribe was removed to Oklahoma in the 1800s. An archipelago of tiny reservations was eventually established for the Mississippi Choctaws. The largest reservation lies just down the road from Philadelphia, Neshoba County's seat and perhaps the most infamous racist stronghold of the Deep South. Philadelphia is the town where civil rights volunteers Michael Schwerner, James Chaney, and Andrew Goodman were murdered in 1964, with the assistance of the local sheriff's office.

Neshoba takes its name from the Choctaw word for "wolf." One can hardly imagine less fertile soil for Native American survival—never mind economic development— than the region's red clay hills. Until late in the 1960s, the Mississippi Choctaws were so poor and isolated that only their nearest neighbors knew they existed.

To those whose knowledge of rural Mississippi is confined to the movies and the national press, first impressions of Neshoba County meet expectation. The red clay is there, all right. Wherever roadwork disrobes a hillside, a rich terracotta loam emerges, flaming under a tedious stratum of tan topsoil. Though colorful, Mississippi red clay is next to worthless—meager to begin with and leached by cotton harvests until it supports nothing but small livestock and stand after stand of pine. The highways are all two-laners, traveled by hand-painted pickups with rifle racks showing through their rear windows. A stranger is sorely tempted to conclude that sharecropping remains the district's economic mainstay, and that all the employers are white.

In fact, a number of those Philadelphia good-ol'-boys now work for Beasley Denson and the five thousand members of the Mississippi band of Choctaw Indians. As secretary-treasurer of the Choctaw Tribal Council, Beasley holds the second highest position in Choctaw government. Over the last seven years, enterprises established by this body have replaced the butt end of the local farm economy with fifteen hundred industrial jobs. The tribe is Mississippi's fifteenth largest employer, and a state whose per capita income is the lowest in the nation takes its leading employers seriously. Mississippi's lieutenant governor, Brad Dye, said, "If the state could get caught up with [the Choctaws] in economic development, we'd get off the bottom."

The bulk of the Choctaw economy lies off Route 16, seven miles west of Philadelphia in the tribe's own industrial park. Its heart is a two-acre expanse of beige corrugated steel called Chahta Enterprises. A Choctaw foreman named Carlton Isaac met me at Chahta's front door. A black breaker of hair curled high above Carlton's face, which bore the contemplative look of a Mexican farm worker. He was wearing blue jeans and a polo shirt with broad, muted stripes.

As we strolled through Chahta's murky, clamorous interior—thick with forklifts and drenched in Joni Mitchell oozing from hidden loudspeakers—Carlton explained the mysteries of wire-harness production. Sometimes by hand and sometimes by machine, Chahta employees cut to size hundreds of types and colors of wire and attach leads to each segment. They combine the resulting cables into the rainbow spaghetti that compose the electrical systems of automobiles and trucks. We passed by one machine that weaves fifty spools of black nylon into a fine mesh cover around a bundle of wires. Its Choctaw operator pulled the bundle up through the maelstrom of nylon fibers as if he were ladling a dollop of licorice from a kettle.

The original Chahta plant, now called Plant I or, more colloquially, the "Wire Harness," presently supplies harnesses for the Chevy V line and smaller harnesses that control mechanisms like automatic windows. Plant II, an extension attached to Plant I, serves Ford Motor Company and Navistar (the successor to International Harvester). The

Navistar harnesses I saw were huge, tentacled masses of wire and plastic hose that bear an uncomfortable resemblance to the anti-hero of the movie *Alien*.

Carlton is one of the Mississippi Choctaws' prodigal sons, lured away from the reservation in the years of tribal destitution. Over an orange soda in a Chahta coffee-break room, Carlton told me about his departure from the Mississippi Choctaws, and about his return. At first, he was reticent and watchful, genuinely surprised that anybody would be interested in his story.

Carlton grew up in Pearl River, in a family of eleven. His father worked twenty years for a paper company in Union, Mississippi, until the plant closed. Like many Choctaw families, the Isaacs, parents and children, ended up alongside Mississippi blacks in the long, seasonal march of harvests to the Delta. As soon as he was old enough, Carlton went into the army. After his tour of duty, its last eight months in Vietnam, he settled in Chicago's north side and for twelve years went from shipping-yard work to assembly lines, to material handling, all the while struggling—along with the neighborhood's poor blacks, poor Asians, poor Indians, and poor Appalachian whites—to raise a family. He was laid off in the late 1970s, and the longer he tried to hang on in Chicago, the better Mississippi looked. "I was afraid of what would happen to the kids if we stayed in the city. The older they got, the more worried about street gangs *I* got. I came down here, and I told the tribe everything I'd done in my life and that I wanted to work."

The tribe employed Isaac in odd jobs for three months, until Chahta began its first round of hiring. He was placed in a "utilities" job, maintaining the equipment and teaching himself to run every station so he could fill in when someone was absent. In four months he was a supervisor. Now he manages some forty line workers, who fondly refer to him as "Coach." His wife, two of his sons, two of his sisters, and one brother all work in tribal businesses.

Back on the shop floor, Carlton showed me how most of Chahta's work is accomplished on assembly lines, where parts march slowly by the flying hands of Choctaw, black, and white workers. (The plant maintains Choctaw preference in hiring, but only in situations of equal qualification.) The workers are casually intent. A General Motors sign hanging from the rafters admonishes them:

> PUSH, CLICK, AND TUG
> CHOCTAW INDIAN
> QUALITY IS NUMBER ONE.

Although Chahta is an independent supplier, some of its clients keep close tabs on the production process. Ford sends an inspector over about once a week. When asked how Chahta weathers these visits, Isaac shrugs. "We've been good for so long that anything under a perfect score is not good enough."

Chahta Enterprises shares the Choctaw industrial park with Choctaw Greetings Enterprise. The "Greeting Card" (in local parlance) is a 120,000-square-foot facility, one of many owned by American Greetings, a billion-dollar corporation that together with Hallmark makes up most of the U.S. greeting-card industry. In addition to greeting cards, American Greetings has created such denizens of Saturday-morning television as Ziggy, Strawberry Shortcake, and the Care Bears, whose first feature-length movie came in second behind Rambo at the box office, according to the Choctaw Greetings plant manager, Joe Young.

A typical American Greetings card travels through five plants in four states before it becomes a salable item. Choctaw Greetings is a hand-finishing plant, which assembles cards that have been printed on big sheets of stock in Ripley, Tennessee, and die cut to individual units in Osceola, Ar-

kansas. "The tribe was looking for a labor-intensive enterprise, and that's what it got," said Joe. "In this market,
people are more efficient than machines. American Greetings has the technical expertise to build machines capable of
handling most of the work, but print runs are short. We'd
practically have to build a new machine for every different
card, and that's not economically feasible."

After the Wire Harness, the Greeting Card appeared
solidly low-tech. The factory is a full acre larger than Chahta
Enterprises, and the lack of noise inside was spooky. I saw
hardly any equipment, and the only discernible noise was
the variable hiss of paper slipping through two hundred
workers' hands. The place looked like a sweatshop but
lacked the feel of one. There was plenty of banter. Joe Young
gave his workers grief, and they gave it back.

One employee was assembling a card containing a silicon
chip that plays an electronic version of "Beautiful Dreamer."

"Do you get tired of the tune?"

"I dream about it every night," she laughed.

Another employee, named Adriana Burt, was working on
a card with a cover that read, "I cleaned my room from floor
to ceiling. Please don't open the closet door." Joe flipped the
card open, and a pile of junk popped up and out. Adriana's
job was to fold these pop-outs, paint a perfect glue stroke on
each one, and slide it into a card.

"Each card has a predetermined production rate," said
Joe. "Adriana's is one hundred and twenty-four an hour."

"How many is that a day?" I asked.

"Nine hundred ninety-two," Adriana answered in-
stantaneously—and broke into laughter again.

"The base salary here is five dollars and twenty cents an
hour," said Joe. "But Adriana's paid extra for every card she
produces over that rate. Last year, she made a hundred and
twenty-seven percent efficiency, so she got a twenty-seven
percent 'raise' for the year. The majority of our employees
exceed one hundred percent."

The Choctaw/American Greetings deal was struck with the help of a Mississippi state revenue bond. Because the tribe has no official relationship with the state, there was no precedent for such an instrument. But tribal officials convinced Mississippi bureaucrats that the state couldn't afford to pass up the jobs. Mississippi allowed the tribe to lease the tribal land under the new plant to the city of Philadelphia, which then petitioned for the bond like any other municipality. In lieu of rent to the tribe for use of the office park, American Greetings is paying off the Philadelphia bond. When it has done so, the land will revert to the tribe, along with the plant American Greetings has built on it.

Choctaw Greetings' personnel director is Henderson Williams, a Choctaw who, like Carlton Isaac, spent some time away before coming back to work in tribal enterprise. Henderson went to college in Chicago and afterward worked in Michigan for an electrical supply company. "The rural people in Michigan were similar to rural Mississipians," he said. "They pretty much let me know they knew I was an Indian— called me 'Chief.' I thought, 'If they keep calling me Chief, one of these days I might actually be one.' I suppose I was out to prove being an Indian was no handicap. Well, it worked. The company saw fit to promote me several times when I was out there."

Like Carlton Isaac and so many other Choctaws who left in search of better jobs, Henderson returned when reservation prospects brightened. He worked in tribal government before coming to Choctaw Greetings and admitted that the switch to business management had been somewhat rough. "In tribal government, I looked at everything from the perspective of people's needs," he said. At the Greeting Card, he sometimes had to turn down needy applicants who failed company standards. "Here I am, an Indian talking to another Indian; if this guy's got twelve kids in the house, his wife's expecting another one, I know he's gotta have a job. I had some problems, until I realized that if we don't fill the jobs with people who are motivated, enthusiastic, ambitious, we won't fill the need of the company, and then the company wouldn't be here to provide employment."

Henderson had also found room for compassion within the confines of business sense. He admitted to sometimes bending work rules around workers' problems. "Most of the people who work here have kids at home," he said. "Their kids get sick, they have to go home and take care of them, and we sometimes get absenteeism. I would respect parents more for going home to take care of their children than leaving them with a baby-sitter."

The first Choctaw leader to greet a white man was the first to be captured by one. In 1540, the conquistador Hernando de Soto—seeking porters, women, and safe passage through Indian country—invited Tashka Losa (whose corrupted name is "Tuscaloosa") to join his entourage, and then kept him as insurance. Tashka Losa, in turn, lured de Soto and his men with the promise of sensual appeasement to the Choctaw settlement of Mabila. After allowing the Spaniards to debauch themselves, Mabila's citizens attacked, liberating Tashka Losa and sacrificing their community to Spanish arson in the process of routing de Soto. Written testimony of a Spanish survivor depicts the cold resolve of the Choctaw combatants, who hanged themselves with their bowstrings rather than be taken captive. In the end, de Soto decided Choctaw Country wasn't worth the trouble and moved on.

Before the European invasion of America, the Choctaws dominated the Southeast, both in numbers and in language, because pidgin Choctaw was the common language of trade among the Creek, Chickasaw, Seminole, Alabama, Mikasuki, and other peoples of the region. On the profits of surplus produce, the Choctaw population radiated from its Mississippi center east to Florida and west to Louisiana.

Although they had their bouts of violent confrontation, the Choctaws generally favored business over warfare: they were the late twentieth-century Japanese of the pre-European South.

There ends any parallel with modern capitalism, however, for the Choctaw economy was entirely communal. There was no private property; the surplus of the able supported the weak. The political culture of the Choctaws was remarkably fluid. There were family lines of leadership, but no divine guarantees of succession. Tribal governance was divided along functional lines of war and peace among several leaders, called *mikos*. Warriors and statesmen had been known to rise on the strength of deeds.

For a century and a half the Choctaws—practical, as always—continued to adopt those European practices they deemed worthwhile. They employed imported horses and new agricultural techniques to enhance further their economic advantage. They even bankrolled missionaries to set up schools in their settlements. The Choctaws were also practical in their political allegiances. During the American Revolution, Choctaw warriors scouted for Washington, while Choctaw statesmen signed treaties with England. In 1783, when the *miko* Franchimastabe went to Georgia to make peace with the new United States, his tribesmen signed a treaty at Mobile with the Spaniards.

As the turning plow augmented agricultural skills, however, cash crops began to supplant, rather than augment, Choctaw subsistence. While chasing after the new American dream, the Choctaws fell into dependency, and when whites began to eat into their land base, the final decline of the Choctaws began. The end came quickly. Through eight treaties over the first three decades of the nineteenth century, the Choctaw universe vanished: 75 million acres—three-fourths of the present state of Mississippi, a goodly chunk of Alabama, and most of western Florida—were signed over to the United States. In return, the Choctaws received paper oaths and property in the Oklahoma and Arkansas territories recently wrested by the federal government from other tribes. A few Choctaws went out to check on the western allotments and found some of them already occupied by white settlers.

In 1824, the *miko* Pushmataha led a delegation of protest to Washington, where he died of a throat infection before he could make his plea. (By some accounts, he was poisoned.) In recognition of Choctaw support in the War of 1812, Pushmataha was accorded a full state military funeral, attended by some two thousand Washingtonians. His grave is in the Old Congressional Cemetery. According to federal records, James McDonald, a mixed-blood Choctaw who lived in the District of Columbia, was left to plead Pushmataha's case with heartbreaking trust: "You cannot persuade all to remove. . . . What will you do with those that remain? What measures will you adopt to improve their condition . . . ? We leave the issue of the question to your wisdom and to the liberality of the South."

Four years later, Pushmataha's old comrade-in-arms, Andrew Jackson, was elected president of the United States. One of his first legislative triumphs was the Indian Removal Act, a campaign to banish to the West any portion of America's Native population that stood in the way of white progress. In 1830, the Choctaws were forced to sign away the last 10 million acres of their land in the Treaty of Dancing Rabbit Creek. The treaty was conducted by the secretary of war. Negotiations lasted two days, but after the first day the majority of Choctaw representatives walked out. The minority who remained to sign the document were primarily mixed-bloods.

As a sop, the United States agreed to reserve allotments for those Choctaws who insisted on remaining in Mississippi. The government expected to grant these to a handful of mixed-bloods. (One of these, Greenwood LeFlore, was a *miko* whose support of Choctaw removal earned him a 15,000-acre plantation, four hundred black slaves, and a seat in the Mississippi senate.) As it was, hundreds of Choctaws applied for scraps of Mississippi. They might easily have numbered in the thousands, except that William Ward, a drunk assigned to administer the allotment program, regularly ducked petitioners and used Choctaw applications for his personal hygiene. In the end, only three hundred individuals were allotted land, half of them white men with Choctaw wives. Several thousand others remained in Mississippi, illegal inhabitants in their ancient domicile.

Some twelve thousand Choctaws took the long walk to Oklahoma. Alexis de Tocqueville was at Memphis to witness their passage across the Mississippi and wrote: "The snow was hard on the ground, and huge masses of ice drifted on the river. The Indians brought . . . the wounded, the sick, newborn babies, and old men on the point of death. . . . The sight will never fade from my memory."

After removal, the landless Mississippi Choctaws lived behind enemy lines, driven farther and farther into the backwoods. The state jailed them whenever it could. A white planter named Joseph Beckham Cobb wrote that the state of Choctaw existence after removal was far worse than that of black slaves. In a splendid example of nineteenth-century doublethink, Cobb justified this state of affairs in a volume called *Sketches*:

> The Indians of our day, besides having a full share of all the lower and degrading vices of the Southern negro [*sic*], such as stealing, lying and filthy tastes, are noted for cowardice, and craft, and meanness of every description. . . . I do not know a negro that would countenance an exchange of situations with a Choctaw . . . as a general thing, these are hardly above animals.

Why would any Choctaw remain in Mississippi under such circumstances? Partly because Oklahoma was no bargain, but partly for the same reason a broken farm family hangs on to the homestead in Wisconsin while factory jobs lie fallow in Detroit. As a Choctaw leader told a federal removal agent in 1843, "Our warriors are nearly all gone to the far country west; but *here* are our dead. Shall we go too, and give their bones to the wolves?"

After the Civil War, the cord of the Mississippi Choctaws unraveled into threads. Even the most meager land scraps fell into white hands. At the turn of this century, the Choctaw community of Tucker consisted of a Catholic mission's tiny congregation, squatting on the mission's grounds. If extinction's failure qualifies as human survival, the Mississippi band of Choctaw Indians survived. Barely. By 1891 the Choctaw population in Mississippi had dropped to 2,000; by 1910 to 1,253. In 1918, one-fifth of the remaining population was killed in a flu epidemic.

The Mississippi Choctaws had bottomed out. Moved at last by this carnage, the BIA established the Choctaw Indian Agency in Philadelphia. By 1930, the number of Choctaw births exceeded the number of Choctaw deaths. By 1944, the federal government had purchased 18,000 acres, apportioned among eight Choctaw communities: Pearl River, Red Water, Bogue Chitto, Tucker, Standing Pine, Crystal Ridge, Conehatta, and Bogue Homa. Together these constituted the Mississippi Choctaw Reservation, one of the poorest sectors of America.

One tribal member remembers Choctaw life then as "a shack in a clearing at the edge of a cotton field, by a grove of pecan trees or pine trees. A dog or two in the yard. No plumbing, no electricity. The man of the family gets up early and gets the fire going. He's a sharecropper. The family depends on the cotton crop to make it for them. If it doesn't make it, then they're in a hole for the winter months. Somehow they survive, probably on credit alone."

In 1945, the tribe voted to adopt a U.S.-style constitution as a component of its official recognition by the federal government. "Constitutional government was alien to us," one Choctaw recalls. "Many thought it was better to run things out of our living rooms, where whites would leave us alone. After the vote came through in favor of the constitution, things ran the way we were afraid they would. The superintendent here called the shots."

To meet the man tribal members call "the architect of Choctaw economic development," I drove beyond the industrial park and took a left off Route 16 at a plain white-on-green highway sign that read CHOCTAW INDIAN RESERVATION. The road wound by a low, white-steepled, yellow brick Catholic church. Across from the church, behind a large playing field, lay the Choctaw Central High sports arena, like the longitudinal half of an enormous corrugated-steel pipe, with WARRIORS painted on it in white block letters. Past the arena, a road forked to the right and into the parking lot of the tribal headquarters. There were big American cars: Cutlasses, Sevilles, a white Ford Bronco. Bordering two sides of the lot was an L of single-storied, brown-stained pine-board buildings. The modest complex was exactly like a national park ranger's station—except for the green-and-orange striped awning over its main entrance, flanked by a sign that read OFFICE OF THE CHIEF.

Inside, the atmosphere was relaxed but energetic. Men and women with chestnut complexions walked swiftly by in slacks and open-collared shirts. Conversations in English were punctuated by brief bursts of Choctaw. Mysterious, almost oriental to my uninitiated ear, the Native tongue seemed to consist of long series of staccato *o* and *u* vowels interrupted by rising whole notes of short *a*s. Well over 90 percent of the Mississippi Choctaw population is fluent in Choctaw; most of them speak it as their first language.

Phillip Martin, chief of the Mississippi band of Choctaw Indians, came out of his office in a light cardigan sweater over a polo shirt and sharply creased brown trousers. He shook my hand and put his arm gently around my shoulders, the better to guide me back outside for a short drive into Phila-delphia and a steak at the Western Sizzlin'. Phillip's Cadillac was in the shop having a new windshield installed, so we took his wife's Buick. Phillip started the engine and donned a pair of designer sunglasses. Above his broad, shallow nose and full, sharp-edged lips, they created the fleeting impres-sion of a Hawaiian tour guide. Moderately tall and comfort-ably trim, with an unlined molasses-colored face, Phillip still looked like photographs taken of him ten years ago.

At the Sizzlin' (a sort of McDonald's that serves steak instead of hamburger), Phillip worked his way through the crowd to an empty table. Mild shouts of "Hey, Chief!" dogged him around the room, some from Indians and some from whites. Phillip responded to all with a lifted hand and benevolent smile.

In thirty years of tribal leadership, Phillip has achieved the stature of elder statesman, known throughout Indian Country—and among a number of major American manufacturers—for his Mississippi miracle. A Native Amer-ican amalgamation of Lee Iacocca and Clark Clifford, an industrialist who advises legislators and bureaucrats, Phillip Martin has done more for his people than any Choctaw leader in half a millennium.

"I have known Phil for many, many years," said Passama-quoddy spokesman Wayne Newell, "and I think he's a very interesting guy. The Choctaws didn't have the money from a land-claim settlement like we did, but I think that Phillip always had a vision of how he wanted things done. He also has the balls to tell the feds, 'You guys help us do it with your resources, but we aren't going to let you screw it up too much.' Federal policy has been nothing but a total disaster nationally. They need success stories. Phil Martin exploits that very effectively."

In answering questions that began over lunch and continued over a period of days, Phillip Martin proved to be more uncomplicated, friendly, attentive, and forgiving of ignorance about his constituents than his position and accomplishments would imply.

The third of six children, Phillip was the son of a janitor for the Philadelphia BIA office. "The agency built a home for us," said Phillip, "which burned down a year after we moved into it." His childhood was meager but happy. "We played with white kids whose parents worked for the agency, and with some black kids who lived nearby. Basketball sometimes, but mostly we played cowboys and Indians. Somehow the white kids used to end up being the Indians."

Phillip told me that early on he "showed potential—for trouble." It is unclear whether this "potential" was a factor in the events that occurred after his father died in 1937. As Phillip told the story, "the agency started working on me to go away to a BIA boarding school in North Carolina. I didn't want to go. My father had just died, and I was eleven years old. But that superintendent kept working on me. I finally told him, 'I can't go. I don't have enough clothes.' 'Don't worry,' he said, 'we'll get you some clothes.' So we struck a deal: the clothes for the trip. The superintendent broke his promise. I ended up in Cherokee with the clothes I had on."

At the BIA school, there were plenty of Indian kids in young Phillip's boat. The school had a program that allowed students to work half a day and attend school the other half. With the pin money they earned they bought clothes from an on-campus army-surplus collection. "I was way behind most of the other students," said Phillip. "My English was really poor, and most of the other kids spoke Cherokee when they weren't speaking English. I had one English teacher, though, who carried me along and worked hard to help me catch up. It wasn't a bad experience. . . ." Phillip lived at school, winter and summer, for six years. He went home to Mississippi once during that entire period. Was he homesick? "Not really. After a while, it got to *be* my home."

Phillip entered the air force as soon as he received his high school diploma. His initial tours of duty were in postwar Europe—France, Belgium, and Germany. "Germany was my best experience in Europe, if you can believe it. The people were determined to build themselves back up after the war. And they were friendly." After Europe, Phillip went on to Okinawa, then to San Francisco with SAC's 3903rd Radar Bomb Squadron, and finally to Bangor, Maine, where he served as a sergeant in an early-warning installation.

In August 1955 he completed his discharge papers and boarded the first in a long, hot line of buses that eventually deposited him at his childhood home in Pearl River. A year earlier, during a rare visit to Choctaw Country, he had fallen in love with a Choctaw woman named Bonnie Kate Bell. They had married, and Phillip had returned to Maine soon after the ceremony to complete his last months of service. He had intended this summer homecoming to last only until he could find work elsewhere and take his bride away.

"I thought maybe I'd find us something in Chicago or back in San Francisco—anywhere but the place I'd come from." He could hardly be blamed for finding little to keep him there. At thirty, Phillip was a citizen of a much larger and richer world than the one to which he had been born. After nineteen years away from the tribe, his Choctaw affiliation was practically nominal. And the aggregate reality of Mississippi Choctaw existence at that time was dismal. Unemployment ranged seasonally between 50 and 80 percent. Choctaw life expectancy was so low that from a population of three thousand there were only two hundred tribal members over sixty-five. As a tribal historian described it then,

"Family life on the reservations is in a deplorable state. . . . Drunkenness . . . and gross sex immoralities prevail. . . . Jealousies, distrust, bitterness, and resentments are common."

This dark Mississippi portrait was common to Indian Country as a whole in the 1950s. The prevailing federal response was to encourage Indians to move off reservations and into the cities, through massive relocation programs. By the late 1950s, up to a quarter of the Mississippi Choctaw population lived in Los Angeles, Chicago, and Cleveland, vanishing with their dreams into the undifferentiated mass of the urban poor. Those without dreams stayed in Mississippi, where farm-wage rates of $2.50 a day put them at the bottom of Mississippi's rickety economic ladder. With an average annual income of $600 per family, they were more properly defined as off the bottom rung.

Their white neighbors, many scarcely better off, were determined to see the Choctaws stay there. Roger Bell, Bonnie Kate's brother and now a Choctaw council member, returned to Philadelphia from an armed-forces stint at about the same time as Phillip Martin. Roger had been stationed in Europe and elsewhere and had grown used to going wherever he pleased. One day shortly after coming home, he walked through the front door of a restaurant in town and was told to "go 'round back." Roger wasn't having any of it, so a scuffle ensued. By the time he drove back home, there were several local police cars on his tail. He was taken in and booked on assault charges. The police made no attempt to prosecute the white men who had been involved.

"All I could see in Neshoba was discrimination, no job opportunities, and poverty," said Phillip. "I was all set to get out and hit the big city, even though I had no specific job in mind." His plans were interrupted when his bride secured a job as a secretary in the Choctaw Agency. "She'd worked very hard to get that position," said Phillip, "and she didn't want to give it up as soon as she'd gotten it. It wasn't a matter of pride, but of necessity. She figured one job in hand was better than none in the bush."

Bonnie asked Phillip to stay. Phillip decided "to give it a whirl." The couple moved into the small house Phillip's mother shared with several other relatives, and Phillip remedied their imposition by installing modern plumbing. He took courses at a junior college in nearby Meridian and found work wiring his friends' unelectrified houses. Eventually he took a job in the maintenance department at the Meridian Naval Air Station, and the family's finances stabilized somewhat.

Still, Phillip could never keep himself busy enough to put the condition of the Choctaws out of his mind. He remembered Germany—an entire society rising from its own ashes—and he began to think that Choctaw circumstances, as bad as they were, were not acts of God but of men, and subject to change.

Phillip began to sit in on the meetings of the Choctaw Tribal Council. The council had no facilities of its own, so the meetings were held in the kitchen of a home-economics classroom in the Choctaw Agency, under the eyes of the local BIA superintendent. Council jobs didn't pay, and having neither time nor energy left over from their day jobs, council members ceded their governance to the eager superintendent. This federal surrogate dominated the lives of the entire Mississippi Choctaw population, because the agency was the sole source of the meager services they received. After observing the farce for a year or two, Phillip decided to run for a position on the council. He was elected in 1957, and two years later he became tribal chairman, the leader of the Mississippi band. Phillip knew that his chairmanship was hollow. He also knew that the local powers-that-be would do precious little to change the status quo. In unconscious emulation of his predecessor Pushmataha, Phillip decided to appeal directly to Washington.

When the superintendent at Philadelphia learned of Phillip's end-run plans, he orchestrated a Choctaw "state visit" to BIA headquarters. As Phillip recalled, "We were driven up in an agency car, and the red carpet was rolled out. The head of the BIA and about twenty-five undersecretaries shook our hands. We weren't used to making formal presentations, and there was this big audience of bureaucrats. It was intimidating, and we struggled through, but absolutely nothing substantial was accomplished."

A second trip to Washington was made, no more satisfying than the first, and Phillip thought, "I've been all over the world. I don't need to be *taken* to Washington." One day in 1959, a Choctaw delegation went up to Washington on its own. "We traveled in one of the council member's cars— Emmet York, Bobby Hickman, J. C. Allen, and I. The superintendent didn't know until after we'd left that we were on our way. We didn't tell Washington we were coming, neither. We just showed up and caught 'em in the hallways. They recognized who we were, and I think they had more respect for us because we were able to do that."

One of the things on the council's agenda was the Choctaw Agency superintendent himself. The Choctaw council hoped to replace him with somebody free from local ties and a lot more sensitive to their concerns. Phillip's delegation persuaded BIA officials in Washington to come to Mississippi and see for themselves the plight of the Choctaws. With typical federal response, a more congenial superintendent was assigned—five years later.

By 1962, the end of Phillip's second term as chairman, the council decided to take full advantage of his brass by making the chairmanship a full-time, paid position. They managed to squeeze a salary out of revenue from the timbering of pine trees on tribal lands, and the job was offered to Phillip— who balked. "I hesitated for about a year, even though the original idea had been mine. You have to realize that we had nothing then, not an office, not a pencil. I just didn't know if we could pull off anything substantial." Finally, in 1963, Phillip quit his job in Meridian to devote himself to the tribal chairmanship.

The timing could not have been less propitious. On June 22, 1964, a few months after Phillip had taken office, several Choctaws found the charred skeleton of a 1963 Ford Fairlane in the swamp of Bogue Chitto. It turned out to be the car that Goodman, Schwerner, and Chaney had ridden in to their terminal midsummer's nightmare. The ensuing storm of publicity sent the town of Philadelphia into such a racial frenzy that according to a citizen who lived through it, there were nights when "if a car had backfired, half the town would have died." The more attention was paid to Neshoba County, the more recalcitrant its white citizens seemed to become. A month after the murder victims were found, Nanih Waiya Church, a Mennonite mission to the Choctaws in northern Neshoba County, was bombed. Nevin Bender, its pastor, thought his parish was singled out because he had enjoyed modest success in weaning Choctaw men from bootleg whiskey and helping Choctaw women duck the imposed affections of the bootleggers themselves.

Philadelphia—which insists it is a city, although its population is seven thousand—still retains the dusty town square and vintage storefronts that were endlessly photographed during the 1960s. The white locals may pronounce their hometown with the cracker crunch, "Fulladeffia," but I left with many impressions that their attitudes had changed. Profoundly. There were black policemen on Philadelphia's streets and families of all colors sharing tables at the Pizza Hut. Lawrence A. Rainey, the sheriff who terrorized the town's blacks during the civil rights war, now works as a mall guard for E. E. McDonald, the black owner of a security service. In 1987, Philadelphia's senior high school class crowned a black homecoming queen. All of these changes are enough to put southward finger-pointing cities like Boston to shame.

Choctaw enterprises currently pump $16 million through 1,200 jobs into Neshoba and neighboring counties. A new Chahta plant, to be erected near Conehatta, and the new Choctaw Shopping Center on Route 16 will eventually produce an additional 220 jobs. The shopping center will also plug a perennial leak in the Choctaw economy. Until now, all of the salaries earned in tribal enterprise have been spent in Philadelphia's retail district. But the Choctaw Shopping Center—with its gas station/car wash, post office, variety store, and a restaurant and laundromat both owned by Choctaw entrepreneurs—will keep more dollars circulating within the reservation.

As early as 1966 a few signs of change had emerged. When the Nanih Waiya church was attacked for a third time in that same year, a group of white Neshobans raised funds to help rebuild it. The evolution of local attitudes helped the Choctaws, but their evolving relations with the federal government affected the tribe's fortunes more deeply. In the mid-1960s, the entire structure of the BIA was recast. In a broad effort to correct the agency's traditional paternalism, meager funding, and feeble service delivery, a host of new initiatives geared toward tribal self-determination and economic self-sufficiency were announced. This revolution from within the federal Indian establishment was augmented by the Great Society programs, which were aimed at all of America's disenfranchised citizens, including Indians. Money erupted from the volcano of the Great Society in a shower of acronyms: OEO (Office of Economic Opportunity), CAP (Community Action Agency), EDA (Economic Development Administration).

Many other Native communities interpreted these initiatives as warmed-over Great White Fatherism and rejected them, but the Choctaws interpreted each expression of federal largess with biblical fundamentalism and went after everything the government had to offer. In 1966 the tribe won a $15,000 grant from the OEO to develop a plan to wage war on its own poverty.

Realizing that destitution was the Choctaws' greatest asset in the quest for federal assistance, Phillip spent part of the grant on a survey of their standard of living. The survey's final report concluded that 90 percent of the Mississippi band lived in poverty, with average family incomes of less than $1,000 a year. The report also strongly recommended the creation of an administrative office that would allow the tribe to tailor federal funds to the specific requirements of the Choctaw community. Later in the year, with the balance of their OEO money, the Choctaw council launched CAP, the Community Action Program.

Phillip stepped over from the tribal chair to become CAP's executive director. Once in place, he decided to deal first with tribal housing. Choctaw generations were living on top of one another in unheated, unplumbed, unelectrified shotgun shacks left over from the New Deal. In 1969, Phillip requested a substantial HUD housing allotment to remedy these conditions. When the funds were secured, he created the Choctaw Housing Authority to administer them.

In addition to his duties at CAP, Phillip became chairman of the housing authority's board of commissioners. The authority founded Chata Development Company, a tribally owned construction firm, which employed tribal members as workmen. (*Chata*—which in other instances the tribe spells *Chahta*—is a closer approximation of the Native pronunciation of "Choctaw.") Chata was up and running by 1969. Its first client was HUD's grant.

Chata won the right to act as a federal contractor by invoking a nineteenth-century law called the Buy Indian Act, which decreed that government agencies on or near

Indian reservations would purchase Indian products whenever possible. Chata's relationship to HUD was the rough equivalent of General Dynamics's relationship with the Pentagon, except that in Chata's case the Choctaws billed the federal government for delivering federal funds to themselves. In essence the Choctaws were able to receive HUD money twice—once when HUD paid for the decent housing that individual Choctaws could never afford, and once again when Chata's employees received their paychecks.

By 1974, Chata had housed half the tribe in modern brick plumbed houses, and had secured government contracts to build community centers in each of the seven Choctaw reservations. In 1975, Gerald Ford enacted the Indian Self-Determination and Educational Assistance Act, which allowed tribes in general to contract federal programs and encouraged them to develop their own delivery systems for these funds. The only stories that made it out of Indian Country to the general public in the years following the legislation were ones of waste and graft, as tribal governments struggled against their own internal politics and bureaucratic inexperience to manage the deluge of mandated generosity.

The Mississippi band avoided these problems with clear and consistent financial, personnel, and election policies. At Chata Development, for example, the company paid no dividends to its tribal board members, so there was no possible conflict of interest to sour the arrangement.

For the Mississippi Choctaws, the Self-Determination Act inaugurated a gradual process, continuing today, whereby the tribe has assumed responsibility for managing its own federally funded programs. In the beginning, the tribe contracted small programs like Head Start, which were easy to manage. The Choctaws who staffed these programs gained the job skills and bureaucratic savvy they needed to take on adult education, employment assistance, and an agricultural-extension program. They also became adept at grant writing and have since grown accustomed to winning in competitive funding situations.

But the real secret of the Choctaws' success was their demand for "indirect costs," a form of unrestricted overhead the tribe had long claimed as a portion of most federal funds it received. This is a common practice among major institutions such as universities, which routinely earmark as much as half of government and charitable grants to pay for in-house operating expenses. The Mississippi Choctaws were the first Indians to qualify for such federal payments, and they have used these funds to hire some one hundred employees to build a strong, professional tribal administration.

In the end, the foundation of the Mississippi Choctaw miracle was a bootstrap. In convincing the federal government to help them and then insisting on being allowed to help themselves, the Choctaws developed their ability to govern and to manage and thereby established a base of economic development.

The Choctaws evolved as a political entity during the decade of Red Power, the heyday of radical Indian politics, but they remained above the fray, avoiding the uncompromising positions of other tribes. In 1969, Emmet York, Choctaw council chairman during Phillip's tenure at CAP, went to San Francisco to meet with the group called Indians of All Tribes, which had occupied Alcatraz. Several times, the activists turned Emmet away from the island's shore because he wasn't on their list of "good Indians." When finally they agreed to give him a tour, Emmet was profoundly unimpressed. He returned to Mississippi and told the tribe's historian, Bob Ferguson, "I don't know what they want with that damned rock."

Neither were the Choctaws managerial demagogues. From the beginning they recruited any expertise they required, regardless of race or background. The Choctaw gov-

ernment still retains a visible representation of white lawyers, planners, teachers, managers, and financial consultants. These nonethnocentric hiring policies have never
diminished the Choctaws' desire for control over their own
destiny. In 1972, the tribe achieved its greatest triumph of
self-determination when the BIA—after first protesting his
"conflict of interest"—finally appointed a Choctaw, Robert
Benn, as superintendent of the Choctaw Agency.

Robert Benn was still in place in 1988, wreathed in clouds of
L & M smoke in a cinder-block, good-enough-for-government-
work office in downtown Philadelphia. Through this man-
made fog, Robert appeared with his neatly combed hair and
powder-blue cardigan wearing a Mr. Rogers smile. He told me
the pile of paper on his desk was the full set of instructions
for handling requests under the Freedom of Information Act.
He answered my questions readily enough, with fine
humor, in a deep, nasal voice.

"For my first BIA job as a housing officer, I just submitted
my application. That wasn't no big deal, 'cause by then the
law said an Indian qualifies for a job in the bureau, he gets
first shot at it. The superintendent thing was a little bit
different, because at that time there was a big debate in the
BIA about whether an Indian should be superintendent of
his own reservation: you know, concentration of power, conflict of interest—those kinds of things. I understand there
was a big fight to clear the way for me here. The tribe went to
Washington to talk to the people who were doing the hiring,
and I think they talked to some congressional people, but I
wasn't involved. Of course, the time was ripe. The atmosphere was beginning to be right for Indians to run their
own lives."

Robert grew up with larger tribal matters. His father had
been a council member and one of the community's lead-

ers in the 1930s and 1940s. "People would always come to
my daddy for advice. I remember as a little kid trying to
sleep while people talked to him about their problems."
After skirting Mississippi's segregated educational system
through several denominational schools, Robert graduated
from Mississippi College in 1956. He was the third college
graduate in Mississippi Choctaw history, and the tribe was
quick to exploit his superior skill in English to write their
council resolutions while he was still in school. Robert went
into the navy after he graduated and came out in 1961.

"I hadn't given any thought to coming back here one way
or another," he said. "But I ended up working for a newspaper in Carthage and, while I was at it, served as a Choctaw
council member. At the paper, I would hear about things
happening elsewhere. I was influenced by the 1960s and the
beginning of Indians doing their own thing."

When Robert was first appointed superintendent, the
majority of the BIA employees were non-Indians. Fifteen
years later, 85 to 90 percent of his staff are Choctaws. "We
stumbled a while because we were training these youngsters
to come up to professional standards. But the kids we hired
took it and ran." In addition to bringing in Choctaw employees, Robert has been an active partner in helping the
tribe contract services from the BIA. In effect, he has slowly
dismantled his place of employment. Half of his original
social-services staffers, for example, now work for the tribe.

He said the only thing that sometimes bothered him was
having to terminate agency positions. "I always believed in
the concept that services should be provided by Indians," he
said. "But when the tribe wins a contract, I have to kick
people off my staff, and I don't like to do that. It becomes
awfully personal. I know these people. I know their families,
their kids. If you're not careful, it'll mess up your mind.
Luckily, most of the people who wanted to were able to
switch their paychecks from the bureau to the tribe."

I asked Robert if he thought the generally negative attitude of Indians toward the BIA was justified. "Well, the BIA
is guilty of a lot of the things they're accused of. And the
easiest way for an Indian guy to get some publicity is to get
some air time and cuss the hell out of the BIA. If you're the
BIA guy, you're the father figure. There's still some people
here who think I can make changes in tribal government, or
the tribe's hospital, or whatever. Oh, I get pounding on this
desk plenty of times. 'You're the Man; go straighten things
out!' " At this, Robert emitted a dark roll of smoky laughter.
"But it doesn't work that way. I work for another government
now. I don't go out and tell Neshoba County or the city of
Philadelphia how to do their business. And I don't tell the
Mississippi Choctaws how to do theirs."

I asked Robert if he hoped to move up in the BIA. "I
thought about going up the ladder to Washington," he said,
"but I'm not sure I'd be happy there. I think it'd be a whole
lot easier job in a central office; *they* go home at four-thirty.
But they live in paper, in statistics. I think that'd drive me
crazy. Here, because you see changes, you feel like you're
part of them, but I *did* promise myself, when this job quits
being fun, I'm walking out of here."

In the spring of 1988, Robert was appointed the BIA
eastern area director, one of twelve senior executive positions a rung or two under the assistant secretary. He moved
with his family to Washington, D.C., and suffered a massive stroke only months after he arrived. Robert is back in
Mississippi now; the prognosis for his recovery is uncer-
tain.


Although they had succeeded in dictating the terms of their
entitlements, the Choctaws in the 1970s had constructed
what cynics might have called a self-governing, imperial
outpost. As Phillip still likes to say, "The Bureau of Indian

Affairs is staffed by government functionaries . . . and it operates under an inherent worry that if tribes become self-sufficient, it will lose the flock it is ministering to." With government money and their own initiatives, the Choctaws had treated their symptoms, working hard to provide the best that public money could afford a deeply disadvantaged people, but their population still lay under Mississippi's economic ash heap. Phillip knew that true self-determination was impossible without economic independence, and that meant business, not make-work projects.

But the circumstances that had drawn the federal government to the Choctaws' aid all worked against success in business, especially in the chronically depressed economy of east central Mississippi. The challenges of the private sector were practically insurmountable for a group of people whose only exposure to a bottom line has been reporting expenditures on government grants.

Phillip was convinced that any successful tribal business would require a relationship with a successful business partner, preferably a large, established enterprise. But what could the tribe offer such a partner? The tribe had no raw physical resources, no guaranteed access to major markets, no investment capital, and few skilled workers. Their business "advantages" came down to a few tax incentives and a great many eager, willing, and cheap laborers. With a 1969 grant from the Economic Development Administration of the U.S. Department of Commerce, Chata Development Company had cleared a thirty-acre industrial park in Pearl River. For the next ten years, the industrial park's sole product was hay.

As economic development stagnated, Choctaw government evolved, through fits and starts. Until the mid-1970s there had been no clear separation between the executive and legislative branches of Choctaw government: the chair's incumbent was elected by the tribal council's vote. Phillip needed more breathing room than that and had pushed through a constitutional amendment to create a bona fide executive branch. The new executive would be called "the chief," and the chief would be elected at large by the entire Mississippi Choctaw population.

The first election under the new rules took place in 1975. Phillip never seriously questioned that he would win, but he was to learn a lesson in grassroots politics. Although Phillip knew his constituents were better off than before he started working for them, the improvements were hard for many Choctaws to grasp, much less eat. Calvin Isaac, a Choctaw with a graduate education and a knack for stump speeches, beat him out to become first chief of the Mississippi band.

For the first time in eighteen years, Phillip was out of tribal office. He set up a consultancy called the National Indian Management Service and soon had clients ranging from several other tribes to the U.S. Department of Education. He also put in long, unpaid hours in his unending quest for Choctaw business partners. Phillip's persistence must have seemed futile; people close to him say he never stopped to consider the magnitude of the odds against him. According to one admirer, "He just didn't know that he wasn't supposed to be able to pull it off."

In 1978, the tribe mowed the industrial park and installed water, electricity, and sewer lines. In addition to the park's new amenities, the tribe could by then offer itself as a minority contractor, which manufacturers with federal customers were eager to hire. Phillip went on the prowl once again. He wrote 150 letters to manufacturing companies and waited for another half a year.

One day a purchasing agent for General Motors's Packard Electric Division, named George Gibbons, came up from Packard's headquarters in the Jackson suburb of Clinton. Packard was seeking to team up with a supplier of wire harnesses. According to one account, when Gibbons saw what the tribe had to offer he likened it to finding "a daughter with a dowry."

Packard jumped. If the tribe could produce workers and a place for them to work, Packard would provide manufacturing equipment and training, sell them the unassembled fragments of the wire harnesses, and then buy back the assembled units for resale to GM. Tribal leaders were ecstatic. And they were scared to death. Everybody knew that a big opportunity like this was a big opportunity to blow it. And a business failure in Indian Country would almost surely mean ten or fifteen additional years of rejection: what one tribal manager calls the "I-told-you-so-about-working-with-them-Indians" reaction would be sure to set in.

The tribe founded Chahta Enterprises in response to Packard's offer. The new company was established as a nondividend-paying corporation with a nonpaid board of directors composed of tribal members. Chahta went to Washington for some working capital and secured another EDA grant, this one for $346,000. With a BIA loan guarantee that allowed them to borrow another $1 million from the Bank of Philadelphia, Chahta had working capital. The new enterprise hired Chata Development to construct a 42,000-square-foot plant, then hired a former Packard employee as its plant manager, who hired a handful of tribal members as prospective supervisors. The group went to Clinton to learn how to oversee the assembly of the wire harnesses. One of them was Beasley Denson, then a young college graduate who had worked for several years as a council member and tribal administrator.

Beasley and the others came back from training and hired the best people they could find in the Choctaw labor pool. As it happened, they had their pick of capable employees because federal funding for CETA (Comprehensive Employment and Training Act) public service jobs on the reservation had just vanished in the first round of Reagan budget cuts.

In much of Indian Country, CETA layoffs simply produced more misery. Among several Dakota tribes post-CETA unemployment runs at 80 percent. But at Choctaw a number of the laid-off CETA workers slid easily into factory positions. Even with this backhanded good fortune, Chahta faced an enormous challenge in creating a factory work force from scratch.

"A couple of Packard people were with us for the first six weeks," said Beasley, "but it was a whole new world. That's the most wires we'd seen in our lifetimes, I guess, and we were working in a confined situation [a shack behind Chata Development] while we waited for the factory to be done.

"We started off with about fifteen people and two utility workers [including Carlton Isaac] who maintained the machinery. We'd go to Station One and say, 'You pick up this wire with your left hand, give it to your right hand. You plug it, and you string it along until you get to this next connector, and you plug it here.' So much for Station One. Everybody enjoyed that. Hey, it looked so easy. But a wire harness is like a railroad track coming into Chicago: all of a sudden, you got tens of railroad tracks coming at you at the same time and you don't know which train is coming on which one. It got to that point at about Station Seven, where each wire had seven branches. Everybody still said, 'Okay, we know it,' but they hadn't worked on a running line.

"The first day we ran the line for real, we decided to start everybody at three minutes. The normal run through a station was supposed to be fifty-three seconds. 'Okay,' somebody said, 'start the line.' . . . And you talk about chaos! In a minute and a half everybody was hollerin,' 'Stop the line! Stop the line!' We were running it in slow motion compared to what I see down there today—but that guy on Station One felt like it was going at a hundred and fifty miles per hour. He panicked, so the next guy panicked. It was a multiplier effect."

When asked how the workers kept their spirits up,
Denson replied, "One of the things around the Choctaw
world is that even in the midst of grief, Choctaws will find
time to laugh. The guy at Station One would be having
problems and everybody'd be laughing at him, and then the
harness would get to [the woman at] Station Three and
everybody would be laughing at her."

The first plant manager, a non-Indian, treated his employees delicately, afraid to ask too much of them. Denson
and his fellow Choctaw supervisor, Edmund Lewis, were left
to push the line workers, perhaps feeling the pressure to
prove themselves. When one of the workers got sick, the
supervisors jumped on the line to keep things going. "It was
May before the line was producing at speed," recalled
Denson. "But we were real good after that." A year after the
plant started up, Chahta had one of the highest quality
ratings of any Packard supplier and had sold $800,000 worth
of wire harnesses.

But the plant was losing money. The plant manager's
financial skills were limited, and with under sixty employees
Chahta had addressed only a tiny fraction of the Choctaw's
massive unemployment problem.

Phillip had by then been reelected as the tribe's leader, and
his position was more powerful than ever. Most of the inevita-
ble turf battles between the new office of the chief and the
tribal legislature had been decided in the chief's favor during
Calvin Isaac's tumultuous term. They had also cost Isaac
most of his support, leaving Phillip to reap the benefits.

Chief Martin's first order of business was to find somebody who could make Chahta a going concern. He found
Lester Dalme.


A large Sheetrock cell in a corner of the original plant consti-
tutes Chahta's administrative offices. Lester Dalme sat erect

behind his desk, confronting forty years of age with a round, boyish face. He was intensely courteous. He leaned forward to listen to my questions, and if he didn't understand one he would say, "Sir?" Gradually, though, he took the conversation's lead. His responses grew more loquacious, and more determined, until they blossomed into sermons on the power of positive business practices. Thus Lester revealed himself as a true believer in free enterprise, spreading his gospel like a backwoods preacher. "I firmly believe that to pull yourself up out of poverty in America you have to work and educate yourself," he said. "Nobody's good intentions will get you out of it in any other way."

A man of strong opinions who sees no reason to keep them to himself, Lester has nevertheless triumphed in a very delicate position. Because Chahta Enterprises is a tribal entity, the company's Choctaw employees are also, in effect, Lester's employers.

Lester has succeeded as a white boss on an Indian reservation in part because he can point to roots that are at least monetarily similar to those of the Choctaws. "I grew up in Bossier City, Louisiana. My mother raised me and my brother on a fifth-grade education, by herself, and she never took a welfare check or a handout from anybody. I've been working since I was ten. I was a telegraph messenger, newspaper boy, grocery-store clerk, construction worker. At fifteen, I was the only white boy working for a moving and storage company. I've worked all over the nation, everything from digging ditches to driving for Allied Van Lines. I worked my way through college on five part-time jobs. When I graduated I'd already had fifteen years of work experience."

When Phillip tracked him down, Lester was comfortably settled as Packard Electric's quality-control manager. Phillip knew after their first meeting that he'd found the answer to Chahta's problems, but it took him a while to convince Lester to leave a pleasant job at a subsidiary of one of America's biggest companies to turn around a start-up owned by a band of Indians.

The story that is now a part of Mississippi Choctaw lore is that Phillip took Lester to the industrial park, gestured toward the uninterrupted hayfields surrounding Chahta's only plant, and described in vivid detail his visions for a major Mississippi manufacturing center—while Lester wondered to himself what the man was smoking.

In the end, as seems to happen to everybody who ends up working for Chief Martin, Dalme's skepticism broke under Phillip's plodding optimism. "What really impressed me was what he was trying to do for his people," Lester told me. "I'd been in middle management for eight years, and it was a great experience. But how many times do you go through the aches and pains of the business world and see nothing but a positive report and a financial statement? Very few people can say they were part of something like this."

For all his professional and personal experience, Lester found he still had plenty to learn. "I thought I'd been raised in meager circumstances. When I came here I realized that in comparison I'd been rich. I wanted to be accepted, and I knew nobody here was going to trust me just because I asked them to. I just tried to treat everybody who came in here with dignity. Basically I told them, 'You are asking me not to stereotype you as drunk and lazy, and I'm asking you to return the favor and not think that just because I'm a white man I'm here to take advantage of Indians. Don't fight me. I'm here to help you.'

"I remember one girl who sat in that chair you're sitting in now. I had to use my secretary as a translator because this girl spoke not one word of English and I spoke no Choctaw. I said to my secretary, 'Will you ask this young lady could I depend on her to be here every day and on time?' My secretary translated that, and the girl nodded her head. And I asked, 'If I put my trust in her to build a quality product, will she do her best?' She nodded again. I said, 'Tell her she's hired.' She's here today and has one of the top ten attendance records in the whole plant."

Lester arrived at Chahta in January 1980. Thirty days later Chahta made its first profit. He now claims it was simply a matter of cutting back on excess overhead. "I took economics in college," he said, "but they never showed me how to take a dollar and stretch every penny of it. My mother showed me how to do that." In addition to good bookkeeping, however, Lester also contributed considerable sweat equity. In the first three years he managed personnel, safety, quality control, production, and finance, commuting three hours from Jackson every day. Often, he would fall asleep on a cot in a makeshift bedroom next to his office, wake up at first light, and take a shower in a tin cubicle in a corner of the plant floor. Once, a supervisor arriving earlier than expected, with employees in tow, forced Lester to make a mad towel-draped dash to the safety of his office.

By 1983, Chahta's work force was approaching two hundred. Lester was beginning to reach beyond the Choctaws to find qualified workers among the general Neshoba population. Phillip decided it was time to bring lost Choctaws home, now that home had something to offer them. He traveled to Los Angeles, Chicago, and Cleveland, roaming through the loose urban communities of Mississippi Choctaw refugees. He would talk, sometimes in group meetings and sometimes door-to-door, telling them that the reservation had jobs if they were up to them, training if they needed it, housing, drug counseling, and—for the destitute— transfer payments that were administered more kindly and more effectively than in any public-assistance office. They needn't answer to "the Man," anymore, said Phillip: back home in Mississippi, "the Man" was now a Choctaw. People like Carlton Isaac and Henderson Williams heard Phillip, and many returned.

Lester now has time, on rare occasions, to lean back and look at how far Chahta has come. As president and CEO of Chahta Enterprises, Lester has great influence and enjoys broad respect among members of the Mississippi band. In nine years, the company's domain has grown to encompass 670 employees: 550 in two plants at Pearl River and 120 in Plant III, which is an extension of Plant II, close to the Bogue Chitto Reservation and adjacent to the city of DeKalb. Plant IV was due to rise in Conehatta in 1989. Lester also helped develop Choctaw Manufacturing Enterprise, a joint venture between the tribe and Richmond Instruments located in Carthage, near the Red Water Reservation, which employs 80 people to produce printed circuit boards and more complex wire harnesses, including several for Xerox machines. Choctaw Manufacturing also produces a component in a widget that measures the weight of railroad cars to control passenger loads on San Francisco's Bay Area Rapid Transit System.

Lester is also Phillip's co-scout for new business ventures and has accompanied Phillip as far as Italy and Germany to hunt for new partners. The two once went to Milan to check out a manufacturer of high-fashion sequined fabric, made of multiple layers of rubberized material—a bit too fancy for the Choctaws at that point. But while the pair was in Europe, they visited an elementary school near Frankfurt, where a group of students had invited Phillip to speak. "We walked in," recalls Lester, "and there—front and center—was a big glass-covered display about the Mississippi band of Choctaw Indians. It just put chills in you. The German children had studied the American Indians much more than our children do, and they asked Phillip all kinds of questions. The only things they couldn't figure out were why he was wearing a business suit and where he'd left his horse. He told them he had three hundred and fifty horses back home, in the engine of his Cadillac."

It is the avowed intention of Lester's masters in the tribal council to train tribal members for Chahta's management, including Lester's job. Lester's all for it. He routinely browbeats his employees to get high school equivalency certificates or to take college courses. A growing number of Choctaws are filling supervisory and middle-management positions, and Lester's hoping to be able to promote somebody to a plant-manager position soon.

Lester is as happy about the future of the Choctaw economy as he is about its present. "Seven years ago it was, 'Oh, you're goin' to be workin' with those Indians? Good luck!' Now I see us doubling our size. I see us become a significant economic factor in the State of Mississippi. I see Chief Martin continuing to lead, and I see future leaders climbing on his bandwagon to continue the tradition. Most important of all, I see the Choctaw people—who are now in high school or going to college—coming home and working with their people. If that happens, then every drop of blood, sweat, and tears that has been shed by everyone to get to this point now will have been well worth it. Anybody who turns the wheel in the opposite direction will have a whole lot to answer for, to their people first of all."

Inside a mustard-colored shed that used to house the tribe's utility commission is an office suite known as the "Plantation," because, unlike most tribal offices, it sports a carpet and new furniture. Its official name is the Office of Economic Development, and its primary occupant is William Richardson, the Mississippi band's in-house equivalent of an investment banker.

A young good-ol'-boy in a white button-down shirt and tweed jacket, William is a venture capitalist's son with connections running from Jackson's real-estate moguls to East Texas wildcatters. Putting deals together is the only part of business that interests him. "If I were a doctor, I'd be an obstetrician," said William. "Just deliver 'em and let somebody else raise 'em." William was writing regional economic-development plans before he was out of college. Soon after he graduated, he helped create a quasi-public entity called a Small Business Investment Company, which leveraged forty dollars of business investment from every dollar the state contributed. William soon left the public sector and plunged into a flurry of deal making—sleeping on corporate jets en route from business dinners in New Orleans to power breakfasts in Houston. He claims he had his mid-life crisis at the age of twenty-seven.

When the tribe's accountant introduced William to Chief Martin in 1983, William had just extricated himself from a moribund oil venture and was making an easy, handsome living as a consultant. Phillip sensed that William could put the tribe on Mississippi's financial map, but William had no intention of taking a job, particularly with an Indian tribe in the Red Clay Hills.

Now, when people ask William why a veteran financier is working for the Mississippi band of Choctaws, he answers with a mildly bewildered smile: "There are no *nos* in the Chief's vocabulary. Phillip came down to Jackson about once a week. He would always invite me out for a cup of coffee and discuss a job offer. A couple of months after he started working on me, here I was, saying to myself, 'Why am I doing this?' I came in November of 1983 and figured I'd stick it out for a month or two. The day after I arrived, I got a note from Phillip saying he'd scheduled me to speak before a conference of applied anthropologists (whatever *they* were) in April of 1984.

"I've been here ever since. In the end, I succumbed like everybody else, to Phillip's infectious personality. And I've learned a lot from him. I've worked with a lot of well-credentialed business types, and Phillip may not have their credentials, but he's incredibly smart about business." (Phillip once proffered his own modest estimation of his uncredentialed talents: "I'm living proof that you do not have to belong to a country club in order to communicate with manufacturers.")

Phillip may, in turn, have sensed in William an optimism as buoyant as his own. Whereas most of today's business news about Indian economic development is about white elephants and bankruptcy, William sees an enormous, untapped opportunity in Indian Country. He is convinced that in twenty-five years the poorest tribes in America can be where the Choctaws are today. "The only reason there hasn't been more business development in Indian Country," he says, "is because most tribes don't know how to attract it. Businesses themselves begin to swarm once a single business makes a tribal commitment.

"Contrary to popular belief, it's a hell of a lot easier to put a deal together in Indian Country than it is elsewhere. There are more opportunities because there's so little business to begin with that it's all a blank slate. You may have nothing to start with, but you also have nothing to work around. Most reservations have an abundant labor pool, due to high unemployment, so you can move most any business at the entry level into a tribe. You can also pick the fruits of the federal tree: loan guarantees and sweet interest rates from places like Farmer's Home Administration, the BIA, the Economic Development Administration, Small Business Administration, and HUD, which all stipulate Indian preference. This sort of money is competitive, but if your project is solid, you'll beat the competition."

William cites as an example the recent creation of Choctaw Electronics Enterprise, a joint venture between the Mississippi band and Oxford Speaker Company, a Chicago firm that makes speaker systems installed in many Chrysler cars. According to William, the tribe financed the deal with a BIA-guaranteed loan from the Citizen's Bank of Philadelphia, which loved the deal because it was virtually riskless.

Oxford Speaker and the Choctaws found each other through a manufacturer's representative who called on both places and knew that Oxford's principal was interested in working with a minority supplier. Like many automotive businesses, Oxford had federal customers, who stipulated a certain percentage of minority suppliers in their contracts. The Choctaws constituted a minority supplier and could also offer tax breaks, granted to tribes to equalize their competitiveness. According to William, the tribe was interested because the deal would introduce the Choctaws to a new kind of technology that would help develop new skills, create more jobs, *and* provide an additional profit center.

"A joint venture is sort of like a marriage," said William, "and there is usually a courtship of sorts." Phillip and Lester were in Chicago and paid Oxford Speaker an informal visit. A plan was subsequently mapped out on a napkin in a restaurant. The Choctaws would bring a building and some working capital to the deal if Oxford would put up a nominal amount of cash, a significant sales contract, and some technical expertise.

From there, according to William, things became "intense, fast, and furious." The courtship had begun in February. Oxford had signed a manufacturing contract with Chrysler to deliver approved products by October 1, so the plant had to be up by June and running by September. It was, and Choctaw Electronics has been busy ever since. "We had hoped to involve Ford as a second customer three or four years downstream," said William, "but they ended up coming on in the first year, too." The business went from thirty to eighty employees in several months.

William will admit that joint ventures have their head-
aches as well: joint ventures by definition require the tribe to
share control with an outside party. (In order to meet some of
the minority contracting requirements of Ford, Choctaw
Electronics has since been restructured so that the tribe
holds the majority interest.) He also warned that the potential for easy profits among Indian tribes has drawn a disproportionate number of snake-oil salesmen into the field.
"There are too many shysters coming through," he claimed,
"and not enough expertise among Indians to evaluate the
deals as to their merit. Tribes spend a lot of time chasing
wild-eyed deals that the pie-in-the-sky guys can draw up
real nice. Every reservation has a story."

One such Choctaw story began in 1984 when Harvey
Greenwald, an entrepreneur last sighted in Dallas, Texas,
made a proposition to the Mississippi band involving a company called Fertyle Mulch. The Choctaws listened politely,
but declined when Greenwald failed to produce anything in
writing. Harvey headed to South Dakota and introduced
himself to the Rosebud Sioux, who entered into at least one
of Harvey's deals.

Within two years, according to the Native American
weekly newspaper the *Lakota Times*, the Rosebud Tribal
Council had issued a $500,000 complaint against Greenwald
for bringing "discredit, loss of reputation, personal hardship, economic and financial harm to the Rosebud Sioux
tribe and its members." During his Rosebud sojourn,
Harvey had apparently swept the tribe up in every project
from meat packing to mobile-home production. When the
dust settled, Harvey was gone, leaving the tribe with a
bloody nose and lighter pockets.

Greenwald seems to have had broad experience evading
the wrath of unhappy business associates. Long before he
showed up in Mississippi or South Dakota, there were law-
suits pending against him from the Southwest to the North-

east. On November 22, 1977, on his way to a New Jersey courtroom to testify about his alleged default on a $7-million bank loan for his Florida real-estate company, Crystal Sands, Harvey was shot three times at point blank range with a .25 caliber pistol. In a *New York Times* account, the gunman was quoted as saying, "This is nothing personal. I'm just doing my job."

Greenwald survived, saved by a bullet-proof vest. He must have started wearing it several months earlier, right after somebody else took a potshot at him outside of his New Jersey home.


Of the 120 people employed by Choctaw Electronics, 105 are tribal members. One of them, Gary Ben, a sincere twenty-five-year-old, holds the company's number-two slot as plant manager. He was wearing a white tennis shirt, ironed blue jeans, dark oxfords, and aviator glasses the day I met him in Choctaw Electronics "executive suite," a large room with gray carpeting on the walls, awash in an odor reminiscent of Duco Cement. His comments were punctuated by the continuous hiss of air drills and an intermittent *wooeeep, wooeeep, wooeeep*, whenever the speaker ranges were tested.

The Ben family has taken full advantage of the opportunities open to tribal members. Gary's wife works next door at the Wire Harness and plans to go to night school at Meridian Junior College. One of his brothers has a business degree from Mississippi State and works at Chata Development, and one of his sisters has a computer degree from Southern Mississippi and works as a computer analyst for Gulf Oil in Houston. Gary's mother is the supervising cook at Choctaw Central High School, and his father, Harrison Ben, recently completed a business degree he began twenty years ago and currently directs the tribe's social services programs.

Gary's father left the reservation for better prospects in the military and raised his family on various air force bases around the country. The Bens maintained their Choctaw ties as best they could, visiting relatives on the reservation at least three times every year. They also tried to hold on to the Choctaw language, although they understood that the language of survival in America was English. "I grew up bilingual until I was in the sixth grade," Gary recalls, "but we didn't speak Choctaw at home after that."

When Gary was twelve, his family came home for good, though at first the Choctaw community of Standing Pine felt very unlike home for Gary. "I was so much into the non-Indian environment that—you know the saying 'All Chinese look the same'?—well, when I first moved here all *Indians* looked the same to me. I couldn't put a face to a name. And my Choctaw was lousy. One of the main ways I got comfortable here was to do the things Choctaws like doing most, and that was baseball and softball. I've seen some put away eating for a weekend to buy a baseball glove. If you played well, they didn't care who you were; they liked you. So I played a lot of ball. I got to know everybody, and everybody got to know me."

Gary went to Southern Mississippi University on an air force ROTC scholarship and took a business degree. When he got out, he went to see Chief Martin. "I was all geared up," recalled Gary. "I wore my only suit. I started off by telling him I had a business degree, and from then on he didn't even look at me or listen to what I had to say. He just picked up the phone. The next day I put my suit back on again and came over here. Two days later I had a job."

Gary's job as plant manager put him in charge of a number of employees who were older than he. At first Gary worried that they wouldn't take him seriously, but his ball-playing abilities ensured respect. "There was one guy, a big old Indian about six foot two, weighed two-fifty, two-sixty.

He used to give me a real hard time on the shop floor. Then
one day we just played softball together, and ever since then
we haven't had any problems."

Gary described manufacturing at Choctaw Electronics as
a long way from the stereotypical shop floor. "It's not manufacturing by hollering," he said. "Choctaws don't holler.
They're shy. They're quiet. And it's a strength. You get a
bunch of people in here not raising their voices, and guess
what? The aggression in the plant is down; the pressure's not
there; people don't get on each other's nerves. Everything we
do in the plant is geared to the group. Instead of taking one
employee out and saying, 'You've got to do better,' we take
the whole group. Now you can hear everybody saying up
and down the line, 'Keep rejects down.' "

Gary's ambitions for his workers are uncommon as well.
"I've encouraged three or four employees to quit and go to
school full-time because they had potential."

Gary and I were joined by his boss, Bob DePerro, the
general manager of Choctaw Electronics. Like Gary, Bob is
smiling, boyish, and sincere. He was wearing an elegant
sweatshirt comprised of aquamarine, light gray, yellow, blue,
and cherry patches. A non-Indian who grew up in Youngs-
town, Ohio, Bob said he learned how to be a good manager
of Choctaws from Gary. "When we first started, a young
woman came to work one day in a T-shirt with something
risqué written on it. I asked Gary if he thought it might
offend some of her co-workers, and he said, 'I can see how it
might. But maybe that's the only shirt she's got.' "

Like Lester Dalme, Bob DePerro knows that his job requires vigilant diplomacy. "Phillip is the chairman of the
board of this company, and if someone in the plant doesn't
like my decision on something, they go to see him. Frankly, I
encourage that. It's their right. If I can't substantiate my
decision, it should never have been made. For the most part,
the Chief backs up my decisions, and the council treats me
really good."

DePerro also understands that his own long-range ambitions must be far different from those of managers in non-tribal business. "I feel my job is to work myself out of a job," he said. "And if I do it in good time, I think they'd recognize it and find me another one."

There is broad consensus among the Choctaws that economic development should not occur at the expense of special cultural distinctions. In a sense, economic development has allowed tribal members to better retain their culture; they can now afford to. The Choctaw language is reinforced in bilingual programs at three reservation schools. Stickball, the ancient Choctaw version of lacrosse, has been revived in a scrappy intramural league.

A carefully chosen, representative selection of Choctaw archives and artifacts are stored and displayed at the tribal museum in Pearl River. Bob Ferguson, the husband of a Choctaw woman from Standing Pine, is the museum's director and tribal historian. This former RCA record producer from Nashville, with two dozen Chet Atkins albums to his credit, has also done graduate work in anthropology and once made movies for Tennessee's fish and game commission. Bob applies these diverse talents to an impressive collection of tribal videos; his twenty-five creations run the gamut from cultural surveys to industrial recruitment.

All communal occasions, from the tribe's Thanksgiving feast for two thousand to ribbon-cutting ceremonies for new plant openings, incorporate traditional dancing and singing. The tribe's crowning glory is the annual Choctaw Fair, which has become a major Mississippi event.

The tribe's latest venture is unindustrial. Choctaw Residential Center, a 120-bed nursing home, is a collage of windows, vaulted ceilings, and courtyards. Its director, Jimmy Wallace, is a comfortably large, sandy-haired smiler, who was careful to point out every amenity on the nickel tour. "Chief Martin wanted a place that was the best in the state, and he got it," says Jimmy. "He went all out to build a facility that would be good for all people—his people, non-Indians, black, white. It didn't matter; anybody can come."

Jimmy showed off the combination dining room, recreation area, and living room. The space is remarkably uninstitutional: an expanse of blond wood, salmon furniture, and aquamarine walls hung with Indian-patterned quilts woven by tribal members. "This is the prettiest room we have right here," said Jimmy. He explained how the view out of the picture window would improve when the center was surrounded by an artificial lake. "You see that gazebo? Well, the water will be right up around it. We'll stock it with fish."

According to Jimmy, the center's primary purpose is health care, but profits and employment vie for second place. About half of the center's eighty employees are tribal members. "We hired some Choctaws who hadn't had a job in some time," crowed Jimmy, "and they're all super." Most Choctaw employees fill entry-level jobs in food services and housekeeping, or as nurses' assistants. "I do have two Choctaw licensed practical nurses," he said. "One of them, Gloria Frazier, finished at the top of her class." The center was about to start a six-month course for Choctaws in nursing assistance, which would be taught by Linda Murray, a Choctaw originally from Oklahoma and a staff member at Mississippi State.

Jimmy's definition of health care encompassed rehabilitation. "Now, we all know the odds," he said, "but we try." A community-action activities coordinator makes sure all patients participate in some kind of activity. "Unless the patient is bedridden," said Jimmy, "we get 'em out to do things—checkers, dominoes, even bingo once a week."

The nursing home had been open only a few months when I visited in January 1988, and was attracting patients in record numbers. While trying to keep on top of the paperwork for new admittals, Jimmy was also trying to catch up on sleep he lost in the final weeks before the facility opened. "One time I worked twenty-nine straight days; I just checked into one of our private rooms."

Jimmy Wallace met Phillip Martin in 1983. At the time, Jimmy was mayor of Carthage, down the road from Philadelphia. He attended the opening of a Pearl River plant, and saw immediately what Phillip was up to. Jimmy recalled asking Martin to consider building a plant in Carthage for the Choctaws of Red Water. "He said he'd think about it," said Jimmy. "The next thing I know, they come up there and want to buy some land in Carthage's industrial park." The upshot was Choctaw Manufacturing Enterprise, the high-tech producer of circuit boards and other electronic components.

When asked how Phillip managed to woo him away from the Carthage mayorship and into a nursing home, Jimmy assumed the same expression of cheerful bewilderment I had seen on the faces of Lester Dalme and William Richardson when I asked similar questions. "Technically, I never asked for the job," he said, "and technically Chief Martin never asked me. It just sort of happened."

When Phillip came up with the idea for the nursing home, he asked Jimmy to serve on the board. The two tried to recruit an old friend of Jimmy's with a lot of nursing-home experience to direct the new center, but failed. "One day we were touring this site," said Jimmy. "Chief Martin said jokingly, 'You might handle this place yourself.' And I said, 'Yeah, I might.' *Jokingly*. Then one day, he called me up and said, 'I want you to think seriously on it for about a week.' I said 'Okay.' Then I had lunch with him. He made an offer, I accepted, and—bam!—two weeks later I was here. I just resigned my position as mayor and came on down."

Jimmy's extra hours on the job may be a form of repayment for an old debt of kindness. Jimmy grew up poor: both of his parents worked and couldn't spare much time to take Jimmy out. Some of his father's Choctaw co-workers at the International Paper Company knew Jimmy liked baseball. They would come and pick him up on Saturday mornings and take him to the reservation, where he would eat lunch with them and watch them play ball. "I remember that," said Jimmy. "I tell you right now that I'm honored to be a part of what these people are doing."


The Choctaw Tribal Council meets quarterly. The public is welcome to attend, so I took a plastic yellow seat—along with a scattering of observers—in a row facing the council bench, which is shaped in a shallow, inverted U. In one corner, an American flag enfolded a pole. The walls were decorated with God's-eyes, multicolored octagonal shields made nowadays by pulling colored yarn in concentric orbits around a hub and spokes made of Tinkertoys.

Most of the council members were male, between the ages of forty and sixty. Two-thirds of the council and most of the observers smoked. The haze defeated the ventilation in half an hour, but nobody noticed. The council members' names were burned into rough wooden plaques resting on the bench in front of each seat: Wilson Dickson, Clay Wesley, Mavis Steve, Johnny Farmer, John Mingo, Luke Jimmy— melodic juxtapositions of Christian names that succeeded the aboriginal Pushmataha, Mushulatubbee, and Tashka Losa long ago.

The council members stood and joined hands while Charles "Doby" Henry, a councilman from Bogue Chitto, recited an invocation. He prayed for the chief in phrases reserved in *The Book of Common Prayer* for the president of the United States, that his leadership might be well guided. He prayed for the council, that their decisions might be just and wisely considered, and he prayed for the present and the future of his people. The invocation, and the entire meeting, were conducted in English, with accents that folded Mississippi syrup into a mild Caribbean burr.

Chief Martin opened the session with a rundown of his own recent activities. He had just returned from a visit to a NASA facility on Mississippi's Gulf Coast, which might provide a new source of business for the tribe. He had also been to Washington, where funds appropriated by Congress to reconstruct the fire-damaged Choctaw Central High School were being held up by a recalcitrant federal agency. Phillip had gone to admonish the agency's senior administrators. While he was in the capitol, he learned that amendments to the 1975 Indian Self-Determination Act he had recently helped through the legislature were so favorable that OMB (Office of Management and Budget) might recommend Reagan's veto of them. "Once again we are reminded," he said, "that the way the federal government goes is the way our fate goes."

News aside, Phillip got down to business. He ran the meeting with decisive, occasionally incisive, good cheer that kept the entire room alert. He would stop in mid-sentence, point to somebody, and say, "Isn't that *your* department? Better get on it." At one point, Morris Carpenter, director of the tribal housing authority, tried to explain why new Environmental Protection Agency standards had raised reservation utility rates. Phillip responded by recounting several complaints he'd received about the quality of the new housing being constructed under Morris's jurisdiction. Morris issued a sullen defense. (Later, I asked a tribal official about this interlude. "Oh, Phillip and Morris like to pick at each other," he said.)

Resolution after resolution was offered, seconded, and passed in voice votes. Should the tribe purchase insurance to bond its work on a state highway project? Aye. Should leases be granted to tribal members who wanted to buy houses in neighboring communities and haul them onto the reservation? Aye. Should the tribe seek funding to broadcast its own programming over the local public-access cable television channel? Aye.

In the end, the Choctaw council meeting was business as would be usual in many small American communities, except that there was so little dissension and so much accomplished. In the last twenty-five years, Choctaw government has boosted the Choctaw people up every indicator in the demographic spectrum. Dependence on public assistance has declined dramatically; life expectancy has increased; suicide and alcoholism rates are down; and young children are far healthier now than in past years. Virtually all tribal members live in houses with electricity and plumbing. In the last fifteen years the number of Choctaw high school graduates has risen from 290 to 1,000.

All the same, as Phillip often says, "There's no middle class on my reservation," by which he means that tribal incomes still trail far behind the national mean. In 1986, the Choctaws' average household income was around $11,000. But a full 40 percent of families earned less than that, and 13 percent struggled along at $3,000. One of the reasons nobody's getting rich is that unlike some other tribes, the business profits of the Mississippi band pay no cash dividends to individual tribal members. In a sense, Choctaw businesses are like state industries. Revenues not plowed back into business development or debt service are remitted to the council, which spends it on programs.

The result is the Great Society come true on a Lilliputian scale: a welfare state of five thousand citizens that really works. Every family who wants a house receives one, eventually, paying either a highly subsidized rent or an extremely favorable mortgage. The Choctaw government provides transportation, job training, law enforcement, day care, Head Start programs, comprehensive medical care, and food programs for the elderly.

Other services are reserved for the one of every six Choctaws who remain victims of chronic indigence and suffer from family problems and alcohol and drug abuse. Choctaws who lived for long periods off the reservation in urban slums compose a disproportionate number of those on the tribe's welfare roles. The tribe deals straight with hard cases and delivers its services with care and efficiency that simply would not be possible in larger and more heterogeneous American communities. In Choctaw Country it's very hard for the truly disadvantaged to hide.

These services are costly, and the cost is still born primarily by the federal government. Also, and in spite of the Choctaws' booming business economy, the tribal government still retains a slight edge as the tribe's largest single employer. Its 430 jobs in government and BIA service contracts run on about $15 million in federal funding each year. The tribe fully expects government funding to diminish relative to its business income. They would love to carry less of the burden of paperwork packaged with all federal outlays, but the leadership understands that total economic independence is a long way off.

In most American communities, government administrations are supported by taxes, but the Choctaw government levies no taxes on its constituents, who in any case have nowhere near the income base to support the kind of government services they require. Even with federal support, the tribe must scrape to cover costs that would be standard in any municipal government. The overhead payments the Choctaws have fought so hard to receive cover business travel, consulting services, and some administrative salaries.

The federal government won't underwrite more than 50 percent of a tribal government official's salary, so the chief and the tribe's secretary-treasurer make up the difference in their own paychecks through the tribe's only other source of elastic money—profits from timber sales and leases on reservation lands. The amount is not substantial, and because it comes from lands held in federal trust, it travels through its own maze of bureaucratic entanglements before it reaches the tribe.

On Sundays, the tribal offices of the Mississippi band are closed, but if Phillip Martin is in town he can usually be found in his office. He greeted me there, leaning back in his chair behind a desk squeezed between the wall and a long conference table that filled most of the room. The dark paneling of the office walls was loaded with photographs and plaques like the office of a Big Ten coach. Phillip wore a blue Dior warm-up jacket with dark blue slacks and white athletic shoes. A small color television was perched within eyeshot. The sound was off, but a football game was on.

For a third of a century, Phillip has moved very slowly, very steadily, and very persistently to enable his people to run their own lives, and he's still at it. When we met, he was negotiating for the tribe to take control of its own schools through a contract from the BIA. His argument was the same one he has used in all previous Choctaw battles for sovereignty: institutions run by federal authorities are unresponsive to the community because they are unaccountable to it. Phillip also wondered whether a federal education would ever prepare Choctaws for the kind of job markets they inevitably encounter. As he says in speeches on the subject, "Schools run by federal bureaucrats produce little bureaucrats."

These days, in addition to the ongoing lobbying for his

own constituents, Phillip spends a lot of time on issues that apply to Native Americans generally. I asked one of his colleagues what it was like to go to Washington with the "Chief." "Tiring," he replied. "When Phillip's lobbying on the Hill he wants to see everybody. He goes into a congressional office, states his case, leaves something in writing, and moves on."

Phillip is particularly concerned with the role of federal government in Indian economic development. Part of the problem, as he sees it, is that federal sources for economic development are spread among a large number of federal agencies. To amalgamate enough federal support to finance a venture, tribes must often mine several different bureaucracies, each with its own rules and regulations. Phillip thinks all Indian economic-development appropriations should be housed in a single federal office—preferably outside of the BIA, because he detects an inverse ratio between the amount of BIA control of a tribe and the extent of its economic development.

Phillip also believes that federal policy is hampered by its failure to distinguish Native Americans from other impoverished citizens. "Economic development in Indian Country is more than just capitalization of businesses," he says. "Although the American philosophy of separation of business from government is sacred (whether the separation is actual or not), it makes little sense to Indian people. There has never been a private sector on most reservations because they have no precedent for accumulating personal wealth for investment. The tribal government is thus the only source of venture and investment capital."

Phillip is also quick to point out that the benefits of successful tribal businesses go far beyond tribal populations. As he once stated to Congress, "I can tell you with some certainty that if we had not developed those manufacturing jobs in our tribal enterprise, you would now find the vast majority of those jobs gone to Mexico or Taiwan. I might also note that the federal investment in our tribal enterprises has had an average payback time in income and FICA taxes alone of less than twelve months."

While Phillip is often strong in his criticism of the federal government, he refuses to relieve tribal governments of their own responsibilities. He believes that all tribal governments are capable of—and bound to provide—stable, responsive, honest, and democratic leadership. Above all, they should conduct business in a businesslike way and in cooperation with their non-Indian partners, including state and local officials. Finally, they should hire managers with the proper expertise, regardless of their ethnic background, and pay them what they're worth. "These things cannot be taught by the BIA," said Phillip. "Tribes need to find their own way, taking advantage of business opportunities according to their own priorities and traditions."

Phillip's way with people belies his strong opinions. He doesn't have time to harbor grudges. He declined to name the former local BIA superintendents who in earlier years had been his greatest adversaries, saying that they couldn't be blamed for their upbringing. Not that he's above taking a potshot at a broad target when one presents itself. A Passamaquoddy remembers an occasion when he and a fellow tribal member shared a cab with Phillip during an Indian Health Service meeting in Nashville. After a series of long stares in the rearview mirror, their white driver finally asked his fares where they were from. The Passamaquoddies, who happened to be light-skinned, said they were from Maine. The cabby seemed to buy that. But when Phillip said he was from Mississippi, the driver could no longer contain himself. "You shore don't look like you're from Mississippi," he said. Phillip smiled, running a finger under his shirt collar. "Maybe that's because I don't have a red neck," he replied.

"Chief Martin is one of a kind," said Jimmy Wallace. "There will never be another person who has done what he has done for his people and for central Mississippi." Which begs a quiet question: Will the tribe fare as well under Phillip's eventual successor, especially considering the demographic challenges that loom? The reservation population is very young: a full 60 percent of the tribe is twenty-five or younger. At the same time, about 250 jobs on the reservation require undergraduate degrees, twice the current number of Choctaw college graduates. The tribe will have to keep on its economic and educational toes if it is going to be able to provide this new generation with incentives to stay home. Will these things happen without Phillip? "At this point," said Wallace, "things are so stable that even a bad chief would do no more damage than a bad United States president: the nation survives anyway."

Beasley Denson is on the short list of possible successors to Choctaw leadership. He has held the tribe's second most powerful position since he was twenty-five, combining the jobs of secretary and treasurer of the tribal council. After his father escaped sharecropping through a job with the BIA, Beasley grew up in Standing Pine, birthplace of Robert Benn and former tribal leader Emmet York. He graduated from Mississippi State in 1972, came home to work for the tribe, and after various administrative positions was chosen for his current job. "Phillip travels all over the country and deals with major issues," said Beasley. "I've kind of patterned my walk after Phillip, so my job is to stay here and sell his program."

On a morning heavy with gray mist, Beasley met me at the tribal offices to conduct a driving tour of the outlying Choctaw communities. Next to his Ford Crown Victoria, he stood about five feet seven in brown loafers, wearing a plaid flannel button-down shirt. Slim, dark, and smiling, he punctuated his comments with a falsetto giggle.

Our journey through the constellation of Choctaw communities followed the most secluded back roads of the Red Clay Hills on rusty macadam so bereft of traffic that the region seemed deserted. A dirt cutoff led to Crystal Ridge, a community of 150 and the smallest, least developed on the Mississippi Choctaw reservation. The landscape was littered with rangy dogs and junk cars, as well as with a number of brand new HUD houses. In front of one of these were three beautiful girls who stared up at the big shiny car as they pursued a solemn game of jump rope.

Like all of the Choctaw reservation communities, Crystal Ridge has a community center—a local seat of tribal government that also provides some social services. The community center at Crystal Ridge is the former home of one Sonny Boy Nowell, an old-time Mississippi white boy who had numerous encounters with David Weaver, a Mennonite minister to the Choctaws. Sonny Boy claimed Weaver was "stirring up the Injuns." Twenty years ago, they would probably have had to grin and bear him. In 1984, when the Crystal Ridge Choctaws grew tired of Sonny Boy's antics, the tribal government simply bought him out and sent him on his way.

A full 30 percent of those employed in Choctaw businesses are non-Indian. Their home in a poverty pocket has proved to be one of the Choctaw's greatest assets, a place where a few jobs can make a big political difference. Beasley was more openly pleased than Phillip with the Mississippi band's local clout, and he related several examples of how the tribe's position as the largest employer in Neshoba County was beginning to show. After habitually relying on the local bank in Philadelphia, he told me, the tribe was courted by a Carthage bank offering a better rate on certificates of deposit. The tribe gave them their business. "Around Christmastime I come home and there's this whole box of oranges, apples, and everything inside the front door. I ask my boys, 'Where'd this come from?' My boys say, 'We don't know; some white man brought it over.' I asked around and I finally found out it was the bank president in Philadelphia."

When I asked Beasley if he thought tribal business would ever be able fully to support the Choctaw government, he shrugged. "Even if we were able to, I think the federal government has an inherent responsibility to provide Indian citizens with protection and service. Indian people can reason as to the government's responsibility. They took the land for a few beads—and that was the weakness of our ancestors—but still I just think that they have a moral responsibility to us. Anyway, I imagine that the federal government has never spent as much money on Indian tribes as they have on non-Indian peoples."

The Crown Victoria rolled on through no-man's-land to Bogue Chitto, which, with its new red-brick three-bedroom houses, looked almost like a suburban subdivision. In his other job as chairman of the board of the tribe's housing authority, Beasley has overseen the creation of these and hundreds of other new houses on the reservation. As he pointed out his handiwork, he explained the intricacies of household finance in Indian Country. "A house on the reservation may be worth twenty thousand dollars on the open market," he said, "but where's your market? Reservation land is held in trust as communal property of the Choctaws. You can't sell it to a non-Indian, and which Choctaw has twenty thousand dollars to spend on a house? Nobody can get a bank loan to buy one because there's no collateral—not even the land it's built on, since that belongs to all of us. That's why HUD housing is essential on reservations. There just wouldn't be housing any other way."

The car made its final stop at Nanih Waiya, a huge earthen mound of prehistoric Choctaw construction and a lodestone of tribal lore. There are two legends of Choctaw genesis. In one, Nanih Waiya is described as the Choctaw Eden, from which the first people crawled as wet clay figures, and on top of which they sunbathed until they were dry enough to walk away. Another tradition holds that two brothers, one Choctaw and one Chickasaw, set out from parts unknown to find a new home. Each night when they camped they would plant a stick in the ground. In the mornings, they would look to see which way it had leaned during the night and make that their compass bearing for the new day's journey. One morning, the stick stood straight up, and the Choctaw saw it as a sign to stay put, while the Chickasaw decided to push on. The place was Nanih Waiya.

There is archaeological evidence that the mound was once surrounded by a walled-in town, producing the hypothesis that Nanih Waiya was the Choctaw equivalent of a medieval castle keep. Other archaeologists, who suspect that the Choctaws migrated to the southeast from the north and west, believe Nanih Waiya is an immense burial ground, the final resting place for the ancestral bones born on Choctaw backs during a long migration.

Nanih Waiya is now part of the Mississippi State Park System. There are wooden steps built into its side, and in deference to his duties as tour guide, Beasley hiked up them to the top of the mound, which is a rectangle whiskered in short grass about a third the length of a football field and forty feet high. He posed patiently for a photograph, with the gray sky and brown vegetation of a Mississippi January behind him.

On the way home over the snaking Neshoba roads, Beasley imparted his vision of the Choctaw future and its distinctions from the American Dream. "We don't want what American society as a whole has. We like your television, we like your stereo, and we like your cars, but we don't want to be you. I'm happy to survive, and I don't need to get rich. I spend my weeks with white bankers, but during the weekend I don't go near them. I have no interest in alienating whites. I just don't want to live in their world."

As he deposited me in the parking lot of the tribal headquarters, he issued a final caution against notions of noble savagery that infect visitors in Indian Country. "I like living in this community, and I like being Choctaw, but that's all there is to it. Just because I don't want to be a white man doesn't mean I want to be some kind of mystical Indian either. Just a real human being."

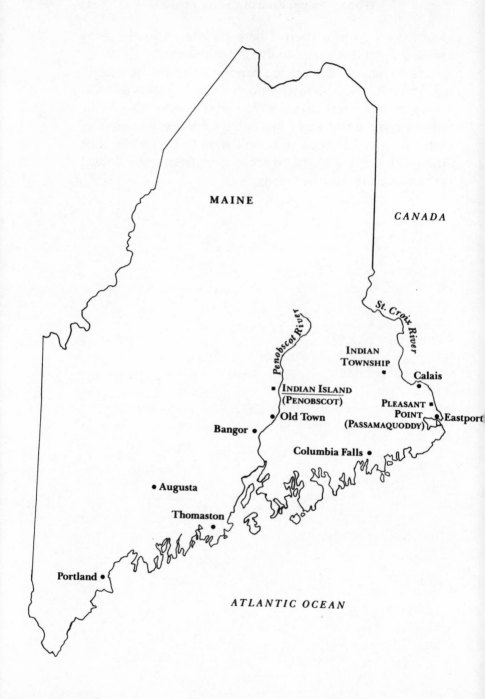

# 3

# The Passamaquoddies: 1988

I returned to Maine and the Passamaquoddies in spring 1988. The coast was saturated in cold mist. The mood among tribal members was not sunny. Passamaquoddy Homes Incorporated, and their new factory in Eastport, had collapsed half a year after its grand opening the previous November. New government regulations on fluorocarbons had doubled the cost of PHI's superfoam panel cores. An untimely Canadian study had shown that the foam lost its insulating qualities over time. American builders were not caring much about energy efficiency anyway, and the new product cost more to make and sold for less than everybody thought it would.

Rob Gips, a partner of Tom Tureen's and Daniel Zilkha's at Tribal Assets Management, described PHI's demise. Rob's manner was friendly but cautious. He carried both law and business degrees from Yale, but his black hair was longer than a regulation investment banker's and parted in the middle to frame dark, penetrating eyes and an arched nose. The first time I met Rob, I mistook him for an Indian; he assured me he was "just a guy from Illinois."

Rob acknowledged that in hindsight, PHI had been a real long shot. "Consider the risks: a start-up, a joint venture, a new market, a new product, a new labor force," he said. "When we saw the business wouldn't break even for years, we advised the tribe to cease operations." There were still some bright spots, according to Rob. PHI's tribal work crews had performed with consistent excellence. All of them, including several who had never worked before, now had a solid year of skilled experience and teamwork behind them. And the tribe still had a first-class manufacturing facility in Eastport, which could be put to other commercial uses.

In general, and on paper, the Passamaquoddies looked "terrific" (a pervasive TAM adjective). Dragon Cement was booming; 1987 had been its best year to date. Northeastern Blueberry was holding its own in a generally oversupplied market. The tribe's overall return on its business investments—even with the demise of PHI—was close to 80 percent. But PHI's failure had been emotionally as well as financially expensive—the kind of false start that had made other tribes walk away from business development altogether.

And there were other problems. After all, the tribe was still dealing with the devastating consequences of two centuries of poverty and neglect. The average life span for Passamaquoddies was forty-seven years, a statistic attributed to the chronic and prevalent diseases of diabetes, heart problems, and drug and alcohol abuse. With the exception of their $1,000 Christmas dividends, little of the tribe's bottom-line success touched the individual lives of Passamaquoddies. Post-PHI, the number of tribal members employed in the businesses they owned was negligible, while unemployment on the reservations was holding steady at around 40 percent.

Heightened expectations, from within the tribe and from outside observers, made all of these problems seem even worse than they already were. Their high-profile business ventures obliged the Passamaquoddies to tackle all of their problems in the limelight. *Maine Times*, a progressive weekly paper that had championed the Passamaquoddy cause in the dark days of the land-claims struggle, had cooled its coverage considerably since the settlement had been won. In a 1986 article on post-settlement Passamaquoddy life, the *Times* seemed to be implying that "white man's" business was unhealthy for Maine's Indians. Tribal members I talked to thought the coverage was simply another form of bigotry.

To solicit an interior perspective, I went to see Wayne Newell, whose speech had carried the day at PHI's opening, and whose articulate knowledge cursed him with a steady stream of reporters, anthropologists, and otherwise malinformed white pilgrims.

I could not have had a better tutor in the contemporary life and times of the Passamaquoddy. Wayne Newell is a political street fighter with a Harvard degree who came of age in the late sixties and early seventies. His English vocabulary shuttles in a rich baritone between countercultural "where-we-are-at"s and sociological polysyllables. His authentic warmth and inexhaustible patience have thawed many a Washington County bigot, and his cosmopolitan manner has disarmed many an urban humanitarian.

Wayne's geniality can be misleading. A former member of the National Indian Advisory Council on American Indian Education and a former board member of the Native American Rights Fund, he is a potent champion of Native Americans nationally. And he rarely allows circumstances to compromise his opinions. Wayne once went to the Rockefeller Foundation to seek a grant for the tribe. He arrived at the New York office and waited an hour for his appointment to return from lunch. When the foundation officer arrived, he was rushed and distracted. He pointed to a stack of proposals on his desk and said, "Those just came in over lunch and they're more than we can fund in a year." Newell straight-faced him and said, "Gee. I guess you shouldn't go out to lunch."

When I met Wayne, he was wearing a purple polo shirt, argyle socks, and penny loafers. His black hair, parted in the middle and looking like it was once a lot longer, capped a serene face and round, squirrelly cheeks. He wore glasses with Buddy Holly frames and bulbous trifocal lenses that compensated poorly for a severe vision impairment. Wayne was born with tunnel vision and no distance perception. His eyes flick back and forth in waking REMs.

Wayne grew up on Pleasant Point Reservation and went to high school in Eastport. "There wasn't much to do then except work in the sardine factories," he said. "My eyesight was so poor I knew I couldn't do that, so I figured I'd better get an education somehow or other." Flouting the tribe's 99.5 percent dropout rate and his own slim preparation in English, Wayne applied and was accepted at Emerson College. "It was my first time off the reservation, and I was living in downtown Boston. Most of the kids there were from high-income families, and their whole way of thinking was very strange to me, as mine—I'm sure—was to them. I was very, very lonely until I met one guy from a poor family. We hit it off right away." Wayne left Emerson after a year and did some additional undergraduate work at Ricker, a college in northern Maine that subsequently folded.

"One of the things I wanted to look at was economic-development projects in Indian Country," he said. "The year the Mets won—'sixty-nine, was it?—I got a Ford Fellowship to travel around to tribes who were getting their acts together. I remember visiting the big resort out in Warm Springs, Oregon. I could only dream that something like that would happen to us someday." Although he never finished college, Wayne was accepted by the Harvard Graduate

School of Education, where he took his master's degree in 1971.

Wayne's history of service to the Passamaquoddies began that year, when he established the tribe's first Passamaquoddy-English bilingual curriculum in the Indian Township school. Since then he has worked as community health director, chairman of the tribe's housing authority, and on the board of the tribe's blueberry company.

"Now my job is turning into public relations," he said, "and it scares the hell out of me." His problem is calibrating for outsiders the gap between multimillion-dollar expectations and the realities of life on the Passamaquoddy reservation. "I've participated in a lot of interviews," said Wayne, "and all I've ever seen as the end result is the glorification of the country's dominant institutions. CBS news just did a segment on us as an 'Indian success story.' The reporters who came up here were great, but by the time the story got washed and pressed by some dude in the editing department, we looked like a real primitive people who had just been blessed by the white man. The point I got out of the footage they aired was, 'All right, we gave the Indians some justice; here's the great thing that we did for them.' You know, we don't look at it that way. We've been fighting all these years because we really believe that aboriginal land is ours by birthright. I mean, the settlement was great, and there's a lot of money now, but we gave up a lot more than we got in the end."

Not that there aren't some satisfactions. "Before, we were just those drunken Indians," said Wayne. "The perception around here was, 'Well, now they'll wreck what they got in the settlement.' But it didn't turn out that way, and now they're saying, 'Wow, we knew all the time you guys could make it!' The other day the mayor of Calais came over to talk about how the city and we can work together for economic growth. The principal of Princeton High School just called me and asked for my help in developing a proposal for bilingual education. I thought, 'Holy cow, we've finally broken the ice.' "

Still, Wayne knew very few things would happen as fast as people wanted them to. "We want to pursue things that will be stable enough to have a true impact," he said. "No temporary measures. No minority status. That means being very, very patient." Wayne said the tribe wanted Indian people managing Indian businesses in the long run, and that several Passamaquoddies were already running tribal ventures. "But we have quite a ways to go before we can say we have all the management expertise necessary to really run our own show," he cautioned. "If we placed Indian people without those skills into those positions now, it would be a disaster. In the meantime we have to entirely trust somebody else, and sometimes that's very frustrating. The hardest thing for outsiders to understand—sometimes it's hard for us, too—is that it is a sign of success, not failure, to attract good managers, Indian or not. I mean, these guys are helping our economy grow. If it grows big enough, there'll be plenty of good jobs to go around."

Although they are now dependent upon outside expertise, Wayne said there is no question among tribal leaders as to who's boss in these client relationships. "A few days ago at a council meeting," said Wayne, "we were wrestling with some new deals that Tom Tureen was handling—a new industry, the purchase of some real estate, some real heavy stuff. We ended up spending most of the time talking about who from the tribe could eventually and realistically become involved in managing these enterprises. Tom was antsy to get back to the bottom line, but he knew enough not to cut into the debate, because we would have jumped all over him.

"I dearly love Tom Tureen, but he has never had to survive under our circumstances. When you have lived it you have a different perspective. He's intelligent enough to know that, but now and then we have to just plain give him hell. You can't get his attention any other way. Then he'll go and think it over, and the light bulb will click."

Wayne is generally optimistic about the tribe's economic prospects, but he told me again and again that "success" in Passamaquoddy terms would have to be much more than a growing collection of white society's brownie points. "There is also a growing awareness that we must renew inner spiritual values," said Wayne, "as corny as that sounds." In Wayne's view, these values are broad and deep, and difficult to identify in a way non-Passamaquoddies can understand. "I think it's a matter of understanding the ramifications of your actions," he said. "Every word, even, that we are speaking now, has implications for years from now. Spirituality, for me, is understanding my obligations to the people and places near to me. It's also a search for balance, in myself and with my surroundings. Nobody here is suggesting that we send back our new houses or that we disconnect all of our utility poles, but there's a real search for perspective on all of this."

I asked Wayne if there were specific traits beyond language that distinguished Passamaquoddies from non-Indians. "Sure," he answered. "But they're subtle. You wear your watch, and I keep mine in my pocket. We've been in contact with the white man since 1600. To survive, we had to prostitute our culture sometimes. For a long time, Passamaquoddies were wearing feathered headdresses like Indians from out West, even though they had never been part of our traditional outfit. But we're still here and still talking about these things. We could have been long gone, like so many other tribes in New England. Our isolation almost wiped us out, but it also probably helped our culture survive. Now our survival is going to depend on how we maneuver through this whole economic maze. If we do it right, we'll come out okay. I am finding that we are all, now, where we are supposed to be."

At TAM, the mood was subdued and a bit defensive. If the Passamaquoddies were learning that the settlement was not a panacea, their investment bankers were learning that not every one of their deals would be as golden as Dragon. Tom Tureen seemed ready to burst out of his office at any moment. On top of everything else, he had given up cigars. As he talked, he paced, marching up to the edge of the carpet and pushing the toe of his shoe against the place where it met the wall molding.

PHI's demise weighed heavily on Tom. Some close friends of his had worked there. Still fresh from the heady experience of the Mississippi Choctaws' more traditional, "community development" brand of tribal business development, I made the mistake of asking Tom whether all the financial ground he was breaking would really bring meaningful change to reservation Indians.

"Why is it that every white journalist who comes around here only looks for snapshots of happy Indians?" snapped Tom. "You're all so impatient, so simplistic!" Having put his audience in its place, Tom launched into a manifesto for the Tribal Assets Management approach. He began by reminding me of the raw resources of many Indian tribes, which together amounted to over forty million acres of land, close to $2 billion in cash, and a vast portion of the nation's mineral resources. "If Indians were anybody else they would be leveraging those assets," said Tom.

Instead, they remained the poorest of the poor, and self-sustaining reservation economies were practically nonexistent. Traditional efforts in tribal economic development focused inward on the reservations themselves, and Tom believed this approach was wrong. Tribes that didn't participate in the outside economy didn't hear about opportunities that might work on the reservations, and they never gained access to the networks that might bring them investment capital.

In the case of the Passamaquoddies, there was nothing to buy on the reservation anyway, so TAM had taken a tact that might seem backward, acquiring a business that already existed off the reservation. Since then, Tom and his crew had been using leveraged buy-outs of off-reservation businesses as a way to jump-start reservation economies. By doing deals to show outside investors that the legal and practical problems of tribal finance could be overcome, TAM was generating the cash to fund on-reservation opportunities.

"I guess it will be some time before we know just how 'meaningful' all of this can be," said Tom. "Off-reservation investments won't immediately create employment, but the jobs they eventually create are more secure, and more rewarding, than make-work.

"There just isn't a substitute for the real world of finance. In any case, we are convinced that tribes will never be able to fulfill their ambitions, or even meet their basic needs, if they have to rely primarily on federal funding. The BIA's got a total of $40 million in credit available annually for all of Indian Country. We raised $60 million for one tribal acquisition last year. The doors being opened by the things we are doing have got to have an impact. Just don't look for it overnight."

In the heat of his impromptu sermon, Tom forgot that TAM *did* have an overnight success to brag about. The partnership TAM helped the Penobscot Nation strike with SHAPE Inc.—Olamon Industries—produced two hundred jobs in two years, bringing unemployment on Indian Island down to only slightly more than the national average.

The Penobscots' economic success had failed to stabilize their polarized government. By the time 1988 was over, then Governor Jim Sappier would be ousted by Francis Mitchell, a contender running on a "get-people-like-Tom-Tureen-out-of-our-lives" ticket. Mitchell would fire TAM soon after taking office, but his mismanagement of tribal affairs would result in a recall election and the rehiring of Tureen and his people.

Despite its whirlwind politics, the Penobscot Nation was maintaining a tribal business that was an almost ideal marriage between employment goals and capital gains. Olamon, in effect, solved the Penobscots' unemployment problem in one fell swoop and became a very profitable business as well. Lately, the tribe has had buy offers from as far away as Hong Kong.

From Portland, I drove north along the coast. In late May, white and lavender blossoms were just beginning to invade the evergreen, along with the lighter deciduous leaves. The odor of paper factories seemed uncomfortably similar to that of the oil refineries of Elizabeth, New Jersey, until my nose found the underlying sweetness of timber.

I drove three and a half hours up Route 1 to Columbia Falls, just south of Machias, and turned into Northeast Blueberry's company headquarters, a large garage of that ubiquitous sky-blue corrugated steel that must be the sole inventory of the region's main industrial contractor. Two tank trucks and a rusty boxcar stood in the sandy parking lot. I found Francis "Bibby" Nicholas, the Passamaquoddy manager of NEBCO, shoulder deep in the engine of a backhoe. He nodded hello and asked me to wait in a small office in the corner.

A few minutes later Bibby entered in black work shoes, jeans, a sky-blue shirt, and a maroon Windbreaker. He was moderately tall and trim, with a handsome, weather-beaten face and thick short graying hair. Bibby was a former Green Beret, with two tours of Vietnam behind him. Given that and his combat-ready physique his voice struck me as surprisingly gentle, almost a whisper. Bibby is a man of stature in the Passamaquoddy community. He was governor of Pleasant Point between 1974 and 1978 and played a major role in the land-claims settlement. Then he came down with angina and, deciding he had served in public office long enough, went to vocational school.

"After we bought the blueberry property, I became one of the board members of the new company, along with Wayne Newell and Bob Avery [CEO of Bar Harbor Bank, then the largest agricultural lender in the state]. One day, Tom and Wayne and I were beating around trying to find the best person to run the company, and Tom said, 'Why don't you run it, Bibby?' I went back and talked to my wife, and I agreed to take it. Then it dawned on me that I would be managing the company I'd just bought."

In 1981 Bibby took over as NEBCO's manager. A blueberry novice, he was grateful for the board's decision to keep the previous owner's staff. "We held on to a guy called 'Mr. Blueberry,' Bud Randall, who's our field supervisor. When I introduce him to people, I say, 'Mr. Randall has over a hundred years of experience.' See, his father worked blueberries for sixty-five years, and Randall's done it for thirty-seven years. As a matter of fact, Randall was *born* in a blueberry patch, in a little shack back out there."

NEBCO owns 2,000 acres of blueberry fields, most of them in Township 19, a wilderness next to Columbia Falls. Half the acreage is in production each year. "We had three terrific years—'eighty-one, 'eighty-two, and 'eighty-three," said Bibby. "Then in 1984 we all started using this herbicide called Velpar to prune the fields. There were so many berries, the bottom fell out of the market. The price dropped from sixty-three cents a pound to twenty-three cents. We'd already gotten back our original investment and then some, so we just coasted from 'eighty-three until this past year. Then a group of growers in Maine and Canada got together and found all these new ways to sell blueberries, and prices began to come up again."

For one of the largest wild-blueberry operations in the country, NEBCO is for most of the year a stingy employer. In addition to Bibby and Randall, there are only four permanent employees, all non-Indians, and even they knock off between November and March. "I spend the winter doing paperwork," said Bibby. "I come down here Tuesdays and Fridays to pick up the mail and check with my bookkeeper."

There is only so much work to do, because the crop is wild. Bibby drove me a mile or two back down Route 1 to the cut-off for the Columbia Falls air force station. There we turned into a maze of dirt tracks through the blueberry stands. The fields lay on high, rolling ground. The day was foggy, and the blueberry patches looked like blooming heather on a Devonshire moor—a sere, crew-cut mat of tightly woven vegetation, lit with lavender blossoms. The pruning season was over and pollination had begun. NEBCO helps this process along with fourteen hundred hives of bees, rented from a Florida apiarist. The hives were stacked four high, like file cabinets. We got out for a cautious inspection. The hives hummed like high-voltage power lines.

During the harvest, in the first three weeks of August, NEBCO's payroll grows from six workers to five hundred. The additions are migrant pickers, mostly Canadian Micmacs. The Micmacs are managed by hired supervisors, called "leaseholders" from the days when landowners actually leased the property to harvest contractors. One of the leaseholders is Ellison Bernard, chief of the Eskasoni band of Micmac Indians in Nova Scotia, who brings 150 of his members down as workers. Herman Paul, another leaseholder, is also an Eskasoni Micmac. He brings 60 to 70 pickers. The workers are paid about $2.50 a twenty-five-pound box, with $.37 going to the leaseholder.

At first glance, such an arrangement might seem exploitative, particularly because the Micmacs bring their children along and sleep in groups of eight in cabins with outdoor plumbing. A notice posted in Bibby's office read:

TO: ALL LEASEHOLD CONTRACTORS/PICKERS
FROM: N.E. BLUEBERRY COMPANY

By law, no children under 12 years old
are allowed to pick berries.

Any parent allowing under 12-year-old children
to work is helping to break the law.

Leaseholders *must* question children and parents
on the age of children.
When in doubt, don't let them work.

A tour of the camp proved that conditions were better than they might be. The cabins were new, clean structures erected by PHI crews in the previous year. We walked into one of them and saw four sturdy bunk beds. A resourceful Micmac artist had turned one wall into a menagerie of Maine wildlife, using knots in the unfinished pine boards as elements of animal drawings: the eye of a snake, a deer's antlers. The outhouses were outhouses, but they were clean and had electric lighting.

"It's a working vacation," said Bibby. "It's a three-week job. They get paid in dollars and take the check home to Canada where it's worth more. They all have good jobs back home. Some of them come in $24,000 trailers. We provide housing, day care, and some schooling for the kids, and we pay 'em a lot better than the previous owner" (around $10.00 an hour). Occasionally, mild but persistent rivalries between Micmacs of the Big Cove band and Eskasoni Micmacs erupt in Saturday-night fisticuffs, but they are resolved in friendly softball games on Sunday.

With twelve thousand members, the Micmacs are one of the largest Indian groups in northeastern America. Although they are generally known as "Canadian Indians," their land and resources were shared with their Native counterparts in what is now Maine. Europeans encountered Micmacs on the mid- and southern Maine coasts in the early 1600s, a time when the tribe had also cornered that region's fur trade.

The Micmacs were members of the same Wabanaki Confederacy joined by the Passamaquoddies, Penobscots, and Maliseets to fight in America's revolution, but the postwar national border bisected their aboriginal territory. British Canada ended up as their legal protectorate. In recognition of their migratory subsistence, however, Micmacs were granted—and still retain—the right to pass freely between the United States and Canada. The twenty-three hundred Micmacs who come south to pick blueberries constitute the largest migrant labor force on the East Coast.

Among the pickers in Cherryfield each summer are Micmacs who reside in Aroostook County, Maine. They belong to a band of some four hundred Maine Micmacs who were excluded from the 1980 land-claims settlement because they had insufficient time to prove their existence to the federal government's satisfaction (a poignant defeat, considering Micmacs in general have a higher Native blood quotient than Passamaquoddies or Penobscots).

The band lost more than cash and federal recognition. In recognizing the other three Maine tribes as its own responsibility, the federal government relieved Maine of any Indian obligations. The state's Department of Indian Affairs shut down, and the state's Micmacs were left with no safety net and a 75 percent unemployment rate. An effort involving the Aroostook Micmac Council, anthropologists, and Maine's congressional delegation is currently underway to bring Maine Micmacs legally and economically in line with the other Maine tribes.

Even in bumper harvests, wild blueberries are a delicacy. "They are smaller and much sweeter than the cultivated ones you get in the grocery store," Bibby told me. Unfortunately for those who would like to taste that wild sweetness, the market for all of NEBCO's fruit is the processor Maine Wild Blueberry, which folds it into products like Quaker Oats cereal and Häagen-Dazs ice cream. Bibby took me down for a quick tour of Maine Wild Blueberry's processing plant in Machias, where I dug my hand into a mountain of last year's flash-frozen crop, hoping to recoup some of the off-the-bush flavor.

From there, we went to lunch at Helen's, a famous old diner for Machias foresters, fishermen, and blueberry pickers. I asked Bibby if he thought when he was growing up on Pleasant Point that the tribe would be doing the kinds of business deals it had done recently. He laughed. "No, no. We were even more isolated back then, because Route One-ninety hadn't been built through the reservation. When you went off the reservation you tried to hide that you were an Indian, but they could always tell by our looks or by our accents."

Bibby told me that although there was very little cash around in those days, their subsistence was adequate. "Everybody hunted," he said. "My father had big gardens and a potato field." I said it sounded almost idyllic. "Yeah," Bibby answered, "but if it had kept up we wouldn't be around anymore. Everybody would have taken off in search of better things."

After three years of high school, Bibby was drafted into the army. "I enjoyed it so much I stayed in for twenty-one

years. Hell, they got me, they were going to keep me."
During long stints in Kentucky and Germany, Bibby gathered certificates of proficiency in everything from intel-
ligence to light weaponry, on a very slim base of literacy.
"Passamaquoddy was my first language," he said. "To tell
you the truth, I didn't know my vowels and consonants until
I got *out* of the army. I made it through by memorization."

Bibby spent his last three service years with the American
Special Forces 203rd "A" Team. Bibby's command zone was in
Vietnam's Central Highlands, which was also the aboriginal
home of the Montagnard tribes. Like Native Americans, the
Montagnards had lived for millennia within the political
boundaries of Vietnam but apart from its mainstream—
alone in the jungle with a dozen distinct cultures and languages. Just as he would later supervise Canadian Natives in
Maine, Bibby was assigned to command Montagnards in
reconnaissance missions.

Bibby returned to Pleasant Point in 1971. He was in his
late thirties. There was so little going on, he thought about
reenlisting. But he fell in love instead, with Julie, a Passamaquoddy woman who had just shed her nun's veil after years
at Pleasant Point's Catholic church. The ex-soldier married
the ex-nun, and Bibby went to work for Georgia Pacific. He'd
been trained in auto mechanics, but the company had no
openings in its automotive department, so Bibby worked as a
laborer.

"That's why I took up politics on the reservation," said
Bibby. "The governorship was a paid position, ten thousand
dollars." Bibby earned his keep. People say he maintained a
very steady, even hand. He ran unopposed for a second
term, which turned out to be the bleak point of the land-
claims case, during the bond issue debacle. For his part,
Bibby was grateful for good legal counsel during that period.

"We were lucky to have Tom Tureen," said Bibby, "very
lucky. Some intellectuals, all they can do is look down, but

Tom could always talk at our level. He would write out on a blackboard the kinds of things that had to happen for the settlement to happen. But he didn't tell us the things he had to go through behind the scenes. Some people didn't trust him. Tom had a skin that was thicker than an armadillo's to take the abuse he did from the tribal members at some meetings."

Bibby now lives in Bangor with Julie and their two daughters. I asked him if he missed living in Pleasant Point. "Well," he answered, "it's hard living in a small area, where everybody knows everybody. You don't have that much privacy. In Bangor, we do what we want to. The schools are better for my kids. Also, our house in Pleasant Point was one of the first ones put up by the tribe's housing authority, and it's got a lot of problems. The contractor had this idea that the houses would be warmer if they were sealed with polyethylene. So the house can't breathe, and the moisture creeps in, and everything inside is rotting from condensation. My wife was so allergic from the mold she could hardly function. Since we moved out, she's been a hundred percent better."

I asked him how different he thought Passamaquoddies were from the rest of Maine's citizens. "In the older generations, when we all had our own language, there was a real difference between us and non-Indians," said Bibby. "But a lot of kids now, they don't know the difference between an Indian and a non-Indian. My kids don't want to go back to the reservation; my oldest wants to go to Harvard and become a lawyer. I'm afraid that in the next twenty-five or fifty years there won't be any Indians. Pleasant Point will just be another Maine town."


Pleasant Point (*Sibayik*, in Passamaquoddy) is a high, thin, hundred-acre land-spit at the mouth of the St. Croix River,

facing Passamaquoddy Bay and the Canadian border. A sign
welcoming motorists to the neighboring town of Perry reads:

WELCOME TO HALF-WAY POINT
BETWEEN THE EQUATOR AND THE NORTH POLE

Pleasant Point is much smaller than Indian Township
and, with the same eight-hundred-person population as the
Township, a good deal more crowded. Through land purchases in Perry, the reservation has recently quadrupled its
size, but the entire community is still under five hundred
acres. Unlike the Township, with its forest canopy, the Point
is treeless and continually scrubbed by the ocean's blow.
Without a camouflage of vegetation, Pleasant Point's litter
becomes a prominent feature of the landscape. Nobody on
the reservation can afford to consign junk to oblivion, because it may someday come in handy, and with basementless
housing, the only room to store junk is out-of-doors. On my
way into the village, I passed a Passamaquoddy teenager
walking along the road, cradling a rifle with a telescopic
sight carelessly in one arm.

There is one industry in Pleasant Point proper, next to the
Sibayik Super Saver. It is owned by a tribal member, and it
predates TAM by several years. A white boy named Peter
Bailey was adopted by a Passamaquoddy couple during
World War II. He went on to graduate from the University
of Maine, came home, and started a business called Passamaquoddy Electric, a supplier that makes cables and fuses
for Digital Equipment and other customers. Bibby Nicholas
sits on Passamaquoddy Electric's board. He had told me
that the business employs tribal members and nontribal
members in a 50/50 ratio, and that the plant's overall quality
rating is steady at 99 percent. In 1987, Bailey wrote bonus
checks to each of his employees amounting to 10 percent of
their salaries.

Cozy Nicholas, the majordomo of PHI's 1987 grand opening, directs the Waponahki Museum and Resource Center. The museum is a small red wooden building that used to be Pleasant Point Junior High School. Nudging sixty-five, Cozy teaches the Passamaquoddy language, sits on Pleasant Point's school board, and serves as the Passamaquoddies' representative to the Maine legislature. "It's a nonvoting position," said Cozy. "Except for that, I'm treated like any other legislator. I can speak out on issues. We lost *that* right for over forty years. But in 1974 I finally got our seat restored."

The museum collection fills two small rooms in an informal, even haphazard array. "Hopefully we will have real, professional descriptions for all this stuff someday," said Cozy. "We can always find some specialist to come in and say what year things were made and so on. Right now, all I'm doing is building the collection. And I'm getting along in years, so I'm in a hurry." The first museum pieces Cozy showed me were sealskin belts his grandfather had made. "Everybody used to say we were just lazy Indians. If my grandfather was so lazy, how come he hunted seal and tanned them himself to make these? How come he traveled from here to Springfield, Massachusetts, to sell them?"

We moved on to some fine old glass specimen cases containing exquisite baskets. "We've advertised locally for donations," said Cozy, "and look what we've gotten. Virginia Pottle, a white woman who told me her grandmother was part Micmac, donated these baskets. Some of them are a hundred years old. She lived right down in Perry, and she had all this stuff. She even gave us the cases. That basket's all birch bark. Someone offered a thousand dollars for the one over there. This is made out of ash. We put the raw material next to it there, so you can see how it was made. The ash is pounded for so many hours it thins out into a sort of thread you can weave baskets with.

"Here is another collection that someone gave us: a canoe, arrowheads. . . . This is real craftsmanship, and we don't do too much of it now. There aren't too many people making baskets anymore, none making canoes or snowshoes. All that stuff is from L. L. Bean now; that is the sad part of it."

Cozy has been resourceful in improvising some exhibits. In one display case is an Indian doll in Passamaquoddy clothing. "Since there aren't any Passamaquoddy dolls around," said Cozy, "we bought this commercial doll, supposedly a Sioux. Ripped the Sioux clothes right off and put her in our style dress." A more genuine sense of Passamaquoddy heritage is preserved in a series of nicely browned photographs. One from the late 1800s shows the tribal council in traditional Passamaquoddy costume. "This gives our kids an idea of how *we* were dressed," said Cozy, "the difference between the headgear of the Indians from the Midwest, say, and these people in the picture. Old Governor Neptune here"—Cozy pointed to the man in the photograph's center—"his three daughters live here now; they're in their eighties. The kids can look at this picture and say, 'Gee, that is what their parents looked like.' "

According to Cozy, the word *Passamaquoddy* is as close as non-Passamaquoddies come to pronouncing the Native *Peskumwokadyik*, which translates roughly into "spearers of pollock fish." (Although they have adopted "The People of the Dawn" as part of the tribal seal, that motto is translated from the word *Wabanaki*, which refers to the larger family of northeastern tribes, including Micmacs, Maliseets, and Penobscots, as well as Passamaquoddies.) Precolonial Passamaquoddies lived on Maine's northeastern coast and riverbanks. Anthropologists hypothesize that the Passamaquoddies wintered in small hunting bands across a broad inland domain and migrated down the St. Croix in the spring, convening in a summer settlement around Pleasant Point.

After thousands of years on their own, the Passamaquoddies treated their new colonial neighbors with remarkable
cordiality. They adopted Catholicism from French missionaries in the early 1600s. "We even fought with the Yankees
during the Revolutionary War," said Cozy. "Our great chief,
Francis Joseph Neptune, shot a British commander right off
his ship in the battle of Machias in 1777. When he dropped
overboard, the Indians whooped so loud the other Brits
thought the woods were full of us and got the hell out of
there."

In return for their revolutionary loyalty, the Passamaquoddies lost half their ancient territories to Canada, and
most of the rest to their former American allies in the treaty
of 1794. By the mid-nineteenth century there were only
about four hundred Passamaquoddies left in Maine, and
tribal members from Pleasant Point walked to Perry every
day to beg for food. The tribe split into two factions. The
"conservatives," who wanted nothing to do with learning
English or electing tribal leaders, abandoned Pleasant Point
for Indian Township and its thicker insulation from missionaries and educators. This split was sanctioned by the state,
which formally recognized two distinct community governments. The rift between the reservations lasted until the
1970s, when the necessity for consensus in the land claims
overrode old animosities.

As the region's white economy developed, the Passamaquoddies were pushed from hunting to craftwork, to blueberry and potato picking, to guiding white hunters, to
welfare. By the 1930s, when Cozy was growing up, the
Passamaquoddies had come full circle to subsistence, hunting to augment Maine's meager welfare rations. "But none
really got starved, because we all looked after each other,"
said Cozy. "I mean, we lived in a shack and my mother was
an invalid, so yeah, there were nights when we went to bed
hungry. But we used to pick berries. We fished. Every family

had a vegetable garden. I wouldn't like to see my grandchild grow up in that kind of atmosphere. But they ought to have the opportunity to learn about it."

Unlike Indian Township's Governor Bobby Newell, who still smarted from the nuns' corporal impatience, Cozy was complimentary about the Catholic church. "The sisters were very interested in us, when everybody else could care less. Matter of fact, one of the nuns, Beatrice Rafferty, is buried in our cemetery, and our school here is named after her. She stayed with us for thirty-five years, and she was something. She knew some of our language and spoke to us in it. She was only a little over four foot high, probably, but in our eyes she was huge. I remember a guy who was probably a little over six foot who had a problem with alcohol. She used to point the finger at him and say, 'I don't want you to drink! You go home and take care of your kids!' He would say 'Yes, ma'am.' "

Like every other eligible male at Pleasant Point, Cozy volunteered to serve in World War II, enlisting in the navy. When he returned, he was worldly and bitter. "I'd fought for this country, and I couldn't even vote," he said. "And we didn't receive any GI benefits, so we were stuck with our cold, crummy houses. I always say we had running water, but you had to run like hell to the well to get it." Cozy moved to Bangor and spent five years there working as a barber and living down his heritage.

"There was a time when I just didn't want to be an Indian," said Cozy. "The forces out there were much greater than I; the movies portraying us as savages. When you are laughed at, you become inferior." But something kept him from putting all of those great-grandparents out of his mind. In the summer of 1965, Cozy revived some tribal habits that hadn't been practiced for thirty-five years. He was inspired by a tribal elder named Mary Moore, who had been taught the old dances by her grandmother, who knew them because she had lived for 105 years.

"We got her to teach us some dances," said Cozy. "Our kids didn't want to do them because as soon as they got into their costumes, the neighbors would come by going, 'Woo-woo-woo' at them. We've held Indian ceremonial days here every August since, and you don't hear any 'woo-wooing' now. We are contributors. We have something to be proud of. People come from all over the place to see us, and they applaud."

Cozy's museum office mate is David Francis, a quiet man of seventy who was a Passamaquoddy governor in the 1950s. Now he is the coordinator of Pleasant Point's language programs. "Passamaquoddy is my first language," he told me. "That is why you hear some breaks when I speak. I am trying to speak in English, and I am thinking in Indian all the time." Dave learned to bridge the gap between Passamaquoddy and English when as a young boy he acted as interpreter between his grandparents and the priest during their confession. "I got to find out how bad my grandparents were," he grinned.

Cozy interjected that there have always been benefits to being bilingual. "I remember one time, some Passamaquoddy was beating the hell out of Hiram Hall [the Indian agent]. That Indian's father was yelling, 'Don't, son!' in English and 'Kill the bastard!' in Passamaquoddy."

Fifteen years ago, Dave worked with an MIT linguist to write a Passamaquoddy dictionary, creating his people's first written language in the process. "We used five English vowels and twelve consonants," he said. From Dave's original typewritten manuscript, he and Cozy have developed a library of Passamaquoddy learning aids, from bilingual textbooks, to teachers' manuals, to language-lab tapes. Their latest venture was a bilingual book of tribal folklore. The three of us sat at a table around the textbook. Dave and Cozy read passages in Passamaquoddy out of a story about the raccoon god, Espons, while I followed along with the concurrent English text:

When he used to roam the earth [Espons] could have at that time changed himself into whatever form he desired. . . . One fine morning he starts walking, having assumed the shape of a raccoon. He goes on until he finds many women who are nursing their children. He tells them they should raise their children faster by soaking them in water all night. That night all put their babies in the water—Espons leaves. The children die.

Cozy found this delightfully funny. I found it a far cry from Mother Goose.

Both men said their greatest challenge was keeping the language in everyday usage, not just in a classroom. As Wayne Newell once put it, "We don't want to preserve the goddam language; we want to speak it." But they are battling against apathy, intermarriage, and television. A blurb in the Passamaquoddy newspaper, *Keq Leyu*, read: "If this is the year you've decided to go ahead and learn your language, please let us know. We're starting with an AD-VANCED class this Thursday evening at the Waponahki Museum and Resource Center. . . . No . . . you adults are not too old to learn to read what you speak; young folks . . . if we don't use it we'll lose it. . . . Come and be a part of the renaissance of our language."

I asked Cozy if he agreed with Bibby that the tribe's economic development would destroy valuable portions of the Passamaquoddy culture he and Dave are working so hard to uphold. "I am not afraid anymore about that," he answered. "To me the culture and the identity are all here. After the settlement, a lot of our people came back from Massachusetts and Connecticut. We have Indians climbing out of the woodwork now. The ones brought up in the city are concerned about Passamaquoddy fading away. They care, and they give more effort in trying to preserve it than I would, because I already got it."

I asked Cozy and Dave to pose for a snapshot. "Give us a really traditional pose," I teased. Cozy obliged with an omnicultural male masturbatory gesture.

"Um, Cozy . . . what kind of tradition is that?"

"Beating my tom-tom, white boy."

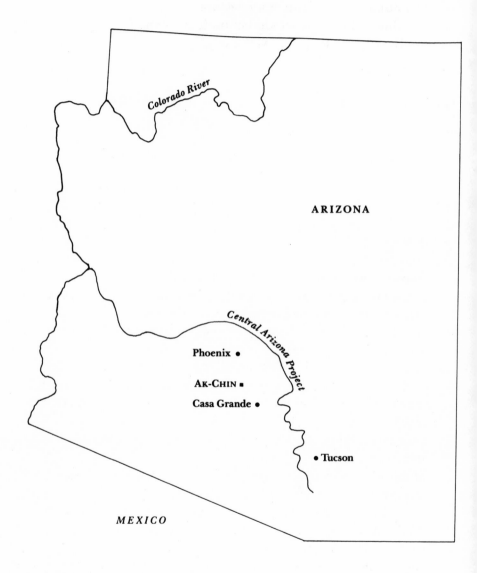

Colorado River

ARIZONA

Central Arizona Project

Phoenix ●

Ak-Chin ■

Casa Grande ●

● Tucson

MEXICO

# 4

## The Ak-Chin Indian Community

Thirty-five miles south of Phoenix, a few members of the Ak-Chin Indian Community still live in "sandwich" homes, framed with railroad ties and walled with mud. When the houses were built, seventy or eighty years ago, the ties were faced with discarded lumber to form the "sandwiches" in which the mud walls were molded. The same color as their sand yards, the sandwich homes look like old Polaroid prints of themselves, left to yellow in the sun.

Cool in the summer and warm in the winter, these dwellings remain practically comfortable in the Arizona extremes of Ak-Chin's desert climate. Until the railroad came to Ak-Chin, at the end of the last century, such one-room huts were framed with the ribs of giant saguaro cacti. Until the middle of this century, more members of the Ak-Chin Indian Community lived in sandwich homes than didn't.

Other signs of a supposedly bygone culture persist in Ak-Chin Village, the center of a diminutive, thirty-four-square-mile reservation shared by some five hundred Papago and Pima Indians. Most Ak-Chin residents now live in sturdy ranch-style contemporaries, however, and there is nothing quaint about the high-tech agribusiness forming the view in every direction. Tractors guided by laser beams grade rectilinear fields as flat as runways. The surgical rows of cotton, wheat, and alfalfa shoot out in perfect lines converging on the horizon. Immense, birdlike robots with wingspans of an eighth of a mile water the crops with an aerosol mist.

On a warm January morning, I met Leroy Narcia at Ak-Chin Farms. Leroy is a farm foreman and former chairman of the Ak-Chin Community Council. Although his dense black hair is cut in a short barbershop style, his brown smooth face with its fine straight nose and oriental eyes comes close to a southwestern Indian stereotype. Leroy smiles slowly but often, unself-conscious about his few cracked teeth. From the waist down, he is an old-fashioned dirt farmer in cowboy boots and jeans, with a wide, figured leather belt. From the waist up he's an engineer, in a spotless, white button-down shirt, complete with a pocket lined with ballpoint pens.

Leroy's job demands more of his upper than his lower half. As he showed me during a tour of the plantation in his green well-dusted pickup, Ak-Chin Farms is so mechanized that most man-hours are spent in the care and feeding of Godzillalike machines. Ak-Chin lies in the Vekol Valley, surrounded by low ranges of desert hills furred with gray-green greasewood. As we drove past the geometric plantations, each a mile long by a quarter of a mile wide, Leroy softly reveled in the farm's efficiencies. "It usually takes five years from the time you dig up some desert to the time you harvest your first crop: we usually do it in about three years. We've already developed ten thousand acres, and we're working our way up to sixteen thousand acres—the total amount of arable land on the reservation."

The main crop of Ak-Chin is pima cotton, the kind that ends up in expensive bath towels and Brooks Brothers shirts.

Leroy explained the cotton cycle on this state-of-the-art spread. The crop is planted around March 15, or a little later depending on the weather. The planter is an obese but gentle machine. As it rolls down the field, its front end scrapes off the peak of each furrow to leave a flat bed on which it drops the seeds; the planter's rear end rebuilds the peaks and covers them over. In a week, the cotton shoots come out. Another machine removes the furrow peaks again, exposing as much of the plant as possible to the sun and to a dose of nitrogen-based fertilizer, shot out of a tractor with an injection pump.

The pima plants achieve their six-foot height in the kiln of the Ak-Chin summer. In September, they are decapitated by another mechanical Leviathan. The tips are taken to a cotton gin, where the cotton is separated from the "trash," and the trash is separated into fertilizer and cattle feed. A mowing machine takes the pima stalks down to six-inch stubble. The stubble is plowed under, and a "ripper" scores diagonal scars across the old furrows to smooth out the field again. A process called "disking" fine-tunes the plowing by pulverizing any remaining dirt clods. The whipped earth and plowed-under stubble are left alone to mulch for the winter months, then bathed in herbicide before the new rows are cut.

Alfalfa serves as a secondary crop, and Ak-Chin Farms charges sheep ranchers a nickel a head per day to allow their herds to graze on its alfalfa fields. The sheep act as lawn mowers, keeping the alfalfa low enough to be manageable but leaving enough growth to enrich the soil before a cash crop. For the past five years, Ak-Chin has also been nursing orchards of pistachios and pecans, which fill in uneven corners of the crop areas.

We drove down one stretch of vegetable plots along the east side of the reservation, close to the state highway. Ak-Chin farms these in a joint venture with an outfit called Santa Rosa Ranches, and the vegetables are picked by migrant workers from Mexico. Leroy stopped the truck, and we got out to stretch. The Mexicans were humped over a huge lettuce patch, with no equipment except for their hands and no shade except for the black oblong cast by a portable toilet. The sight gave me a touch of vertigo. Vegetable picking was the only back-breaking work left on Ak-Chin Farms, as far as I could see. I wondered if the Ak-Chin had some fellow-feeling for these workers, who are as powerless and as destitute today as the Ak-Chin of only twenty years ago. I wanted to ask Leroy if it made him feel strange to think that to the Mexicans he was the "Man."

I didn't know him well enough to think of a fitting way to pose the question. As I was ruminating, Leroy reached down and said, "Look, we have carrots. I hear they're sweet." He yanked up a root with a two-inch diameter and handed it to me, then pulled another for himself, wiped it off on his pants, and took a bite. I glanced down at my freshly laundered jeans and did the same.

Leroy grew up in a mud house, at a time when Ak-Chin had few jobs and few prospects. Now he works ten hours a day, seven days a week and hasn't taken a vacation in three years. Space-age machinery notwithstanding, Leroy's work remains tough, hot, and dirty—not the kind of job you'd put up with unless you owned the place. Ak-Chin Farms—its products, its profits, and its labor—belongs to Leroy Narcia and all other members of the Ak-Chin Indian Community. Everybody here, from the newborn to the elders, owns an equal share of the tractors, the land, the crops, the homes. As Leroy told me, "Everybody is a one-hundred-percent owner."

Ak-Chin is the smallest Native American community I encountered, and its people maintain the simplest economy: Ak-Chin Farms. Period. The farm employs 80 percent of Ak-

Chin's working population and bankrolls the other 20 percent, who work in the community's government to provide the free housing and other benefits available to every Ak-Chin member. "Once a person gets a home, it's theirs for life," says Leona Kakar, executive director of the Ak-Chin Community Council. "We pay no rent, we get free maintenance. If you work for the community or the farm at least fifty hours a week, your gas and electricity are paid for."

Besides creating the Ak-Chin job market, the farm replaces federal outlay to cover the costs of these tribal benefits. Any Native American community Ak-Chin's size qualifies for millions of federal dollars, but in 1987 the community accepted only $22,000 from the BIA. When it comes to national largess, Ak-Chin leaders prefer to play dumb. When Leona Kakar claims, "We don't know what they're talking about—all the intricacies of government funding," she means she simply can't be bothered. "As long as we pay for it, we don't have to go through all that red tape with the government. I mean, take HUD. HUD regulations, some of them—and you can quote me—are downright ridiculous."

Underwriting 97 percent of its own budget, Ak-Chin is about as self-contained as an American community of any kind can get. Ak-Chin provides a job for any member who needs one. It builds and maintains its own roads and its own water and sewer systems. Its workers receive private health insurance as part of their benefits package. Ak-Chin Head Start, a community-funded preschool program, is so popular that it must now turn away a line of neighboring non-Indian children waiting to attend.

Not that life at Ak-Chin is lavish. The median family income in 1986 was $9,000. One might expect the higher wage rates of nearby Phoenix to fuel an exodus from the reservation, but the community has seen an influx of its own people over the past decade. Combined with skyrocketing birthrates, these repatriates helped boost Ak-Chin's population from 389 in 1981 to 580 in 1987. Self-sufficiency, it seems, is worth more to Ak-Chin Indians than certain material advantages.

Ak-Chin is known throughout Indian Country for the extent of its disengagement from the apparatus of federal Indian policy. And yet, Ak-Chin's self-sufficiency remains fundamentally dependent upon the federal government for protection of its only resource—water. Ak-Chin is an enormous sandbox. Even the mesquite and greasewood grow sparsely. Without water, Ak-Chin Farms would dry up, along with Ak-Chin's economy.

Ak-Chin's inhabitants refer to themselves as an Indian community rather than a tribe because they are descended from Papagos and Pimas who have lived together at Ak-Chin for more than a century. Through the years they have developed a joint dialect. "The Pimas say we talk like the Papago," says one community member, "and the Papago say we talk like the Pimas." In either language, *Ak-Chin* translates as "place where the water spreads out." The term came to mean a type of farming that depended on "washes"—seasonal floodplains created by winter snows and summer rains. Both groups employed this natural form of irrigation by planting downslope from a wash, allowing the floodwaters to slide over their plots of corn, beans, and squash.

Archaeologists generally assume that Ak-Chin was settled by a group of Papagos who migrated from the village of Kaka, thirty miles to the south, to farm on the Vekol Wash, an "ak-chin" for the Santa Cruz River. The year 1875 is communally remembered by the Ak-Chin as the year of the settlement, and a federal report issued in 1911 described the community as two hundred Indians farming about one hundred acres.

As Ak-Chin was being settled by Papagos, so was the

adjacent town of Maricopa being settled by white immigrants. In 1878, Southern Pacific Railroad laid tracks across one end of Ak-Chin Wash and sold its surplus federal land grants to speculators and cattle ranchers. It was clear from the beginning that the area's natural water sources would never support a large population. In 1914, Charles A. Engle, a federal water engineer, wrote of settlers lured into Casa Grande Valley: "With these people the appearance of a green plant is a memorable event, and the glad tidings are heralded throughout the neighborhood with exuberant joy."

Nevertheless, federal officials tried to accommodate the daydreams of new arrivals by asking the Indians at Ak-Chin to relocate, either northeast to the reservation established for Pimas in Gila River, or southwest to the Papago Reservation (now called the Tohono O'Odham Reservation). But the farming at Ak-Chin was good, and the Indian settlers had outgrown their original tribal affiliations. They insisted on staying put. Their first water dispute with their non-Indian neighbors erupted immediately thereafter. A Colonel William C. Greene built a dam upstream on the Santa Cruz, diverting water away from the Ak-Chin plantations.

To secure Ak-Chin's land base (and in gratitude to the Papagos for helping U.S. troops rout the Apaches in the 1800s), President Taft created a reservation at Ak-Chin in 1912. His executive order, issued on May 28, set the size of the reservation at 47,600 acres. Ten days later, as compensation for actions like Greene's dam and against future encroachment, the Indian Service filed a water appropriation claim on Ak-Chin's behalf. The appropriation called for annual deliveries to Ak-Chin of 10,000 acre-feet from the Vekol Wash and 60,000 acre-feet from the Santa Cruz: 70,000 acre-feet all together. (An acre-foot is the amount of water needed to cover an acre one foot deep—about 326,000 gallons.) This was all too rich for the blood of the settlers, whose ire traveled quickly back to Washington. Four months after he established Ak-Chin's boundaries, Taft issued a second order reducing the reservation to 21,840 acres, less than half its original size.

To honor its promise of water, the federal government made a halfhearted attempt to build an irrigation system for the reservation. Instead of bringing water to the plots chosen by the Ak-Chin themselves, the project confined watered acreage to a square mile of land called Section 32. A Rube Goldberg arrangement of dams, canals, reservoirs, and tanks produced a trickle, enough to irrigate 2½ acres of land per person. In explaining his failure to irrigate the full 160-acre allotments officially designated for each Ak-Chin member, the federal engineer declared, "It would be useless to do so, as the Indians could never cultivate it."

So the Ak-Chin Indians, who had been farming successfully in the natural irrigation of the Vekol Wash, ended up with a system so contrary to the habits of the local geography and climate that it was regularly destroyed by them. Vekol overflows regularly swamped Section 32, ruining crops, irrigation equipment, fences, and homes. The more absurd the arrangement proved to be, the more vigorously officials enforced it. Ak-Chin tribal members were jailed for attempting to expand their meager domain. A 1919 report from Arizona Congressman Carl Hayden to the commissioner of Indian affairs reads:

> I beg to advise you that while I was in Phoenix, a very intellegent [sic] Indian woman from the Maricopa Reservation complained to me about the allotment of lands on that Reservation. As I understand the situation the allotment agent has so distributed the allotments that a number of the Maricopa Indians have been compelled to give up lands that they have cultivated for a number of years and allotments that they do not desire have been forced upon them. This Indian

woman said that a number of Indians have been arrested and taken to Sacaton because they had planted wheat on their old lands and not on the lands allotted [*sic*] to them. She also complained because poor Indians who had no money to buy wire with were compelled to fence their allotments and if they failed to do so they were ordered to jail.

Federal remedies had forced the Ak-Chin into the barest poverty, and they didn't like it. In the 1930s, generations before the self-determination policies officially sanctioned by federal authorities, seventeen Ak-Chin members wrote to the House Appropriations Committee about their plight:

Since 1914 we Ak-Chin Indians have had some land and water, but not near enough to make us self supporting. Only about half of us Indians have an allotment of 2½ acres. . . . During the past 15 years we have often been in great want.

It was impossible for us to make a living on our very small farms and inadequate water supply. At times when we could not get work on the white man's farms far away we had to go hungry.

We herewith request that each Indian be given 10 acres of land with water. . . .

Men acquainted with the cost of drilling and electrifying wells and subjugating land, assure us that $75,000 will be required to carry out our plans.

Therefore we petition you kindly to obtain for us this amount and we on our part guarantee you, that we shall be self supporting and never again appeal for help if this request is granted.

The letter went unanswered. Ak-Chin farmers remained confined to six hundred acres through World War II. In 1946, the BIA determined that because the Ak-Chin had been so mysteriously unsuccessful as farmers, the agency would lease their land to non-Indian farmers nearby. According to Ak-Chin Executive Director Leona Kakar, the leaseholders were supposed to improve the land by adding water wells. Instead, most of them drilled wells on their own farms and piped their water—for a fee—to the land they were leasing from Ak-Chin. The BIA leases were so undervalued that several leaseholders made a handsome profit subleasing Ak-Chin land to other farmers at market rates. Leona tells a story of one farmer who was paying $10,000 for Ak-Chin acreage and subleasing it for $50,000, all with the knowledge and tacit approval of the BIA.

"After 1946, we were all working for non-Indians," said Leroy Narcia. Into the early sixties—as the civil rights war broke out in the South, and Jack Kennedy announced his promise to beat the Russians to the moon—the Indians at Ak-Chin were still living in their sandwich homes, without electricity or running water.

"The only beef we ate we stole," said Leona Kakar. "Every couple of years or so a stray cow would wander into town from some non-Indian ranch. The men would hide under the mesquite trees, and on a dark and rainy night when nobody was up and about they would slaughter it. The next day you would see beef jerky hanging on the clotheslines."

The Ak-Chin Indians survived by hunting quail and jackrabbit, and by cultivating family orchards of pomegranates, apricots, figs, and grapes. When a few wells were finally installed, everyone grew sugarcane. "It was the little green kind," recalled Leona, "just to feed the livestock. But we used to steal the cane as kids. We'd ride on through and pull out clumps of it. The farmers would yell and throw things at us, but what could they do? We were on horseback. We were just like wild Indians, I guess, we kids back then. . . ."

Leona shared these memories while gazing out the

Levolor-shaded window of her office in the building that houses both Ak-Chin's government and the management of Ak-Chin Farms. (The two entities are so intertwined that they share a single receptionist.) The Ak-Chin Indian Community and Farms Office is a square doughnut of spacious cubicles, whose inside walls are faced with clear glass overlooking a core of secretaries, computers, and photocopiers. On my way to see Leona I passed one office displaying a picture of Curly from the "Three Stooges," a clock with Native American patterns on its face, and a bumper sticker that read I'M A PAPAGO INDIAN AND PROUD OF IT. In another office, bare except for a folding table and upended computer boxes, was a white man with a distinctly New York City accent reciting numbers into a telephone. Ak-Chin had hired him to audit the community's accounts.

The carpet in Leona's office was the color of sand. The furniture was teak with rounded corners, and there was a wall system loaded with Papago basketry. On the walls, papered in a pattern of small mauve clouds, were a Western Machinery Company calendar, a framed formal photograph of her children, and a framed lavender lace doily. There was also a map showing the original Ak-Chin Reservation, before President Taft halved its size. "It makes me mad every time I look at it," Leona said.

She was wearing a lavender pantsuit with a black vest, a thin watch, a large silver bracelet, a large silver ring, and dangling black-beaded silver earrings. Her face looked more tan than brown, and the close curls of her hair were streaked with gray. In her sensible glasses, she looked a little like a town librarian.

An hour's conversation with Leona convinced me that the librarianisms were deliberate, as were several other personas she adopted depending on the topic. Over politics, especially federal politics, she sounded more like a one-woman special-interest group. "I was going to throw my shoe at him, right there on the House floor," she said of a congressman who once crossed her, "but my lobbyist stopped me." Of a BIA official with whom she fought a long battle and whom she eventually befriended, she was all girlish giggles. "That Joe, he was a tough nut to crack," she recalled. "He was next to bones, he was so thin. We would take off at lunchtime to get a nice hot meal, and he'd open his briefcase and dig out a little sandwich and an apple."

As the surviving member of a family that re-created Ak-Chin in its own image, Leona Kakar is effectively Ak-Chin's matriarch. She has worked for the community for twenty-five years and led it for almost a decade under the guise of several official capacities. She has served as the chair of the community council and is now the council's secretary and the chairman of the board of Ak-Chin Farms. Ak-Chin is so dependent on Leona's leadership that after the community's 1988 election, when she lost the council chairmanship to her niece, Delia Antone, the council quickly passed a resolution creating a position for Leona called "executive director," in effect Ak-Chin's CEO. She was appointed to the position in June 1988, and her term of office is indefinite.

Her responsibilities seem to weigh lightly on Leona. She is remarkably comfortable with herself and as easy with her Indian constituents as she is with her non-Indian business managers. Her serene confidence follows decades of experience in leadership, but a portion of it may be attributed to her own complex heritage.

Leona's mother was half Papago and half Swedish. On her father's side, she traces her roots directly to Maricopa's founder, an English-Irish immigrant named Perry Williams, who in the 1800s built the town's first hotel, first house, and first school. Perry Williams eventually married a white woman from back East, and brought her to Maricopa. Leona believes her grandmother was his only child, though, because he made sure that her son (Perry's grandson and

Leona's father) was allowed to attend public school in Maricopa. "We have a picture of my grandfather in the school yard, surrounded by all these white kids," said Leona.

Leona's father, Hiram Carlyle, was chief mechanic for a local division of Caterpillar Tractor Company in the nearby city of Casa Grande, where his family lived much as their non-Indian neighbors did. At Ak-Chin, though, Hiram was called "Chief." Smart, skilled—a man who got things done—Hiram had inherited the mantle of Ak-Chin's predemocratic executives, when leadership was the result of natural selection. In 1954, when Hiram was in his early forties, he had a premonition that he would not live long. He moved back to Ak-Chin to spend his last years at home.

Four years later, after reclaiming an old family farm, Hiram died. His death left his eldest son the chief's burden. A high school graduate and Korea veteran, Leona's brother Richard Carlyle was scraping by on his own ten-acre plot. His modest success within this tiny resource made Richard keenly aware of the obvious potential in the agribusinesses surrounding the reservation. He wondered what would happen if the Ak-Chin Community became an agribusiness of its own.

If only there had been some community land. In the 1950s, the bulk of Ak-Chin farmland was still out of Ak-Chin hands. BIA leases to non-Indian farmers had grown to 11,000 acres, and after the lease money had passed through the maw of the BIA, what remained for the tribe was a pittance. The bureau's lease management "was lousy," Leona told the *Arizona Daily Star* in 1983—"the worst they could have done."

Disincentives built into the leases, including a clause that reserved a percentage of farm yield on tribal land for Ak-Chin, resulted in gross inefficiencies. "The yield that they made off the lease land was a bale and a quarter to the acre on cotton," said Leona, "while the yields they made on their own land just across the fence would be more like four bales to the acre. We could see what was going on, but the BIA never moved on it. 'You are doing fine,' they said. 'You're getting ten thousand dollars a year.' Yes, but the bureau was collecting that as payment for the federal pump we used for our domestic water and a little bit of family farming in the village."

Richard was given the political means to confront these inequities in 1961, when Ak-Chin adopted its first constitution. "Before then, there was really no Ak-Chin Community government to speak of," said Leona. "Buddy [Richard's younger and Leona's older brother] got hold of some constitutions from other tribes, so we picked out what we needed." On December 20, the community approved the document in a referendum, and soon after elected the first Ak-Chin Community Council.

Although now official, the council had no place to convene. Sometimes they met in an old "ladies' club," where the community's jail compound now stands, and other times they sat under a tree. During these meetings Richard convinced the new leadership that Ak-Chin farmland would yield exponentially more to Ak-Chin members if they farmed it themselves, reaped their own harvests, and plowed the profits back into their own community.

Richard was a practical visionary. He understood that even with the will to do things for themselves, his people had neither the capital nor the managerial experience nor the technical expertise to pull it off alone. Ak-Chin's leaders would have to practice what Richard often preached to his own children: "Do the best you can, and learn from them"— meaning white people.

There was one white farmer who held a lease on Ak-Chin land who hadn't abused the arrangement. His name was Wayne Sprawls, and he had once been married to a Choctaw woman. Now semi-retired, Wayne divides his time between a home in southwestern Oregon and a thousand-acre spread in Cibola, on the Arizona-California border. I'd been calling him for months when he finally bothered to pick up a fuzzy-sounding portable phone at his Oregon retreat. In a deceptively low and gentle voice, he spent an hour describing his first encounter with Richard Carlyle, and all that came afterward.

Wayne is the kind of man who would last less than a minute in a federal agency or an academic symposium or a political action group for Native American interests. For one thing, his opinions are politically "incorrect." He told me that thin leadership in Indian Country today is the result of all inherently aggressive Indians being wiped out during the Indian wars. "Only the weak are left," said Wayne. "Maybe they'll breed back out of it, but you know what I mean."

Not a man who would come first to mind as a pioneer of reservation economies. But Wayne was the one who would awaken Richard's dream. "I had a lot of friends who were Ak-Chin," said Wayne. "A bunch of them had been working for me for years, and I knew Richard's dad real well. When Hiram retired from Caterpillar, I was the only guy he'd freelance for."

One day in 1962, as Wayne was walking across the reservation, he was hailed by Richard, who was drilling a new well for village tap water. "I hadn't met Richard until that very moment," said Wayne. "But Richard had heard about me, and he'd been planning this all along." Wayne came over and asked how the well was progressing. The two small-talked, and then Richard asked Wayne a point-blank question: "What would you do with this place if you owned it?"

"I'm a farmer," Wayne replied. "I'd farm it."

"Then let's work out a deal, and you can farm it for us."

"I thought for about a minute," recalled Wayne, "and I said, 'Okay.' I thought it was just a lark. I mean, there was just a bunch of mud huts down there at Ak-Chin, and people said we couldn't do it, so I decided to see if we could.

"But Richard, he cared only about helping his people.

The farm was just a vehicle. He was truly an Indian, even if his family was about half white. He'd go down to the Papago reservation a lot, and talk to the old ones down there. Richard was more of a thinker than a doer, but he could get people to do what he wanted them to do."

Richard brought Wayne back to the council, and a community meeting was held to present the plan. Richard told his constituents they would still go out and work the fields but that instead of working for other people they would be working for themselves and working their own land. His audience seemed to like the concept, but then someone asked, "What would you do if we got drunk and didn't show up on a Monday morning?" Wayne answered that one. "That cotton won't wait until you sober up, so we'll just have to go off reservation and get whoever we can to do the job." Relieved to know that the success of their new venture would not depend on them exclusively, the people of Ak-Chin voted to take over their leased land and go ahead with the farm.

Sprawls handed the day-to-day oversight of his own farm to a foreman and dug in. "As far as I was concerned, there was no financial risk. Ak-Chin Farms was a dead-sure thing, if we could get the bureau out of the way."

I asked what kind of restrictions the BIA tried to impose.

"Oh, about ten years of bureaucratic red tape, and then they would have killed it."

And how did they get around the bureaucracy?

"We didn't. Richard went up there and told that superintendent if he didn't get out of his damned way he was going to kill the son of a bitch."


In 1961 or early 1962, the Ak-Chin Indians began to recapture their land. When the leases came due, the community simply refused to renew them. The leases were good for ten years, and it took five years for the entire lot to expire. "Every time a lease came due, we'd lose a friend right there," Leona recalled. "When we told our ex-tenants we were going to farm the land ourselves, they were furious. Who could blame them? Water was cheap in those days; everybody was making a fortune out of the farming. We were the most unpopular people that you ever heard of."

As Ak-Chin was busy securing its landholdings, the council approached the BIA for start-up funds and was refused. "They told us we didn't know what we were doing," said Leona. "We told them to go to hell, we were going to do it anyway."

Private money sources were as unhelpful. Banks wouldn't offer financing, because as trust land the Ak-Chin holdings couldn't be held as collateral. The community was finally successful when they did what their competitors did—finance everything through a cotton gin. In 1963, Wayne Sprawls convinced a ginning operation called Western Papago to finance the first crop of Ak-Chin Farms. The community configured the loan by offering the *use* of their land as collateral. As Leona explained it, "If we didn't pay off our loan, they could come in and farm our land to get their money back. They could never seize the land itself, but they could always use it to cover their losses."

Leona was hired as the farm's first bookkeeper, and for a while wished that she had never taken the job. "We've never failed to pay back our loans. But in that first year, 1963, it sure was a near thing. If we didn't tell some fast stories! I'd tell some seed dealer, 'Oh, I thought I had paid that bill,' and we'd go back and forth and back and forth until I found some cash to pay him off. I dreamed that someday we would have enough money to pay our way and never owe."

Ak-Chin Farms's first office was an uninsulated, unair-conditioned shack with no plumbing. "I remember every time a car went by, the place rattled and made all sorts of strange noises. It was so cold in the winter, and in the

summertime we would just about boil to death. If I had to go
to the bathroom, I had to walk five minutes down the road to
my mother's and use her outhouse."

If the facilities impeded office productivity, Leona's office
mates sometimes obliterated it. Richard and Wayne fought
loudly and constantly. "He was always on my case with new
ideas," said Wayne. "Richard, he was a great big fella, and I
used to get so mad I'd tell him, 'You big Indian son of a
bitch, you let me alone and let me farm!' Yeah, I just cussed
the hell out of him. One day we was in the office fighting,
and Leona was in there typing and stuff. She wasn't listening to us, 'cause she heard it all the time. And there was
some salesman in there, a friend of all those white farmers
who hoped we'd go under so they could go back to farming
our land on the cheap. So anyway, I told Richard off, and I
walked out. Then Richard walked out. That salesman—he
was as happy as he could be. He said to Leona, 'Are they *mad*
at each other?' Leona said, 'What are you talking about?' She
hadn't heard none of it."

Leona's powers of concentration must have been un-
canny, which didn't surprise Wayne. He was, and is, convinced that Leona is psychic. "She can read *my* mind. When
she was my secretary, I didn't have to take phone calls or
nothing. She'd give out my own answers, even when I
hadn't told them to her."

Ak-Chin Farms managed to turn a tiny profit in 1963 and
immediately received an earful of loud kudos from the BIA.
According to Leona, this was a reflexive attempt by the
bureau to claim the Ak-Chin's success as its own, but it
served to notify the community that the traditional balance
of power had tipped in Ak-Chin's favor. When the community council decided to spend some farm proceeds on worker
housing, the BIA tried to stop them. According to Wayne,
"Housing was supposed to be a federal responsibility, and
since all the bureau people cared about was justifying their

existence, they needed to say *they'd* done it. So we put some federal housing funds into the farm's bank account and built the houses ourselves. As long as the feds paid the bill, it was a feather in their cap. We didn't give a damn who's cap the feather went in, as long as we could get what we needed to do done."

"From then on," Leona told the *Arizona Republic* in 1987, "we would ask [the BIA] for support, but if they said no, we'd just go ahead and do it anyway. When you have your own money, you can do what you want."

In 1964 Ak-Chin Farms's net profit was $21,000. On Easter Sunday, 1965, Richard Carlyle died in an automobile accident on his way home from a holiday visit with relatives in Gila Bend. He was thirty-three years old. "Richard was our first real leader," said Leona, "the first to really bulldoze his way through. When he died the people were just lost. They didn't know what to do."

Wayne admitted even he was dazed. "I used to get so mad at Richard because he was always pushing me, but it was almost like Leona said—preordained, you know? He was going to die, and he had to do all this stuff before he died, so he was in a hurry and he was punching me to get it done. I was just trying to be a businesslike farmer, but Richard got me interested in helping the people. The only reason I stayed on after he died was to carry on what he'd started."

Buddy, Richard's younger brother, shared Richard's qualifications of education and experience. He was Richard's natural successor to Ak-Chin leadership, but he was also battling a titanic case of alcoholism. "He had a problem that just wouldn't quit," said Leona. "He'd disappear for a week and surface in Tucson, or L.A., or New Mexico." Wayne attributed Buddy's problem to conflicting heritage. "Buddy was a dual personality: a white man and an Indian, and they fought each other. That's probably what his drinking was about."

After Richard died, perhaps because Richard died, Buddy came home and halfway settled down. "He still had his drinking problem," said Leona. "When we had important council meetings scheduled, I sometimes had to call the police to throw him in jail and keep him there until the meeting began. The first time I did that I thought he was going to kill me when he got out. I told him, 'Well, who was going to run that meeting if you weren't around?' When he figured out I was going to keep doing that, he began to straighten out. Whatever he thought of me, he never said it." Buddy held the throne; Leona acquired the power behind it.

By 1968, Ak-Chin Farms had a brand-new office, with its own bathroom inside. Leona had gone from bookkeeper to council's secretary to a council member in her own right. The Farms were netting $1 million annually. After investing half of that back into farm capital and maintenance, the tribal council spent the remaining $500,000 on housing and other community services.

Some community members thought that profits should be distributed as annual cash payments to individuals. Certainly from a mainstream American perspective, the Ak-Chin government's withholding of cash in lieu of services it decided were good for all of its constituents would seem patronizing. But by the early 1970s, the Ak-Chin were farming 11,000 acres, as many as their non-Indian tenants had farmed before them. Unemployment was no longer an issue: the Farms had jobs for every Ak-Chin member looking for one. Less than 2 percent of Ak-Chin's entire population depended on government assistance. "If we'd divided our profits into per-capita payments," insisted Leona, "we would have nothing right now."

In a dozen years, Ak-Chin had saved themselves from poverty, perhaps from extinction. They might have lived happily ever after if their non-Indian neighbors hadn't begun literally to undermine them. The problem was water. Less than eight inches of rain falls on Arizona in a given year. Since World War II, Arizonans have been drilling for water like Texans drill for oil. These wells have drained underground water tables to deeper and deeper levels, sending many Arizona communities—rural and urban—in search of other water sources. Phoenix sprinkles its golf courses and cools its Palo Verde nuclear power plant with recycled water, called "effluent." The state has forced developers to limit the size of artificial "lakes," which decorate new housing developments, to the dimensions of Olympic swimming pools. Big cities regularly try to buy out rural farm holdings for their water rights alone. Drastic, sometimes bizarre measures, like weather modification, are routinely proposed.

Non-Indian water pumping was so heavy around Ak-Chin that an enormous cone had formed deep underground at the north end of Ak-Chin's water table. Dubbed the "Maricopa-Stanfield depression" by hydrologists, this man-made cavity had reversed the natural flow of local groundwater. Water that had once traveled north under the reservation toward the Gila River's underground streams had begun to head south into the Maricopa-Stanfield depression, draining the reservation's aquifer.

Ak-Chin Farms scrambled to dig new wells, but their output and income were rapidly diminishing. Wayne Sprawls was doing the best job any businessman could do under the circumstances, but Ak-Chin's problems were rapidly becoming legal and political. Ak-Chin remembered well the 70,000 acre-feet of water promised them in 1912, and decided it was time to hold the federal government to it. The council hired Burton C. Hirsch, a former Phoenix city judge, to advise them on how to pursue a legal claim.

Wayne disagreed with the whole legal approach. "I had another ranch on the Colorado River, in Cibola," he said. "I knew there were fifteen thousand acres down there they could have bought for about five million dollars. I told Buddy and Burt Hirsch they woulda had to move some workers two hundred miles up to the new farm. They coulda done it themselves, without government aid, and kept their damned self-esteem. But Buddy wanted to go on a begging spree; he said he wanted to milk the government cow. I said, 'To hell with you.'"

Wayne left his job as Ak-Chin's farm manager in 1972, but he never shook the bug he caught from Richard Carlyle. Since then he has helped three other Native Arizona communities—on the Salt River, Colorado River, and Mojave reservations—start their own commercial farms.


In 1976, Buddy testified before the Senate Committee on Interior and Insular Affairs, requesting that the federal government honor its old water guarantee. In concluding his remarks, Buddy told the committee:

The people of the Reservation are not asking for gifts. When the Reservation was created in 1912 . . . enough water was reserved to make the land liveable. Aside from two abortive attempts in 1912 on the part of the Government to appropriate water for the Reservation, nothing has been done by the Government to provide any water whatsoever for the Reservation. . . . Ak-Chin seeks not money but water—water that allows it to lift its head high and say, 'I made it!'; water to which it is entitled by law; water to sustain and improve the very quality of their lives; water which cannot be denied.

Buddy's testimony was part of an effort by Senator Edward Kennedy to clear up the water claims of five Arizona tribes—Ak-Chin, Fort McDowell, Gila River, Papago, and Salt River—in one piece of legislation. The plan proved to be too complex and too costly, and it died on the Senate floor.

In 1977, Ak-Chin hired Forrest Gerrard, a member of the Blackfeet tribe, as a legislative consultant. They chose well. Forrest had just left his position as a staffer on the Senate Interior Committee and would soon be tapped by Jimmy Carter as the first assistant secretary for Indian affairs. In his former capacity, Forrest had once given Ak-Chin legislation poor odds of passing because it had not been generated by his committee. As their consultant, he was more optimistic. Along with Buddy and tribal attorney Hirsch, Forrest convinced Arizona's newly elected Senator Dennis DeConcini to push for separate legislation to address the Ak-Chin claim.

DeConcini agreed and introduced a bill that spring that would authorize the Department of the Interior to drill for enough water on nearby federal land to supply Ak-Chin with 70,000 to 100,000 acre-feet annually. DeConcini called his measure "an opportunity for all parties—federal government, Indians and non-Indians—to fashion a solution based on concessions." Arizona Congressman Morris Udall introduced a companion bill to the House, saying that the Ak-Chin had achieved "what we all are seeking for all tribes, economic self-sufficiency and independence."

The tribe was a model case in point. Employment on the reservation was virtually full in 1977, despite the water shortage. "Some people get the idea that because we're Indians on the reservation that we live off the government," Buddy told the *Casa Grande Dispatch*, "but there's a lot of BIA services available that we don't use. . . . We're making it on our own. We're not the richest, but we're doing well living on what we make."

Ak-Chin was all for a legislated settlement, but while the bills were pending, the community prepared a protective lawsuit against the farmers who had been mining Ak-Chin water. The farmers called the suit an attempt to wipe them out. John E. Smith, president of the local farmers' water district, told the press that the Indians were trying to corner all the water in Arizona and that the federal government was using taxpayers' money to "harass and intimidate" citizens. He added, for good measure, that Indian reservations were a failure and should be eliminated.

One Ak-Chin member tells a story about sitting in a bar with his best friend, a non-Indian, while the suit was pending. His friend filled a paper cup with water and proposed that everybody join him in a toast to Ak-Chin, "since I guess this water's yours," he said. Ak-Chin, in turn, gently reminded its neighbors that at the rate the water table was dropping, local water would soon be too expensive to use. In eight to nine years, not only the reservation but all the local farmers would be wiped out.

Meanwhile the legislated solution had run into an unexpected roadblock named Jack Cunningham, a freshman congressman from Seattle. Cunningham was pushing hard for an amendment that would loan Ak-Chin the money to dig more and deeper wells rather than tap water under nearby federal land. "He was real nasty," recalled Leona. "We later found out that he owned some property in the area they were going to take our water from. During one House session, he said Ak-Chin's counsel had agreed to settle for money. Well, our lawyer had never said any such thing. I was in the balcony when Cunningham came out with that, and I almost threw my purse at him. Thank goodness Mo Udall was there to smooth things out." (An article on Congressman Cunningham by columnist Jack Anderson supports Leona's story. Apparently, Cunningham's family owned a thousand acres in Yuma County, which they irrigated with federal water that might conceivably have been assigned to Ak-Chin under the proposed settlement.)

Cunningham notwithstanding, the legislation passed in the summer of 1978 as PL 95-328. Ak-Chin's new attorney,

William Strickland (Burt Hirsch had gone to prison, convicted of conspiracy to murder), called PL 95-328 the first legislated—not litigated—Indian legal claim.

The law carried a $43 million price tag to bankroll the Department of Interior's efforts to find a permanent 85,000-acre-foot supply of water per annum for Ak-Chin by the early twenty-first century. Some of these funds were meant to pay for interim supplies from temporary sources. The law further stipulated that if the government didn't come through with the water in full and on time, it would be obliged to make cash compensations. In return, the community agreed to drop all claims to groundwater under Ak-Chin land.

For the next five years, Interior experts spent $29 million of the $43 million searching for water under the Vekol Valley before deciding that the search was futile. The only source they found would last but a hundred years, and drilling for it would lower the water table on the Papago reservation to the south.

As the feds toiled along, non-Indian resistance to the bill congealed. Calling the settlement "the worst piece of legislation ever conceived," Don Walter, a Scottsdale dentist—who, like Cunningham, owned land in Vekol Valley—said the government should have invested the $43 million appropriation at 10 percent and paid Ak-Chin per-capita dividends. If Walter's sentiments represented those of his Scottsdale neighbors, then at least a few of Arizona's white citizens were beginning to realize what had been the case since the state's conception: a third of its land was Indian Country—and subject to broader laws and deeper values. Buddy Carlyle, then Ak-Chin chairman, made a swift, angry, and remarkably candid response to Walter's proposal. "If we got money, we would kill ourselves," he declared, implying that without work, his people would drink themselves to death.

By 1979, Ak-Chin Farms shriveled to 5,000 acres. In 1980 President Carter cut PL 95–328's annual appropriation out of

the federal budget and brought work on the Vekol well field
to a halt. The money was restored before the end of the
budget process, but by then estimates of the project's eventual cost had almost doubled.

The mounting disappointments of the settlement began
to take their toll on Ak-Chin's leadership. Buddy, who had
quit drinking in 1977 and finally come into his own as an
effective leader of the community, now began to falter.
Council Chair Delia Antone, Buddy's niece, remembers him
as "so bound and determined to see that act through, he
ignored his own health until it was too late."

"I should have seen the signs," sighed Leona. "He had
diabetes and poor circulation, and his legs were giving out.
There were times we had to carry armfuls of handouts door
to door on Capitol Hill. Near the end of a day like that,
Buddy would sit down and say, 'Why don't you finish, and
I'll wait here.' I'd drop him off in his hotel room at six
o'clock, and I wouldn't see him until the next morning."

One day in 1980, Buddy gave Leona a file folder. "When I
die," he told her, "just look in there; it'll tell you what to do."
He died a few months later, after gallbladder surgery. He was
forty-seven. "I thought that was terribly young," said Leona.
"I was so sad it came so soon after he had worked so hard to
get sober and help his people." After the funeral Leona
retrieved Buddy's folder. In it she found detailed instructions
for the disposition of bank accounts and family property.
"He'd even ordered his headstone and the inscription," said
Leona. "All I had to do was sign it and send it in.

"Richard got us started, and then he left us, and Buddy
got us over the hill, and then he left us. The men in our
family just didn't live long."

It was Leona's turn to run Ak-Chin, and the timing
couldn't have been worse for her. She and her second husband (both of her marriages have been to non-Indians) were
trying to raise fourteen children—four from her previous

marriage, nine from his previous marriage, and one of their own—in a three-bedroom house. Leona's sister had just moved in with two of her kids. On top of her own dire financial straits, Leona was beginning to feel the political pressure of the community's dwindling funds.

"We were using farm proceeds to pay for the settlement fight. That money had to be drawn from other community services. For a couple of years, we couldn't build any community housing because all our profits were going to lawyers, consultants, and trips to Washington. It just went on and on. I would come home from a trip to D.C. and all I'd hear was, 'Where's our house? You say we're finally going to get water, and meanwhile we don't have any housing, the farm's drying up, and we're slipping back into the old days.' "

In Washington, the water battle had reached its most frustrating stage. "Our consultants and our attorneys and Interior's consultants and their attorneys would go at these piles of paper with their red pencils. And the arguments that followed! We would all stay at it 'til we were buggy-eyed, and then we would go to bed and get up in the morning and start all over again. The same pieces of typed paper, pages and pages and pages.

"Every time we thought, 'This is it; we are going to get this passed,' somebody would come along and mess it up. If those old war-horses like Goldwater and Udall hadn't been with us, I don't think we would have made it. Senator John McCain got in there, too, and really pushed for us. He was young, and he'd just gotten elected and he was out to do some good."

In 1982, the farm was able to scavenge only 30,000 acre-feet of water, barely enough to irrigate 4,000 acres. Because Interior had failed to find water, and because the department was required to pay Ak-Chin for its failure, it looked for a while as if the government would follow the Scottsdale dentist's lead and settle for cash. Leona stood firm. "The tribe needs water, not money, to survive," she told an Indian newspaper. "Farming is the tribe's only source of income, and if we lose the water . . . we'll be a basket case. If we're not trained to get jobs, we'll have to go on welfare. They're hoping we will reopen negotiations, but we will hold them to it. We may dry up and blow away trying, but they owe us something."

During the month of March 1983, Leona practically lived in Washington and was so exhausted she seriously considered resigning Ak-Chin's chairmanship and moving away from her home. "Just when I'd reached the end of my tether, we made a trip to Washington to see Secretary Watt and a bunch of his people. They said, 'We have a new plan.' I thought, 'Lord, deliver us.' But the more we talked about it the better it sounded."

For decades, the federal government had been building a massive water-delivery system called the Central Arizona Project—CAP, for short. CAP is a canal that draws water from the Colorado River along the state's western border, at Lake Havasu near the Parker Dam. The water is pumped straight up and over the Buckskin Mountains and travels due west to Phoenix, where it angles southeast. Scheduled to reach Tucson in the 1990s, the CAP canal had already come close to Ak-Chin's latitude. The Department of Interior discovered that 58,000 acre-feet of CAP water had escaped allocation to the legion of municipalities and farming districts that had already laid claim to theirs. A four-mile extension to the aqueduct would bring CAP water to a place called the Maricopa-Stanfield turnout, where it could be "wheeled," or delivered, to Ak-Chin.

CAP water constituted a permanent source, and it would arrive in 1988, fifteen years ahead of the original date legislated for permanent water delivery to Ak-Chin. "They tried to get us excited enough about those points that we would forget they were still thirty-five thousand acre-feet short of the eighty-five thousand we'd settled for initially," said Leona. "We haggled over that for the longest time. They said, 'You don't really need eighty-five.' I finally decided we could drop it to seventy-five thousand if we were absolutely promised that water, even before other CAP users."

Interior persuaded another irrigation district called Yuma Mesa to sell a portion of its CAP allotment to satisfy Ak-Chin's demand, but then continued to dicker. "It finally got to the point where we were haggling over five thousand acre-feet. Bill Strickland said we should settle there. I said no. Even Forrest Gerrard (he'd left the BIA and was back consulting with us) said it would be enough. I said no; I would not go back to that council and tell them that I just gave away another five thousand when I'd already given away ten. The attorney and the consultant asked one more time, 'Are you really going to hang tight on this?' I said yes."

The department came up with the final 5,000.

"I won!" said Leona. "It made me feel so great I decided to hang in there and not quit."

Ak-Chin and Interior drew up an "agreement in principle" for a revised settlement. The agreement reduced the original settlement's annual 85,000-acre-foot allocation to 75,000 but guaranteed that amount forever. It also guaranteed that during droughts Ak-Chin would receive its water first, before Arizona municipalities and industries. In lieu of damages already owed to Ak-Chin, the agreement gave the community $15 million to buy water for the interim.

The agreement was co-signed by Leona and the secretary of the interior in September 1983. It was one of Watt's last acts before leaving office, and Leona worried that he would resign before the agreement was secure: "I mean, I didn't always *like* the man, but this was one time I wanted him there."

One October morning in 1984, Goldwater summoned Leona and her fellow council members to Capitol Hill. "When we got there, he told us, 'This thing will go through sometime today, but I'm not going to be able to tell you exactly *what* time.' We were up in that balcony all day long;

we waited and waited. It got dark. Goldwater kept coming into the chamber and looking around. Then he would sit down and vote on something else. We found out later that he was waiting for some senators who were opposed to the agreement to leave. One of the council members fell asleep. I said, 'Okay, let's go home.'

"Just after we left, Goldwater railroaded it through. The phone rang just as we got back to the hotel. It was Forrest Gerrard telling us it was all over. I think I slept all night that night."

Ronald Reagan signed PL 98-530 into law soon after its congressional ratification. In addition to $15 million in monetary compensation, the law also gave Ak-Chin a $3.5-million economic-development grant and $25 million for the leveling, canal construction, and soil conditioning required to prepare Ak-Chin Farms to receive federal water. The total cost of the new agreement was $40 million. The bill for the original settlement, had it been honored, would have topped $100 million as early as 1985.

The agreement also stipulated that the CAP extension to Ak-Chin would bring federal water to Ak-Chin's neighbors, the farmers of the Maricopa-Stanfield Water District. I spoke with Van Tenney, who succeeded John E. Smith as head of the district. Tenney was considerably higher on Ak-Chin than his predecessor, although his members consider the arrangement a mixed blessing. "The water table was dropping here," said Tenney, "and if Ak-Chin hadn't pushed for a settlement we'd still be pumping. Some acreage hereabouts had already been taken out of production. Of course, some farmers believe they could have pumped forever, and they resent having CAP's high prices foisted upon them. I think CAP water is cheaper today than their pumped water would have been had it continued at the old rate.

"White farmers, and I would say particularly the ones who live nearest to Ak-Chin, admire the Indians. Still, if you asked them if they thought Ak-Chin's farming with free water gave them an unfair competitive advantage, they would probably say yes."

Leona went home. "They told me I had to keep my mouth shut until January 1988, which was when they promised to deliver the first water." On June 27, 1987, an Ak-Chin farm foreman named Butch Cannon stuck his head into Leona's office on his way down the hall and said, "Guess what? CAP water is running on the reservation."

Leona couldn't believe it. "That was the only time I ever knew a federal agency to beat its own schedule. I didn't know whether to jump in that water or get down on my knees and pray to it. I decided to pray because I can't swim; I was never around enough water to learn. But that water looked so good."

Within a month, Ak-Chin Farms was irrigating its fields with CAP water. On January 9, 1988, the Ak-Chin Indian Community formally celebrated the water's arrival with a twenty-four-hour party. Invitations to the "first negotiated, legislated water settlement in contemporary history" were sent to all Ak-Chin members, most of their neighbors, other Arizona Indian tribes, visiting dignitaries, and to everybody—official and otherwise—who had in any way been involved in the settlement negotiations.

Three hundred people came. The festivities started at 9:30 A.M. with the (American) National Anthem and a flag-raising ceremony under a huge canopy tent, sixty by ninety feet, that Ak-Chin had pitched against the January sun. "With all our fields in production, it was real dusty," said Leona. "So we had our celebration in the village, not down by the reservoir. We had to pretend we saw the water rushing around." A non-Indian farmer named Joe Turner laid down the olive branch on behalf of Ak-Chin's neighbors, saying, "Without the continuous efforts of Ak-Chin, CAP water would not have been available to anyone in the Maricopa-Stanfield area. The good work done by this tribe benefits everyone."

Assistant Secretary Ross Swimmer, then head of the Bureau of Indian Affairs, surprised everybody by making a cameo appearance to call Ak-Chin "an example to all of Indian Country." What type of example—economic acumen or determination in the face of federal sloth—remained unclear. The most poignant speeches were made by Ak-Chin members honoring council members like Richard and Buddy Carlyle, who could not witness this glorious end to their mortal struggle.

After a barbecue lunch, the music and the dancing began. Men from the Tohono O'Odham Reservation performed the "Pascola" dance, with bags of seed on their ankles recreating the sound of rattlesnakes. Then they invited everybody to dance "Chicken Scratch," a two-step barn dance with Mexican overtones. "The invitation said, 'Continuous entertainment, two P.M. Saturday to seven A.M. Sunday,'" said Leona. "I lasted 'til three-thirty in the morning."

Leona's niece, Delia Antone, looked out her window at 7:00 A.M., and the dance was still going strong. "I felt good because it had finally happened," she recalled, "but I felt sad because my father and my uncle weren't here to share in it. I decided I was being selfish; they were probably up there somewhere having their own all-night dance."

The community's newspaper reported the event this way: "The cold night did not stop people from celebrations, and another historical day passed in the self-sufficient village of Ak-Chin."


During our tour of the farm, Leroy and I followed the trail of settlement water as it flows from its storage reservoir in the southwest corner of the reservation. The reservoir is elevated, and the water runs out from it through a pipe that extends in a nine-mile diagonal across Ak-Chin's landholdings. From the main pipe, the water shoots out into long troughs called laterals, which border every field. We passed a couple of people who were cleaning the laterals; I wondered if theirs was the only handwork left for Ak-Chin farmers. Barely a drop of the precious resource is wasted. The "tail water" missed by siphons in the laterals flows to the corners and is consumed by the strategic pistachio and pecan plantations.

At full production, the current farm expansion to 16,000 acres places Ak-Chin Farms among the larger agribusinesses in the area. The community expected its farm income to level off at about $2 million (1988 dollars) a year. "A farming venture of our magnitude," boasts the *Runner*, "will take us into the economic mainstream of the nation."

Farm revenue has allowed the Ak-Chin government to create a life for its members that is secure but spare. The community's self-sufficiency is authentic but bought with hard, hot work at low wages—a price few communities, Native or otherwise, would be willing to pay. John Artichoker, a Sioux who directed the BIA's area office in Phoenix, once said of Ak-Chin, "In my years of experience . . . I have never seen a group of people so self-sufficient and independent as they are. The Ak-Chin have transcended the need for many services that most reservations require. There are no BIA staff located . . . on the reservation."

Which begs a question of the chicken-or-the-egg variety. Ak-Chin members believe the roots of their independence can be found in their geographic isolation from federal assistance. The nearest BIA office is the Gila River Agency, an agency primarily for Pima Indians, twenty-five miles east in Sacaton. Ak-Chin was too small a reservation to impel the bureau to establish a physical presence there. "We've always been far enough away from the federal government that we've had to fend for ourselves," Leona said.

Self-sufficiency has evolved into the credo of Ak-Chin government. Ak-Chin maintains its own police force, its own fire department, and its own day-care and preschool facilities. Members have full medical coverage through the community's self-insurance plan (although some community members, particularly the elders, still insist on going to the Indian hospital at Sacaton, out of long habit).

Self-sufficiency is promoted—some would say enforced—among Ak-Chin members through the community's employment policies. There are jobs in Ak-Chin even for people who in other communities would be listed as unemployable. Ak-Chin Farms has an ingenious program called the "Goofy Gang." "This is where you go when you hit bottom," said Leona. "When you can't get a job on the tractors or the pickers, or something a little steadier, you get on the Goofy Gang. We created it shortly after we started the farm because we had so many people who needed a job but could not stay with it permanently.

"There're six people on Goofy Gang, and they work five days a week unless there's something that we really need them to do, then we work 'em Saturdays. They are revolvers. Five will work together for a stretch of three weeks or so. Then one of the five will fall off the wagon and won't show up on Monday morning, so Number Six will take his place. Then somebody else falls off. They know the rules, and they don't argue. If you don't show on Monday, somebody gets your place. It just goes around and around."

The Goofy Gang might appear to be a cavalier solution to the ravages of alcoholism, but it is immediately practical. Nor is Ak-Chin's steady work force tempted by the Goofy Gang example; an announcement from the community council attached to recent paychecks warned that farm employees faced "automatic dismissal when work is missed because of weekend or evening drunkenness."

The Goofy Gang excepted, Ak-Chin farmers work steadily and long: their minimum work week is fifty hours. With 97 percent of Ak-Chin's working-age population holding down jobs, unemployment is no longer the problem. The community is now trying to focus on creating Indian managers. According to Leona, "There are still too many white-eyes in top jobs; we're looking for some Indians to balance them out. So far, we've placed one overseeing the laser-leveling crew, one with the regular foreman for the overall farm, and one in the irrigation department."

Leona has had no luck so far in locating an eventual successor for Don England, the farm's current, non-Indian, general manager. "We've been trying to get somebody trained for years and years, but nobody wants the responsibility. Indians are funny. They won't listen to another Indian sometimes. You know the attitude: 'Why should we listen to you? You're just one of us.' We are crazy people. We resent it when one of our own gets into one of the top jobs. They don't mind foremen or assistants, but at top levels there is always jealousy."

Wayne Sprawls agreed. "Indians don't like Indians getting ahead. I trained one Indian farm manager up at Colorado River. In ten years he got to the point where the farm was doing so good he was pulling down two hundred thousand dollars a year, and that was too much for an Indian to be making, so the tribe fired him. It was perfectly all right for somebody like me to make that kind of money, but not one of their own."

Ak-Chin may be slow to award ability in part because the community has been so successful in addressing need. Ak-Chin treats its few destitute members the same way it treats its handful of indigents—as family. "We have a standing order with the BIA people at Sacaton," said Leona. "If any of our people show up over there looking for a handout, the agency tells them, 'Sorry, but Leona says you have to go directly to her.' When they get here, I say, 'Oh yes, we'll give you money. And a job to go with it.' I've gotten cussed out a lot of times, but that's the way it works here."

The community's housing program moves doggedly toward free housing for all Ak-Chin members, although that end is still out of sight. A growing population—partially fueled by off-reservation Ak-Chin who have decided to return *because* of the free housing—makes the promise of universal housing more and more burdensome. "We're frustrating a lot of people," conceded Delia Antone. "Right now, some homes have three or four families living in them, sharing three bedrooms and one bathroom. They've had to wait twelve years for the settlement to come through, and now we tell them they have to be patient for a couple more years before they get that new house."

Ak-Chin augments these internally funded services through a few federally funded programs, although it forgoes many other entitlements and accepts its relative pittance with some misgivings. Ak-Chin members firmly believe they deserve government support, but they hate the restrictions that come along with federal largess. As a case in point, the $11,000 that Ak-Chin receives annually from the BIA to transport its elderly members to meal programs and hospital visits covers only two-months worth of the actual transportation costs.

"We finally bought our own van," said Leona. "It has a hydraulic lift that can haul wheelchair patients up into it. We paid for it ourselves because it was so much easier than buying through a government grant. You can't get rid of publicly funded vehicles when they wear out. You have to get permission from some bureaucrat to junk the thing."

Ak-Chin-funded services are also free of ups and downs in federal-funding levels. Delia recalled hearing a tribal member from the Gila River Reservation agonizing about the 1988 presidential election and what the BIA budget would look like under the winning candidate. "I just kind of sat back and was glad that we don't have to go through that anymore."

Ak-Chin's economy has effectively freed it from federal solutions to social problems, but not from the problems themselves. A single measure of the challenge is life expectancy on the reservation: only twenty-five members of Ak-Chin's five-hundred-person population have lived past the age of fifty-five. Community officials blame these foreshortened lives on diabetes and alcoholism. Leroy Narcia, who is in his mid-forties, found out he had diabetes a few months before I met him. As he was dropping me off at the community office after our farm tour, I told him I might be coming back, and he answered, "I hope I am still here when you come."

Diabetes is epidemic among the Pimas and Papagos. The reasons for this remain unclear. The effects of alcohol consumption on diabetics are conclusively disastrous, however, and according to Leona, somewhere around 35 or 40 percent of the people at Ak-Chin drink, some heavily. The community provides free access to alcohol counseling in the city of Casa Grande, twelve miles away, but she would like to have a recovery unit on the reservation.

Leona would also like to have a nursing home at Ak-Chin for the handful of elders. "We've had to send some of our people to a nursing home in Laveen, run by the Gila River Agency. It's too lonesome. They don't know the people up there. We just sentence them to death by sending them away, but they're at the stage where they need to be watched over. One old man of ours used to just wander off into the desert, and we'd have to send people after him on horseback."

The five members of the Ak-Chin Community Council are better suited than most public servants to develop long-term solutions to complex social problems. For one thing, they know all of their constituents by their first and last names. For another, the structure of Ak-Chin's government and its ownership of the only employer in town gives this handful of men and women extraordinary political power. There are few structural restrictions to keep their power in check. The distinction between legislative and executive functions is blurred. The council selects a chair and vice-chair from their own number, and the collective view of the council as a whole dictates policy. "I may be chairman of the council, but the council is still above me," explained Delia Antone.

Council members receive only a three-hundred-dollar monthly stipend for their services, so they take other jobs to make ends meet. Often those jobs are within the community's administration.. On top of her duties as tribal chair, Delia serves as the community's assistant coordinator, which she says covers everything, including cleaning bathrooms. When I mentioned a conflict of interest between legislative and administrative commitments, Leona reminded me that Ak-Chin was drawing from a very limited pool for administrative skills. "We're such a small group that we just ignore things like that here. Our way of avoiding nepotism is to try not to have somebody working under you from your immediate family."

Ironically, Leona's current situation represents the one separation of power in Ak-Chin governance. Her position as executive director allows her to make a broad range of unilateral decisions without the council's consent, just as a president runs a company between quarterly board meetings. Leona runs the community, even though she holds no elected position.

"These people are tribal people, not democratic people," contended Wayne Sprawls. "Our system don't work with 'em. When they try to put it on, they end up with people like Peter MacDonald at Navajo, who are just in it for themselves. Take Leona's father. He wasn't the chairman or nuthin' like that; he was the chief. These people need to be led, and that's why Leona's running everything. Those official titles don't mean nuthin'. She's the chief."

The result of such intimate, concentrated leadership is

reflected in Ak-Chin's house organ, the *Ak-Chin O'Odham Runner*. For the most part, the *Runner* reads like many small-town papers. Recipes for Green Chili Corn, Cheesy Skillet Lasagna, and Edna Lou's Sour-Cream Cake vie for space with columns like "Search the Scriptures," by "Rev. and Mrs. Bud Fisher." The Fishers' Protestant evangelism competes, in turn, with a front-page story about eighteen Ak-Chin children receiving their first communion in the Ak-Chin Catholic church. The paper is ecumenical, if heavily religious.

The *Runner* also addresses social problems, however, and in these cases the tone—at least to the non–Ak-Chin ear—has a touch of Big Brother in it. An article in the December 1987 issue urging Ak-Chin G.E.D. students to complete their course work listed every candidate by name. The piece continued:

> Students should be in the Center library from 3:00 P.M. to 7:00 P.M. In keeping with Tribal policy of continual self-improvement and self-sufficiency, we urge you to continue with this portion of your education. If illness or family emergency prevents you from attending courses, please contact Ms. Smith, and convey any special requests. If you are a family member or friend of an enrolled student, please do your part in encouraging study and class attendance. We will all profit from a better-educated community.

There is an odd hint of relief in this and other public exhortations. The impression at Ak-Chin is that the big battles are over. Even chronic social problems are simply matters of fine-tuning. Indeed, Ak-Chin has toiled to perfect its ideal of a social economy to such an extent that the community all but ignores the larger economic transformations in its own backyard.

The town of Maricopa, next door to Ak-Chin, retains some of the true grit of a frontier settlement. This is still the desert, after all, with average summer daytime temperatures over 100 degrees and a recorded maximum of 122. Every time a car pulls out from a dead stop, it drags a quarter mile of dust behind it. I saw a boy driving a huge tractor down Maricopa's main street kick up as much dust as smoke from a forest fire.

Maricopa smells of manure and seems to enclose more of its residents in mobile homes than in houses. Every intersection is four straight lines to a ten-mile horizon. Against the surrounding uninhabitation, Maricopa defends itself with establishments like Harold's Club (BEER WINE & COCKTAILS), Maricopa Mercantile, Headquarters Buffet, Southwest Body Shop, Richard's Hay Barn (FEED/VET/SUPPLIES/TACK/RENTALS/WELDING/MATS, NEW AND USED), the Church of Jesus Christ of Latter Day Saints, and the Assembly of God.

Maricopa's heart beats at Pella's Place, with its sign bearing the promise of HOME STYLE COOKING and a picture of a coffee cup. I ate a lunch at Pella's Place, at a table next to a blond seventeen-year-old boy wearing a hundred-gallon black hat, a vest, a red kerchief, and wire-rimmed glasses like those favored by John Boy Walton. He was chuffing on a Marlboro and blowing smoke rings against Pella's window. As I considered this callow throwback, two fighter jets struck sparks off Pella's roof as they thundered on low trajectories into Luke Air Force Base, about thirty-five miles north near Sun City.

Bob Pella looked like Lee Van Cleef packing half a mile of mustache. He and Arizona Pella run the place. (I later discovered that Ak-Chin owns it.) No one at Pella's seemed to be conducting business or eager to get back to it, except for one young fellow who was doing business over Pella's pay phone. His name was Rick Scott, and he ran Trail's End Realty out of the Maricopa Business Barn, an establishment of corrugated steel across the street.

I asked Rick how the real-estate business was going in Maricopa. He produced a smudged Xerox with a dream on it, a 42,000-acre residential and commercial development only a few miles away from the reservation. Rick wanted to bring jobs, employees, and homeowners to town, all at once. The community will be called the Stanmar (i.e., Stanfield-Maricopa) Valley Consortium.

Most of the Stanmar land base has already been sold to investors, though there has been little actual development. But Maricopa just voted to approve a plan to widen the two-lane track connecting Maricopa with the main highway between Phoenix and Tucson. Change will come. Unlike Ak-Chin, which has first dibs at CAP water if things get dry, the farmers of Maricopa and Stanfield have to wait until the cities and towns are watered before they get theirs. "We've currently got more than we can use," said water-district head Van Tenney, "but push will eventually come to shove. At that point, all of us farmers are supposed to turn into real-estate developers. When you think about it, we're only an hour from Phoenix, which makes us a potential suburb. A four-lane from Route Ten will move things along considerably. I think in five to ten years this place will look a lot different."

If the future is just around the corner for Stanmar, it has already arrived just down the road in Casa Grande, where in 1987 alone the population grew a full 7 percent, from 17,500 to 18,600. A brochure issued by the Casa Grande Chamber of Commerce reminds one forcefully of the area's future. The city is hell-bent for light industry. Already a company called Hexcel, which makes "honeycomb products for aircraft," employs four hundred Casa Grandeans. Ross Laboratories employs 265 to make Similac baby formula, and the 270-employee Frito-Lay plant is, according to the Chamber, the "most modern snack food plant in [the] nation."

I asked Delia Antone if the Ak-Chin had considered what

would happen if the farm economy was superseded by another. "It's hard to picture what we can do when farming is all we've ever done," she answered. "I just keep my fingers crossed. To be honest, I'm against real-estate development. I know progress has to be made, but why can't we keep some of what we have the way it is? I can't picture this place filled up with homes. I've seen it over in the Sun Lakes area, because the Gila River Reservation borders on the backyards of a lot of those people. There are the little reservation homes, and—*whoosh!*—there are these fancy mansions. We can almost see the lights of Phoenix now, and Casa Grande is growing all the time. We're going to lose our openness."

Not all Ak-Chin members have such cloudy opinions about the future. An Ak-Chin fifth-grader, asked to make a poster of his dream for the community after the water settlement, drew a shopping mall with a shoe store, a movie theater, a mall, a motel, a Pizza Hut, and the "Ak-Chin World's Indian Rodeo."

With a view toward diverging from pure agriculture, Ak-Chin has reserved a 109-acre industrial park from its farmland. The park has three tenants: the Pinal Meat Packing Company ("a custom-kill processing firm"), Arizona Grain Storage Company (an Ak-Chin operation), and Grande Machinery, Incorporated (an Allis-Chalmers dealership). Leona thinks the park would do a lot better if the BIA wasn't involved. "All our leases have to go through the bureau because the land is held in federal trust. They get real cruddy about it sometimes, just pushing their weight around."

On the other hand, the tribe recently received some welcome federal assistance in the form of a $1 million UDAG (Urban Development Action Grant) to fund a joint venture with Calfonic, a Japanese car-parts manufacturer. Calfonic built an eight-mile test track along Ak-Chin's southern border, where the company subjects radiators and other components to the Ak-Chin elements. "They wanted the hottest, dirtiest site they could find," said Leona, "so they came here." The $20-million bond Calfonic was able to float with UDAG's cash and Ak-Chin's tribal status didn't hurt either.

In return, Calfonic pays Ak-Chin interest on its $1 million and gives community members first crack at nontechnical jobs. Already some Ak-Chin members serve in Calfonic security and maintenance positions. (Leona told me that "security and maintenance" means chasing coyotes and tumbleweed off the track, so the cars, coming around at 180 miles per hour, won't flip.)

Wayne Sprawls thinks Ak-Chin lacks any incentive to diversify its economy. "They got the CAP water forever," he grumbles, "and as long as you and I [the taxpayers] are paying their water bill, they'll do just fine." Indeed, Jim Hartdegen, Casa Grande's state representative, has speculated that Arizona agriculture may someday be an exclusively Native American industry.

When Ak-Chin received water, it also received its first ancient history. As a condition of water delivery, Ak-Chin commissioned an archaeological survey of the land the CAP canal would traverse. The archaeologists found something they thought deserved a closer look. Ak-Chin Farms' engineers were itchy to clear the land, but Leona held them off long enough to give the archaeologists a second shot at the sites. They struck a Hohokam site dating back to A.D. 300, unearthing a factory's worth of potsherds, intact houses, and human remains: "About twenty-six-people's worth," said Leona. "They're all the ancestors we have, and we didn't know what to do with them, so they sat in my office for about three months. We've finally decided to bury them in a common grave. I hope and pray to God that they all belonged to the same tribe, because I would hate to have them fighting in there for the rest of eternity."

Almost two hundred acres of Ak-Chin Farms have since been set aside as archaeological sites, and Ak-Chin is planning a museum to preserve their findings. They hope the museum will display or document everything that occurred in Ak-Chin Village from prehistory to post–water settlement. Leona invited me to sit in on a meeting of the Ak-Chin Museum Board, which was held in the community building's conference room, with its light brown carpet and long high-gloss table. The table was littered with aerial photographs of the reservation, and around them sat Ak-Chin's newly formed museum board and several council members.

For a group of people who had lived and worked with one another all their lives, the assembly was a study in individuality—in hairstyles alone. Leroy Narcia, who serves on the museum board, sported a "vanilla" barber's cut. Joseph Smith, a stocky council member who looks to be in his late thirties, wore a 1980s version of the old DA; and Norbert Peters, another council member and the youngest person present, wore a shag with a long, thin braid sneaking out of one side.

Charlie Carlyle, Ak-Chin's court jester and jack-of-all-trades, was there in his jeans and boots, wide belt and sport shirt. Leona's eldest son (who was raised by her parents), Charlie, coordinated a grant to the museum from the Administration for Native Americans. Forrest Gerrard, who is still on retainer as Ak-Chin's Washington consultant, was present, looking more like an artist than a lobbyist, in a green-tick designer shirt.

Presiding over the meeting was Nancy Fuller, an assistant director of the Smithsonian, donating time to the Ak-Chin project. Her first questions were pecuniary, and they sent Charlie in search of his secretary.

"Carol's got the exact figures on this. Where's she at?" asked Charlie.

"Doing the payroll," answered Leona.

"Well, leave her to it, or we'll all go hungry."

Many Ak-Chin artifacts are being held at Arizona State

University, and that makes Leona nervous. Ten years ago a group of archaeologists raided the tribe's archives. "That was in 1969, before the Antiquities Act made robbing Indians such a big thing. We lost a whole bunch of stuff. That's the main reason we wanted to build this museum, so we could have our things here with us."

The discussion moved to the preservation of the village and what sorts of accommodations the community might develop for visitors.

"Maybe you'd like to have some objects that children can pick up and play with," said Nancy.

"How about cactus?" suggested Charlie.

The talk moved into larger issues of culture than could be encompassed by a museum. The language of the Ak-Chin is dying, and the group wondered how it could be preserved. "My oldest two kids can speak Indian," said Leona, "but my youngest and my grand-kids speak none at all. I'd like to see a good school system and a real good Indian-language program, starting with preschool and going up through the first few years. If we don't, we'll lose the language to our TVs."

Leona was named Maricopa's citizen of the year in 1986, and Delia was asked to make a speech in her honor. "I told a story I had heard, that Leona and her sister used to scavenge wild birds' eggs and cook them up in a can with some grease and water. I said, 'She took chances eating those eggs, and she's still around. And she took chances with Ak-Chin; and we're going strong.' "

Leona Kakar turned fifty-three in 1989. As I was leaving her office, she announced to me, with the calm certitude that amazed her old boss, Wayne Sprawls, that she would live to be seventy-five or eighty years old. "Which is fine by me," she said. "I've got that much to do."

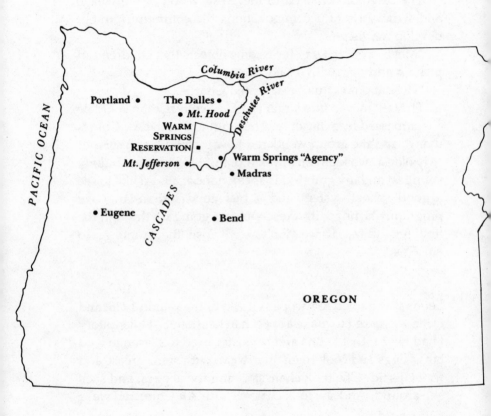

# 5

## The Confederated Tribes of the Warm Springs Reservation

My first phone call to the Confederated Tribes of the Warm Springs Reservation in Oregon was shunted to a tribal government staffer named Jeff Sanders. I told him about my book, and that a chapter on Warm Springs was almost obligatory given Warm Springs's reputation as Indian Country's "Big Daddy" of economic development. Jeff was silent for several moments.

"Hello?"

"I'm here," Jeff answered. "We have our own gas station."

"A gas station. That's nice to have."

"It's all right, I guess. Oh yeah, we also have a hydroelectric plant. It doesn't employ but two people."

"Is it profitable?"

"I guess so. We netted about four million dollars on it last year."

"Anything else?"

"Let's see . . . we have our own timber and sawmill operation. Got hundreds of people working there, actually. And we do about thirty million dollars in sales. We have a new sewing plant, which makes apparel for companies like Nike.

Oh yeah, I almost forgot Kah-Nee-Ta. You know, one of those four-star resorts—golf course, swimming, fishing, horseback riding, tennis, what have you. . . . "I guess you should know: we're the largest employer in central Oregon. We just don't like to brag about it."

Jeff said that if I was planning to come out, the confederation could arrange a discount rate at the tribes' resort. I asked him for directions.

"That's easy enough. Fly to Portland. Ask the rental-car place how to get on Route 26. Follow it up over the Cascades and down into the desert on the other side. Drive for about an hour until the road drops into a canyon. At the bottom of the canyon there's a blinking yellow light. If you took a right there, you'd be in Agency, what we call our main town. Take a left instead. Drive another twenty minutes. You'll be at Kah-Nee-Ta."


Several weeks later, at dusk on a Thursday night in one of the coldest Oregon Februaries on record, I crested the Cascades, skimming over sand-fine snow in a weightless Subaru Justy. The Matterhorn peak of Mount Hood appeared in a brief spotlight of sunset, then vanished in the dark and a persistent snow squall, while the Justy switchbacked down its eastern slope.

The desert was there, at the bottom of the foothills. The road drew itself into a taut line; the pines turned into sagebrush. Except for the temperature, I might have been in Ak-Chin, Arizona. At the end of a thirty-mile beeline, the road sank into the promised canyon and reached the blinking yellow light, the first traffic signal since Route 26 shed the Portland suburbs. The road to the left wandered up into a new set of hills. I turned on the radio and heard the quavering, falsetto shouts of traditional Native American song, accompanied by heavy drumbeats. Finally I reached Kah-

Nee-Ta, a gigantic arrowhead of lighted windows cut into the side of a steep bluff. The lobby was severe and grand, with high cedar walls decorated in tribal motifs. A sizable and pungent tree trunk smoldered in the middle of an open fire pit as big as a pond.

I ate a late dinner at a table covered with pink cloth in a dining room lit by two dozen globular chandeliers suspended in small constellations from a vaulted ceiling. My waiter had a dark, full-blooded countenance, but his accent and demeanor were in keeping with a trendy restaurant on Manhattan's Upper West Side. He introduced himself as André and served me broccoli soup, a grilled salmon steak, wild rice, ratatouille, and a flap of hot, remarkably delicate frybread with homemade huckleberry jam.

The food was delicious, but the space was like a stage set. I was the only customer in a room that could accommodate 140. In heat and light alone, it must have been costing Kah-Nee-Ta thirty dollars a bite to feed me. Was the lodge a going concern, or a showpiece? Tribal leaders, as I would discover, had recently asked the same question of themselves.

Three Indian populations compose the Warm Springs Confederation—the Wascos, the Warm Springs, and the Paiutes. In 1988, there were three thousand people on the tribal rolls, about twenty-three hundred of them living on the Warm Springs Reservation. Before American legalities lumped them into "tribes," the people who came to be known as Wascos and the Warm Springs Indians lived for ten thousand years in extended-family villages up and down the Columbia River. The Warm Springs spoke Sahaptin and occupied the middle longitudes of the state, while the Wascos spoke a Chinook tongue and lived further west toward the Pacific. The combined aboriginal territory of the Columbia River people covered 16,000 square miles, a sixth of present-day Oregon, bordered by the Columbia in the north and reaching as far south as the city of Bend, as far west as the Blue Mountains, and as far east as Mounts Jefferson and Hood.

On June 25, 1855, four years before the Oregon Territory earned its statehood, General Joel Palmer, the territory's superintendent of Indian affairs, gathered an arbitrary representation of the Columbia River tribes and bands under an oak tree in Wasco, a settlement near The Dalles, where the Columbia narrows. His mission was to clear the way for the final limits of the westward expansion, securing incoming homesteaders from Indian attacks.

Dubbing the river people Wasco and Warm Springs Indians for the occasion, Palmer urged the group to sign a treaty ceding their 10-million-acre habitation in exchange for a 600,000-acre reservation a hundred miles south of their Columbia homelands. The Indians were in a poor bargaining position. Between 1750 and 1800 imported European diseases had reduced their original ten-thousand population to about two thousand. Palmer sweetened the deal with $150,000 in cash and promises of farm equipment and a newly constructed town, complete with white tradesmen who would teach their skills to Native apprentices. The Wascos and Warm Springs signed.

By 1859, all except for a few holdouts had moved to the new reservation. Although their adopted territory was mostly unfamiliar to them, the Indians were mollified by a treaty provision that guaranteed them the right to continue to draw food from "all other usual and accustomed stations," including their old salmon fisheries on the Columbia. No provision had been made, however, for the event that these "usual and accustomed stations" would soon belong to white landowners, who couldn't abide Natives on their riverfront property. A supplemental treaty, drawn up in 1865, soothed white settlers with a stipulation that Indians could not leave the Warm Springs Reservation without a permit. Their new home had become a prison camp.

The treaty of '65 was never successfully enforced, but in the autumn of 1879, thirty-eight Paiute Indians were carried to Warm Springs from Fort Vancouver as prisoners of war. Hunter-gatherers from the Great Basin, the Paiutes represented an entirely different culture from the Wascos and Warm Springs, and were sometime enemies of both. The Paiute prisoners at Warm Springs were later joined by relatives and friends fleeing other reservations.

Somehow this conglomeration of mutual strangers surmounted their differences, and the Confederated Tribes became confederated in more than name. They were forced together in part by their isolation. The first paved highway didn't make it into the reservation until after World War II. Unbothered by outsiders, a number of people at Warm Springs were still living in tepees in the 1920s.

Jeff Sanders brought me up to date on Warm Springs history in a spacious office he had commandeered from an out-of-town colleague in the Tribal Administration Building. Outside its plate-glass wall, a hunting red-tailed hawk was glued to the gray sky above an arid landscape. Faced with the same cedar lap siding as Kah-Nee-Ta lodge, the administration building is a large, low, striking piece of architecture, completed in 1977 with $1.5 million in FHA financing. Its interior is carpeted in earth tones and separated into working spaces by movable partitions dressed in abstract orange and plum designs.

Jeff is a Wasco Indian. His graying black hair hung down either side of his face to chin level. He sported mutton chops and, in line with his fifty years, a minor gut. He wore tinted aviator glasses, a white shirt, gray tie, and a cardigan sweater. When talking or listening, Jeff leaned forward on his elbows, his forearms flat on the table and his hands clasped together, twiddling his thumbs.

"Warm Springs has been a very closed community," he remarked. "We haven't been willing to share anything with the rest of the world until recently." Requests for public information are not assigned to any one person but passed like hot potatoes between several busy administrators. Jeff got me. He works on the staff of the Confederated Tribes' general manager (Warm Springs's CEO) and lives back up Route 26 in the Cascade foothills, where the only noise he hears is made by coyotes. If a truck goes by at night, it wakes him up.

The cold snap had frozen Jeff's water pipes the night before, and his Bronco had failed to start that morning, but Jeff was gracious. He also managed to present an enormous amount of information about his people in a very short time, without seeming to hurry. A self-described "high school dropout," Jeff has served the tribes as public works manager, by overseeing housing, utilities, a community center, and recreation programs. For a decade before that, Jeff was chief of the Warm Springs police force, having worked his way up from a weekend substitute back when his regular job was pumping gas at the tribes' garage.

"Not twenty years ago it was still like the Wild West around here," he said. "We'd have our summer tribal celebrations, and when the drunks got too out of hand, I'd just haul 'em over to a skinny tree and handcuff 'em to it 'til they sobered up."

Jeff grew up in a one-room house with a dirt floor and no plumbing. "Up until World War Two there weren't *any* houses on the reservation with running water," he said. "We would live on timbering jobs or follow cash-crop harvests like Hispanic farm workers now. In the spring and summer and fall we'd pick strawberries and raspberries in the Willamette Valley [below Portland], hops in the Salem area, and up to The Dalles for the cherry and apple crops. We used to bury some of the potatoes we picked in our cellars. I don't remember too many trips to the grocery store."

Like all of the children on the reservation, Jeff boarded at the BIA school, even though he could see his family's house through the classroom windows. "The poverty here was to the point of food shortage, so really the parents had no choice," he said. "If you wanted your kids to eat, you sent 'em to school." The BIA also provided the students with clothing—all identical. Boys wore white T-shirts and Levis, and girls wore white blouses and blue jumpers. They all wore black high-top shoes. Students were also issued a "Sunday best" uniform, because on Sundays, in a triumph of church over state, all students were required to attend Catholic or Protestant services.

Jeff's mother was a Wasco from Agency. His father was from the Siletz Indian Reservation on the Oregon coast, a logger and welder who came to Warm Springs in the depression as a worker in a CCC (Citizen Conservation Corp) camp. Sometimes the family would go up to the Columbia River to fish in a shantytown on the site of the Wasco's ancestral home. Jeff remembers seeing signs in restaurants near there saying NO DOGS OR INDIANS ALLOWED.

In 1938, the year Jeff was born, the Confederated Tribes established a formal, democratic government under the Indian Reorganization Act. In addition to adopting a constitution, the confederation also formulated a corporate charter, which authorized the tribes to engage in business enterprises as a corporate entity. Later Warm Springs generations would see these two documents as the bases of Warm Springs's eventual and remarkable success. At the time they meant little at all. As with Ak-Chin and the Mississippi Choctaws, the BIA in that era had total control over Indians' lives, and the Warm Springs Tribal Council's members had so little to attend to that they met only once or twice a month.

For a century after their relocation, the inhabitants of Warm Springs had remained powerless. And poor. And their imposed home was perhaps the richest territory in the state. Two-thirds of the Warm Springs Reservation—more than five hundred square miles of it—is covered by forests of commercial-grade pine and fir. A third as much timber as on International Paper Company's celebrated million-acre Maine timber empire stood untouched on the reservation's hills and mountainsides. "We were all scratch farmers, we were all broke, and we were all sitting on a gold mine," said Jeff. "Only it hadn't turned into gold yet."

The first council member to develop Warm Springs's economy was the first Warm Springs Reservation Indian with a college education. His name was Vern Jackson, a member of the Wasco tribe. In the 1950s, when timber revenue began to trickle through the BIA into the tribal coffers, Vern Jackson was a young, impatient leader. He harped on education as an essential tribal bootstrap until his fellow council members told him to practice what he was preaching. Vern took a leave of absence and went with his family to the University of Oregon, where he graduated with a business degree in 1958 at the age of forty.

When Vern returned, the council created the first executive office for him: secretary-treasurer to the tribal council. Vern was in essence Warm Springs's CEO, with primary authority over the tribes' assets and resources. The council removed itself from Vern's day-to-day decisions but reserved the right to fire him if he screwed up.

As it happened, Vern's first economic break came with the destruction of one of Warm Springs most cherished assets. In spite of intense non-Indian pressure, the Warm Springs Confederation had defended for a century its treaty rights to take salmon from the Columbia. But though they had held their own against white landowners, they were no match in the end for the federal government. In early 1957 the U.S. Corps of Engineers completed The Dalles Dam at Celilo Falls. The reservoir filled by the dam submerged the old fishing grounds of the Warm Springs and of the Yakima and Umatilla tribes along the Columbia's northern shores in Washington State. In 1958, the same year Vern was appointed secretary-treasurer, the Confederated Tribes received a backhanded windfall: a federal cash settlement as compensation for the Native equivalent of Noah's Flood. (As a friend of the tribes put it, " 'perpetuity' took on the value of $28 million.") Warm Springs's portion of this was $4 million—far short, they claimed, of the lost food and commercial value of the salmon.

But $4 million was something. While the Yakima and Umatilla atomized their settlements in per-capita payments, the Warm Springs Tribal Council—on Vern's strong recommendation—reserved most of their money for investments that would benefit the Confederated Tribes collectively.

Like the Mississippi Choctaws, the Warm Springs Indians spent their first discretionary income on a written report. Not long after the settlement money arrived, the tribal council commissioned Norman McCowen, an economist at Oregon State University, to conduct a $100,000 study on tribal resource development. McCowen's research team, at times forty strong, swarmed across the reservation. They were led by Jim Rock, a Ph.D. candidate who produced as his doctoral thesis a five-volume economic road map for the Confederated Tribes called the "Comprehensive Plan."

Based on countless interviews with tribal members and detailed surveys of natural resources, the Comprehensive Plan examined every aspect of Warm Springs life, from timber resources to educational aspirations. "Cash. Jobs. Homes. College," a tribal councilman told me. "Everything—but *everything*—was part of the plan."

Jim Rock is now a D.C. lobbyist for Montana Power Company. Thirty years after the fact, he remains deeply moved by his experiences at Warm Springs. "Vern's father, Charlie Jackson, was tribal chairman then, and he treated me like family. When I got my degree, the entire tribal council showed up to see me pick it up." Not surprisingly, Jim agreed to stay on at Warm Springs to help realize the vision he had codified from their dreams. Only after he began trying to make the plan stick did Jim begin to understand the cultural divide between mainstream and tribal attitudes.

"It took a year to get the people here to accept the project," said Jim. "We would meet in the Agency Long House [a place where traditional tribal ceremonies are held]. The Indians sat according to seniority, the men along one side and the women along the other, the elders closest to the front. I noticed in all the meetings where nothing seemed to happen that the seat closest to the front on the women's side was always empty.

"One Sunday a woman named Mary Wilson took that seat. She was ninety-two years old, the oldest person living on the reservation. I gave my two-minute summary of what we were trying to accomplish, which took about ten minutes to be translated into Sahaptin. When I was done, Mary Wilson stood up, and it got real, real quiet. She stared right at me for a minute, and then she spoke. When she was done, the translator put her words into English: 'You have saved the lives of my grandchildren,' she said.

"That was all it took. I went by the tribal office afterward, and all these tribal members who'd been stonewalling for months were waiting outside, itching to go to work. On a Sunday afternoon.

"That's when I decided that Warm Springs was a matriarchy."

Thus began what Vern Jackson would later call "a transition to the white man's way of looking at things." A footnoted oracle, the Comprehensive Plan predicted the value of timber, the potential of tourism, the potential profits of water power. Tribal members believe it would not be stretching the point to say that the first twenty years of the Warm Springs boom boiled down to filling in the blanks of the plan.

The Warm Springs people I talked to also attributed their half-century rise to long and careful sight of the tribal council. This group of eleven men and women bear a grave responsibility, because there is no complete separation of powers at Warm Springs, and everything flows to and from them. Council members tend to be chosen for their common sense rather than their technical proficiencies. Jeff Sanders told me that the council's average educational level has remained steady at the fifth- or sixth-grade level for decades. As their success has proven, however, these people are perfectly capable of making sound decisions. They simply delegate chores requiring formal academic or business skills in the way corporate executives delegate typing and accounting.

Council pay rates are set by tribal referendum. Council members are not paid salaries but fees set at a flat rate for the days they are present. One council member told me that his average annual income was $6,000, and his tribal duties allowed no time even to consider moonlighting. Warm Springs, one of the most prosperous communities in Native America, which pays its top business managers nationally competitive executive salaries, is governed by the hearts and minds of people who are poor.

Under certain conditions, steam from the Warm Springs sawmill generates its own weather conditions in the Deschutes River valley. The thermometer sat on four degrees the morning I arrived, and an otherwise dazzling central Oregon morning was dim and cloudy for a mile around the plant.

The effect was a bit unsettling, but the manufactured

cloud cover was clean. Benson Heath, the tribes' personnel director, remembered working at the mill one summer in the 1960s. "That was pre-EPA standards, and we burned all of the mill's refuse in an open pit. Soot was on everything. By the end of the day I looked like a coal miner. A couple of months of that was a great incentive to stay in college."

The tribes' timber processing operation is called Warm Springs Forest Products Industries (or by its ungainly abbreviation, WSFPI). The sawmill's personnel director, safety director, and man-about-town is Lewis O. "Woody" Wood, and he didn't laugh when I cracked a joke about his name. A non-Indian, Woody is a small, neat man with a gray mustache and wire-rimmed glasses.

I met Woody in his office, a sort of in-house storefront of sawmill supplies that looked like an auto-parts shop, except for a copy of the *Kiplinger Washington Letter* on the counter. Woody told me he had worked this mill for twenty-one years, since before the tribes bought it in the 1960s. His first job was as millwright, the keeper of the plant's machinery. Woody still knows hundreds of pieces of equipment inside out, and his tour of the mill was a short course in the art of timber processing.

A good portion of the operation occurs out-of-doors or in unheated spaces. Woody and I were underdressed—he in a red-and-black checked woolen jacket and I in a Windbreaker—but neither of us was about to admit it. As the morning wore on, and the temperature failed to rise, we both developed a hunched, stiff-legged gait. Woody is a ferocious smoker, like a lot of people in Warm Springs. He rumbled along in front of me, billowing smoke and frosted breath like a steam engine.

Our first stop was the lumber mill, where Ponderosa, white pine, and sugar pine logs are turned into the boards that account for 40 percent of WSFPI's business. The early stages of lumbering are largely mechanical. The workers—

evenly divided between Indian and non-Indian, according to Woody—emerged from the shadows of the machines like friendly ghosts, waving and smiling at Woody and pantomiming their reaction to the weather with exaggerated shivers. Raw logs are loaded onto conveyors and passed through a barker, which denudes them with rapid chain lashes. After scanning the scoured logs with its electric eye, a computerized buzz saw like a jumbo pizza wheel attached to a long handle slices the logs into exact lengths, cutting through twenty inches of tree trunk with barely a whistle.

The uniformed lengths run along another conveyor, which rolls them onto the scaffold for the head saw. This stainless-steel beast squares them off, discarding the round outer layers for wood chips, then passes lengthwise through each log to cut as many boards of a predetermined thickness as each length will yield. The fresh lumber that results is sorted by hand. The three graders (as the sorters are called) on shift during my visit were all non-Indian. Woody told me that whites, by virtue of experience, still dominated the grading positions. In two seconds, with the kind of smooth speed that mimics slow motion, each grader checked everything about a board, from its knots to its grain pattern, and scored it according to its particular market and price bracket. Between them, the three graders were sorting dozens of boards a minute.

Stacks of inspected boards are built into six-layer ricks, then conveyed over a short railroad track to a warehouse-size oven to be steam dried. As Woody and I hoofed it from the mill to the drier, we saw a tribal member on a steam shovel digging out some frost heaves that had grown up between the tracks and backed up the boards' migration.

Most of WSFPI's boards are sold to manufacturers, who make windows, furniture, and toys from them. Most of the lumber is sold to Oregon companies, though some of it finds its way to Florida and Georgia. Tribal harvests of Douglas fir, western larch, hemlock, spruce, cedar, and other timber species go directly from the forest to the veneer plant.

Veneer is the base material for plywood, pared from whole logs in long sheets. Each log is maneuvered into place against a sharp straight edge and whirred against it so the veneer peels like paper towel off a roll. In a matter of seconds a twenty-inch trunk is reduced to a lamppost, while out of the peeler's backside shoots a long, flat sheet curling at the edges like a papyrus scroll. The machine can peel sheets as thin as a tenth of an inch. The peeling process heats the green wood, making steam that rises to the ceiling, where it forms into clouds. Woody had seen it rain inside there on a hot day.

The most back-breaking work I saw at WSFPI was the sorting and stacking of fresh veneer sheets as they came barreling down the line. A deceptively slight tribal member hauled unwieldy four-by-eight-foot flaps of the stuff off a rushing conveyor belt and pumped them into a rick behind him. Woody told me the worker would do that for two hours straight, then take a fifteen-minute break, which must be why jobs at WSFPI are described as "working the green chain."

Once the veneer has been sorted and stacked, it is turned into plywood. On that day, the plywood operation was making three-ply, five-eighths-inch plywood. A machine spread glue on a four-by-eight sheet, which passed on to a station where workers placed smaller strips of veneer crosswise on it. Another machine glued a second four-by-eight on top, and the assembled plywood rolled along conveyors into a three-hundred-degree oven to bake for an hour until the glue set.

All of these processes produce leftover wood chips. WSFPI sells them to Crown Zellerbach for paper. Sawdust and other wood trash are dubbed "hog" fuel and used to fire the operation's own power plant. The hog is blown through air shafts to the "cyclone," a centrifuge through which the fuel is sifted, like brown snow into a furnace, to explode in almost total, smoke-free combustion. The conflagration drives boilers that produce steam to dry lumber and power electrical generators. Woody explained this process to me in a huge black room in the bowels of the power plant. He pulled a large bung out of a hole in the wall and exposed a roaring maelstrom of fire. Then he pointed to the floor, where I could see hell light shining through the cracks between the steel plates under our feet, and he winked at me.

Woody proudly displayed his set of three-story boilers. They were already thirty years old and stranded in Alaska when Warm Springs bought them in the early 1970s. Persh Andrews, the former sawmill manager, decided they were still a bargain—in good shape and a tenth of their original cost. Woody himself shepherded them down to the reservation—boilers, turbines, generators, piping, housing, substation and all—by railroad to the Alaska coast, on barges to Seattle, by railroad to the reservation border town of Madras, and on trucks to Agency. In 1987, the WSFPI powerhouse generated 22 million kilowatt-hours, used almost 21 million, and sold the remainder to Pacific Power and Light, netting ample savings in overall operating costs.

WSFPI jobs are among the most coveted on the reservation. Nothing except construction pays better, and those jobs are even harder to come by. Woody told me that the waiting list at WSFPI is three years long. When workers quit or get fired they go to the back of the line to reapply. As Woody put it, "The job market at this skill level, in this neck of the woods, is tight. If you lose your job, you don't work."


Kah-Nee-Ta may be Warm Springs's showpiece, but timber is the key to Warm Springs's prosperity. In 1987, WSFPI escorted more than $21 million through the reservation economy. The mill bought $10-million worth of Warm Springs trees, generated $3.7 million in wages to tribal members, and remanded $1.3 million in net income to the tribal government. The timber is harvested from tribal holdings by fourteen private contract loggers, nine of whom were tribal members. In 1987, the loggers' collective earnings totaled $6 million, paid by the tribes at prices negotiated with WSFPI.

The general manager of WSFPI is Bob Macy, a tribal member who grew up within sight of the mill. Bob looks like a swarthy John Updike, handsome and strong-nosed with his thick black hair roughly parted far to one side. When I met him in the mill's office building, Bob was wearing a maroon sweater, brown suede athletic shoes, and half-glasses around his neck on a black lanyard. He smoked tidily and continuously, and was quick to respond to questions with thorough, clear answers. We were joined by Bob's administrative assistant, Ralph Minnick, who recently held the Confederated Tribes' highest executive office as secretary-treasurer of the tribal council. In that capacity, Ralph was in effect Bob's boss. Now the roles are reversed, although neither of them made anything of it.

Except for its punctuation by the locomotive whistle of the mill's shift alarm, my conversation with Bob and Ralph was surprisingly like conversations with Tom Tureen and Daniel Zilkha, the Passamaquoddies' Ivy League investment bankers. They were a couple of pros, happy to share their experience, interrupting each other with lively sarcasm, amused that anybody would be interested in their jobs, showing none of the anxious earnestness of people over their heads.

For the last year or two, Bob and Ralph had been on an international shopping spree, looking for a new mill. "We went over to West Germany to look at one system that would do a beautiful job," said Bob, "but it cost sixteen million dollars. When the tribal council heard *that* price tag, they about shit in their knickers. So we scaled back our ambitions and came up with a new estimate from the West Germans and another from a U.S. company, each about fourteen million. Then we got 'em down to about twelve million."

WSFPI needs a new mill because the enterprise will have to be able to process small logs more efficiently to remain profitable. Most of the larger trees in the Warm Springs forests are gone, and the tribe is rapidly approaching its "target forest," a static number of trees harvested each year to sustain a permanent timber supply. "Log size is crucial," said Bob. "We're walking away from three, three and a half million dollars a year trying to run small logs through an ancient mill. We did an in-house study and found that we could lose six hundred thousand dollars in one day trying to feed our old system small logs."

The new mill, which would produce dimensional lumber like two-by-fours, represents a sizable investment of tribal funds, but it is far from a luxury item. Twenty-five Oregon mills shut down in 1988. Some of these closings were due to rising exports of unprocessed logs and environmentally driven restraints on harvesting of public forests. (The U.S. Forestry Service had restricted cutting of older conifers to protect spotted owls, and a sign posted outside of a mill that closed in February 1989 read, THE OWLS WON AND IT'S OVER!) A large part of the problem is overcutting of privately held acreage. Warm Springs has avoided serious trouble in this regard because tribal members in charge of other tribal resources, like water and game, have forced down WSFPI's annual allowable cut. "They came up with a recommendation that our cut be reduced by sixteen million board feet," said Bob. "That's a seven-million-dollar drop in income, so there is a financial price to pay."


Until the 1940s, all of the timber in the world wouldn't have helped Warm Springs compete with the forests near major markets in Portland, Corvallis, and Eugene. Transportation would have been expensive even to nearby customers, because there was only one road in or out of the reservation, a one-laner from Madras that dead-ended in Agency. Like all timber on Indian reservations, the Warm Springs trees were managed by the BIA, which only harvested a few trees each year for reservation projects like housing, the school, and the health center. Then came the war, and the price of timber took off. In 1942 the tribes convinced the BIA to lease some of their timberland to a company called Tite Knot Pine Mill, which had mills in Sisters and Redmond. The tribal council trusted Tite Knot because tribal members who had worked for the company had been treated fairly.

A year or two later, Sam O. Johnson, sometime state representative from Redmond and a land baron who owned a company called Jefferson Plywood, was granted permission to build a mill where WSFPI now stands. The Jefferson mill cleaned up through the war years and extended its reach when a wider, paved Highway 26 came into the reservation in 1956. "Some of the things that have happened here we've had help with," said Bob Macy. "Sam Johnson was a good friend of Warm Springs, and really the first major employer of tribal members." Like Wayne Sprawls, Ak-Chin's first farm manager, Sam Johnson believed the Indians of Warm Springs could handle the mill themselves and it was he who made it possible for them to buy it.

In a reservation-wide referendum in 1966, the Indians of Warm Springs authorized the Confederated Tribes to finance their own forest-products complex. "When the people voted on this enterprise," said Ralph Minnick, "they also set up the two documents under which this place operates. One created a separate board and a business manager, which put the enterprise at arm's length from tribal government. The other created the cutting contract, which sets the terms and the price of timber that the enterprise buys from the tribe, within the BIA's forest management rules."

Current estimates of the original purchase price of Johnson's mill vary between $2 and $6 million. "I'd say the *total* purchase price of the mill was about five point two million dollars," said Bob. "But that was some time ago, so we're taking these figures off the skin of our butts." The tribes had to borrow the full amount, so Sam Johnson set about convincing funding sources that they were a good credit risk.

"The biggest problem was collateral," said Bob, "since there's a quirk in our constitution—"

"Not a quirk," threw in Ralph, "a provision!"

"All right, a provision, which says that the tribes can never sell any of their assets. But we *could* mortgage the cutting contract because it was separate from the actual forest resource. The way we finally set it up, if we defaulted on our loan, the bank had the right to come in with their own people and operate the plant until they had recouped their investment."

In 1967, with several bank loans and some cash fronted by Sam Johnson himself, WSFPI bought the local Jefferson complex, including the sawmill and the veneer machinery in Warm Springs and a plywood factory in Madras. Jefferson's management (all non-Indian at that time) remained in place under contract to WSFPI. Four years later, WSFPI had paid off its loan. Shortly thereafter, the tribal enterprise terminated its contract with Jefferson and hired Jefferson's managers onto WSFPI's own payroll. In the early seventies the enterprise was put on notice that its plywood factory in Madras was subject to state tax, because the plant was off-reservation. WSFPI hauled the entire operation up to Warm Springs, retaining the Madras site as a private railroad depot.

I asked Bob how his life prepared him for the biggest job in the tribes' economy. He answered that his parents were Warm Springs's first entrepreneurs. Macy senior founded Macy's Store, the only retail business in Agency. All of

Bob's siblings followed their parents' lead into business. One of his brothers now runs Macy's, and another, Richard, owns an Agency restaurant called the Burger Inn. A third brother runs a cable television system. "And I have an older brother, Danny, who's an engineer in offshore oil exploration for Texaco," said Bob. "He's based in New Orleans and goes 'round the world, swapping information with Texaco's foreign business partners."

"What a great job," I said.

"Yeah. Danny really enjoyed Angola," said Bob, and he and Ralph cracked up. "He told me all you saw around there was Russian equipment driven around by armed Russians. He spent his free time playing tennis with Russian engineers, and there'd always be a KGB guy sitting on the sidelines like a referee."

Bob grew up around the store and worked after school in a little jukebox room his parents had set up for youngsters. "The kids from the boarding school would come down to buy candy twice a week—fifty to seventy-five kids at once to get bubble gum and pop," said Bob. "The grown-ups would often pay for their groceries with firewood, and then we'd resell it. When I was about fourteen, I used to haul that wood to customers so I could drive my father's truck. It's amazing what you'll do to get behind the wheel when you're fourteen; I'd load a whole cord on board for a two-mile ride."

Bob graduated from Oregon State in 1963 and worked for five years as a BIA forester on the Colville Indian Reservation in northern Washington State. "When I was growing up, *I* stereotyped Indians, because all the people that ran anything around Warm Springs—besides Macy's—were white. Colville changed my mind, since up there everybody in charge was *Indian*, not white. By the time I got back here again, a lot of our own Indians had gotten into traditionally white positions."

Bob came back to Warm Springs to work at Macy's and

was elected to the tribal council. "This was 1971, four years after the tribes had bought the mill, and we council members were trying to get WSFPI's bosses to move tribal members into management. I was working in the store one Saturday, and Persh Andrews—the mill's manager then—came in for some coffee. I guess he must have been a little tired of hearing the council push for more tribal workers and administrators 'cause he said to me, 'You have a background in forestry. You think it's so easy, why don't *you* come over and try it?'

"So I did, in 1972. I started out as an all-purpose helper. Then in 'seventy-six our accountant left us to go work for a tribal logger who'd bought a couple of restaurants in Portland. Before he took off, I remember going in and asking him how he came up with the figures I was using to write up a project for precommercial forest thinning. His answer was to clean his desk off onto mine and say, 'The best way to learn the books is to do 'em. You got any questions, here's my number in Portland. Call me.'

"He was gone a couple of days later. Somehow me and the girls [the mill's bookkeepers] managed to get out the next monthly report and the one after that. By the time we got to the annual report, we'd made all the mistakes we were going to make in the monthlies and we just readjusted them."

In 1978 Persh Andrews retired, and WSFPI picked up a general manager named Ralph DeMoisy, who had just retired from Fiberboard Corporation in San Francisco. DeMoisy was hired on a short-term basis as Macy's mentor, working Bob into his job.

Bob has four children. Three are in college—one in Eugene, one in Springfield, and one at San Diego State. "There's lots of pressures here that keeps kids close to home and out of college, lots of temptations to find anything that will let them stick around. It was the same when I was growing up. I've told my kids, 'Don't tie yourselves to any particular locality. You can always come back. We'll always be here. But don't sell yourself short just to stick around.' "

Nineteen eighty-seven was the twentieth anniversary of WSFPI. In that time, the mill had purchased almost 2 billion board feet of reservation timber and paid the Confederated Tribes $130 million for it. It paid out $38 million in wages to tribal members, spouses, and other Indians, and another $70 million to tribal loggers. And it remanded net profits of $24 million to the Warm Springs government, which spent it on services for its constituents.

A decade's worth of WSFPI books were audited by Coopers and Lybrand for the anniversary report. Their analysis showed an interesting pattern. Between 1978 and 1987, despite a flood tide of cash flow, overall business income dropped from $14 million in 1978 to $12 million in 1987. Part of this sluggish earnings report was due to the 1980s collapse of the housing market, followed by a collapsing lumber market. Prices had begun to pick up in 1988, but WSFPI still faced an operating loss of $1.5 million for the year.

The root of the 1988 shortfall was a strike, which presented WFSPI's management with an unprecedented challenge and broke new ground for the tribes' jurisdiction. Since 1958, before the tribes took ownership, WSFPI workers had been unionized. The contract came up for renewal in August 1988, and negotiations broke down. The union staged a walkout and set up a picket line in front of the mill entrance. The tribe ordered the union off the reservation, forcing the picketers across the Deschutes River, half a mile down the road. The order was enforced by tribal police. Indians who would not comply were jailed in Warm Springs, and non-Indians were jailed in Jefferson County's slammer.

In their now-distant picket post, the strikers weren't visible enough to make an impression on scabs. The union took the case to the National Labor Relations Board, which ruled that indeed it had no jurisdiction on a reservation and that a

Warm Springs tribal enterprise was exempt from U.S. labor laws. As strikes go, WSFPI's experience was relatively short and sweet, lasting only a few weeks. The tribe issued a letter to all employees saying those who wanted their jobs still had them. In the end, the mill only lost ten workers. According to Woody Wood, the benefits and wages at Warm Springs today are in line with those in the region.

Bob began to talk about WSFPI's dreams of moving into remanufacturing, using the shop materials produced by the mill to make merchandise like door- and window frames, which would create more jobs and another profit center. A phone call interrupted him, and Ralph Minnick took me down the hall to continue the conversation in his office. Ralph wore steel-rimmed glasses and sported a practical haircut, gray flannels, short boots, and a plaid shirt with a white undershirt showing through an open collar. He had never been to New York and was rather proud of that. But he couldn't have pulled off the role of a country bumpkin if he tried. With his mild, cosmopolitan smirk and conspicuous intellect, Ralph resembled a pretenured college professor.

As our conversation evolved from business technicalities to broader concerns, and as he warmed to my dawning understanding of his point of view, Ralph emerged from his laconic shell as a man with a powerful imagination who has dedicated his considerable talents entirely to the Confederated Tribes. He started working in tribal administration in high school as a summer go-for. He took an undergraduate business degree at Portland State and went on to serve as the tribes' financial administrator and health manager, before being appointed to a four-year term as secretary-treasurer in the early 1980s. As Bob's assistant, he had been crunching a lot of numbers associated with the small-log facility and tuning up personnel policies in the wake of the strike.

Ralph's background in tribal governance frames his evaluations of WSFPI's performance. "We're an enterprise," he said. "We're expected to make a profit. But how much of a profit are we supposed to make? Who are you going to measure us against? From a purely economic standpoint, we should have had that small logging mill in here three years ago, but there are all these other considerations to take into account. As managers, we are insulated from the tribal council by our board of directors, but when you get right down to financing, we compete for money that belongs to all of us as Warm Springs people. The council needs to know what's going on and to make sure that what we're doing is correct.

"Bobby and the previous manager have both done a tremendous job of increasing the percentage of tribal members employed in this plant, from the teens to almost fifty percent. In order to do that, we've had to overstaff a bit, to cover ourselves when some of the boys get a touch of the weekend flu. But that's significant growth, and some of those guys have moved into the skilled positions. How do you equate that sort of accomplishment with Joe Blow over the hill who says, 'I've got to get a twelve-percent return on my money.' If we don't achieve twelve percent, are we worth less? More?

"What do you expect as a return on your money in Indian Country, knowing the social environment you're working with? If the tribe puts its money in the U.S. Treasury, we get seven percent. Maybe that's how you determine economic success in Indian Country: anything better than the feds can give you. I'm never going to get eighteen percent if I keep giving some guy one more break before I let him go, so maybe Indian Country can't compete on a national level now, but then we're playing a different ball game."

When the tribes undertook the first major revision of the Comprehensive Plan for its twentieth anniversary in 1980, the task approached the revision of the King James Bible.

"Point 4" of a report issued on the revision reads: "If the Tribal Council reaches a decision which is contrary to the Comprehensive Plan, the council will first amend the Comprehensive Plan as necessary to conform with its decision."

Thirty years later, the modified plan continues to hold sway over major tribal decisions, and today the Confederated Tribes employ 1,200 people: 340 work at WSFPI; 75 to 175 at Kah-Nee-Ta (depending on the season); 50 with the Bureau of Indian Affairs (80 to 90 percent of whom are in forestry); 40 in a new sewing factory; a considerable number employed by independent tribal loggers; some entrepreneurs in Native arts and crafts; and around 600 in tribal government. Together with the jobs generated for contractors and nearby retailers, the tribes are now officially the largest employment center in central Oregon. The Central Oregon Economic Development Council, which represents the communities of Bend, Sisters, Redmond, and Prineville, reserves two seats on its board for Warm Springs Indians.

As an organization, Warm Springs has become a sizable corporate-government hybrid, employing four CPAs and the services of several investment firms to manage its assets and its cash flow. With its ambitious range of functions, from psychiatric services to road maintenance, Warm Springs resembles at different times a municipality, a county seat, or a federal agency.

Tribal enterprises generate almost $80 million in operating revenue each year, most of which is plowed back into the businesses themselves. But $2 million a year is devoted to tribal government programs—law enforcement, utilities, road maintenance, electrical power, early childhood programs, elderly programs, scholarship programs, public housing. Although the tribes receive some $5 million in federal program contracts, none of the services listed are covered by federal dollars. One wonders how the people of Warm Springs would fare on federal support alone.

In my room at Kah-Nee-Ta was a brochure on the resort's amenities. In a coy appeal for corporate business, its cover featured a daguerreotype of a nineteenth-century Warm Springs Tribal Council over the caption: "Kah-Nee-Ta: Successful meetings for over 3,000 years."

I read that the lodge has 139 rooms ("each with private balcony"), rising in three levels from a central core surrounding a swimming pool. In addition to the Juniper Dining Room (where I took my first meal), the lodge's amenities include a coffee shop, a gift shop, the Eagle's Nest Lounge, and a floor of meeting rooms. Down the hill at Kah-Nee-Ta Village is a huge, hot swimming pool fed by the warm springs that give the reservation its name. There are also private mineral baths, the River Room Restaurant, the Pi-Um-Sha Game Room, tennis courts, trailer hookups and camping spaces, a snack bar, miniature golf, a craft shop, a riding stable, twenty-four "Nee-Sha" rental cottages, and an eighteen-hole golf course, which traces the banks of the Warm Springs River. As the brochure instructs Kah-Nee-Ta's guests: "Mount up at our stables and enjoy a guided trail ride. . . . Trout fishing here is superb. During summer, you can also experience the thrill of whitewater rafting on the nearby Deschutes River. . . . And don't miss our traditional Indian salmon bake: huge fillets skewered on cedar sticks, cooked slowly to perfection over glowing alderwood embers."

One can also "take the tribe camping in an authentic Indian teepee [*sic*]." There are twenty-one tepees (with cement floors and fire pits), which sleep up to ten people each.

Kah-Nee-Ta was the first tribal enterprise of the Warm Springs people, who regard it as a love child. In terms of income and employment, Kah-Nee-Ta pales in comparison with the subsequent success of WSFPI, but it remains the most visible manifestation to the outside world of Warm Springs's clout and sophistication.

Long known to the tribes and long used as a public bath by them, the warm springs had been taken out of tribal hands in 1935, when a white man named Freeland bought it from a tribal member for $3,500. Conflicting accounts refer to Freeland as a doctor or a preacher. He built a small spa around the springs and brought his followers up from Portland for the cure. In the 1950s, Freeland sold the springs to a consortium associated with a famous Portland sporting-goods store called Smith's. This group made a halfhearted attempt to develop a resort around the springs, but by the late 1950s not much had come of it.

The Comprehensive Plan targeted the springs as an economic resource, and in 1961 the tribes bought it from the Smith's group for $165,000. Ed Manion, a non-Indian married to a tribal member and now the Warm Springs government's community-services director, was given the job of developing a new resort. "When we started working on the place, it was really outdated," said Ed. "We totally redid it. We had the big pool put in. We built ten little rental cottages and a dozen cabanas for camping. We installed trailer hookups for water and electricity, and we leveled an open field for people who wanted to pitch their own tents."

The resort was named Kah-Nee-Ta, after Xnita, the Warm Springs woman who owned the land before it was lost to Freeland. Ed and his wife, Urbana, devised an emblem for Kah-Nee-Ta that displayed three stylized tepees, one for each Warm Springs tribe. The emblem now appears on most tribal literature and is embossed on tribal business cards.

Initially, Kah-Nee-Ta employed only half a dozen people—lifeguards and maintenance workers for the pool area, and workers at a concession stand. The small enterprise was an instant success. The tribes did no advertising, but word of the springs had gotten around Portland when the Smith's group had owned it, and in 1962 the ten-mile track from Route 26 to Kah-Nee-Ta was paved. "We made a profit right from the beginning," said Ed, "and we stayed profitable until the late sixties, when we decided to expand."

Tempted by a $5-million low-interest loan from the Economic Development Agency, the Warm Springs people voted to invest an additional $750,000 in tribal funds to build Kah-Nee-Ta lodge. The lodge, completed in 1969, was the project that had taken Passamaquoddy Wayne Newell's breath away when he had visited Warm Springs on his Ford Fellowship. The new facility bumped Kah-Nee-Ta's staff to over forty people. "I think that was the largest payroll the tribe had at that time," said Ed. "Seventy-five percent of the staff were tribal members, and many of them had never had a job, so it's not really surprising that we had problems making ends meet. But I've watched the people who've gone through Kah-Nee-Ta from the time it was opened. And the people I deal with in upper-management positions in the tribal organization now are people I worked with at one time at Kah-Nee-Ta. To my mind, it was a costly investment, but worth it."

Like all of Warm Springs's business boards, Kah-Nee-Ta's is a blend of local talent and professional experience. Its chairman, Michael Clements, is assistant secretary-treasurer of the tribal council. Kah-Nee-Ta's secretary-treasurer is Robert Hull, the non-Indian president of a Eugene-based consulting firm that has advised hotel developers from the Northwest to Hawaii. Board member Zane Jackson is chairman of the tribal council; Gordon Shown, a non-Indian, is a former oil executive and commissioner for Jefferson County; and Clyde Persell, the board's vice-chair, is the (non-Indian) co-owner of a big restaurant in Bend.

In its 1988 annual report, one year shy of its twenty-fifth anniversary, Kah-Nee-Ta's three major objectives were listed as: "1) Maintain the quality facility of which the Tribes can be proud. 2) Provide Tribal Members with employment and

training opportunities. 3) Secure an optimum economic return for the Confederated Tribes." Kah-Nee-Ta has fulfilled
the first two objectives since its birth. At times in its short life
the resort has earned five-star ratings in the *Mobil Guide* and
is renowned through Oregon as being too good (read "too
expensive") for anyone except out-of-staters.

Despite this ambitious range of attractions, Kah-Nee-Ta
has yet to secure a decent return. The board has just hired a
new general manager, Ron Malfara, a twenty-year veteran of
the resort business; he spent ten of those years running
Sunrise Ski Resort at Fort Apache Indian Reservation in Arizona. During Ron's tenure, Sunrise went from three lifts on
one mountain to eleven on three mountains. As Jeff Sanders
said, "We go to the marketplace for our managers."

Over coffee in his aerie on the executive floor of the lodge,
Ron presented a decorous, ex-athlete's appearance, with his
light curly hair, well-groomed mustache, gold-rimmed aviator glasses, and spit-polished tassel loafers. But his disposition reminded me of Wayne Sprawls, Ak-Chin's brusque
farm manager. Ron shared Wayne's pugnacious impatience
with careful white expressions of concern for Indians. His
response to my question about his relations with Warm
Springs workers was "*I* don't give a *damn* if you're Indian *or*
white, long as you do your job."

Ron began his career in 1968 as a ski bum in Oregon. He
migrated to Arizona on the Sunrise ski patrol, where he
eventually graduated to mountain manager, in charge of
everything outdoors from chair lifts to snow. After some
time out in Idaho, he returned to Sunrise as assistant manager, rising to general manager in the mid-1970s.

"Sunrise was so federally dependent when I got there that
things weren't getting done and we were lagging behind our
competitors," he said. "By the time I left, Sunrise was one of
the biggest resorts in the western states; we'd tripled our size
and had a big profit margin." Ron worked closely and com-

fortably with Ronnie Lupe, then chairman of the White Mountain Apache Tribal Council. Lupe's political opponents within the council were hard on their relationship, sometimes implying it might be too comfortable. "I think they got tired of paying me so much, even though they couldn't say I wasn't worth it. It got to the point where it looked so easy I think they said, 'Hell, we can do it ourselves.' " Ron left in 1986; Sunrise has had its problems since.

Ron had been at Kah-Nee-Ta for a year when I met him, and he had a good grasp of the resort's history, particularly from the point where its initial financial success began to sour. "Kah-Nee-Ta has provided the tribes with employment and training," he said. "But they've had to pull money out of their right pocket and put it in the left pocket to do it. That's not good enough anymore. I've sliced management in half and installed one or two of my own players. Now there are three and me—a rooms manager, a chief engineer, a food-and-beverage manager, and I'm managing recreation. I've also taken a firm stance on drugs. Last July I popped my head chef; he was stealing from me to support a three-hundred-dollar-a-week habit. It was almost suicidal to fire him at the height of the season like that, but it stopped outsiders who were dealing on Kah-Nee-Ta property, and sent a message to employees."

Recalling my solo dinner in the Juniper Dining Room, I asked Ron how he expected to increase the number of Kah-Nee-Ta's off-season guests. He answered that the resort's current deserted state was purely a marketing problem. This was the first winter Kah-Nee-Ta had been open since the tribes abandoned the season a decade previously. Few prospective customers realized it was open year-round again.

Ron said that despite Kah-Nee-Ta's reputation as being too fancy for in-state customers, most of the resort's clientele were Portland residents. For them, Kah-Nee-Ta's main attractions, in summer or winter, were sunshine and golf. The current cold snap notwithstanding, daytime temperatures in most Warm Springs Februaries range from thirty-five to fifty degrees. Ron was sure that once word got out that the course was open for business, a steady stream of overcoated golfers would follow. He was also dreaming up ways to expand winter business by covering the lodge pool, installing an ice rink, adding condos, racquetball and squash courts, an outdoor amphitheater, even a helicopter landing pad.

Kah-Nee-Ta's revenue had risen 18 percent under Ron's regime. "We put a lot of little things in to keep up revenue," he said, "and they didn't cost much." Ron had also cut costs by $500,000. "I always say let's poor-boy ourselves. How would you do it if it was your money?" With those savings, Ron added to the lodge a fitness center with a Jacuzzi, sauna, weight machines, exercise bikes, tanning rooms, and rowing machines. To the village, he added new volleyball courts, a three-mile raft trip on the Warm Springs River, and mountain-bike trails. He remodeled the restaurant and added a driving range.

The resort hoped to break even in 1989, for the first time since 1967. "Next year this will be a five-million-dollar operation, and I'd like to return ten percent to the tribes," said Ron. This is all good news to the Confederated Tribes, which have taken a quick shine to Ron. The feeling is mutual. "I detect an air of optimism—wanting to expand, wanting to achieve things," said Ron. "I'm also overwhelmed by the business acumen here. Tribal assistance has been *assistance*, not resistance."

Jeff Sanders took me to lunch at Deschutes Crossing, a diner owned by the tribes and leased to a tribal entrepreneur. The restaurant was busy. The crowd was mainly Indian, and the attire was motley for a small-town eatery. In one corner was a young man who wore his hair down to the base of his back.

His hawk's face and flowered headband evoked distracting
Hollywood images of Indian Country. The tribal bureaucrats, Indian and otherwise, were buttoned-down. Jeff was
looking Texan in boots and a string tie.

Russ Winslow, the manager of Warm Springs Apparel
Industries, joined us for lunch. A silver-haired native of
Pennsylvania, he wore a white shirt, dark trousers, and no
tie. Warm Springs Apparel (or WSAI) was the confederation's new sewing factory. Like Ralph DeMoisy at WSFPI,
Russ was hired by the tribes when he retired from a career in
garment manufacturing. The tribes get Russ's experience
and his commitment to work a tribal member into his job.
Russ is bound by no long-term commitments, which suits
him fine, because he has his own garment company in Hood
River.

Russ had been a plant manager for Jantzen Industries, a
major apparel manufacturer. He seemed relieved to be working for a smaller outfit. "Jantzen had been LBO'd [as in
"leveraged buy-out"] twice," he said. "Under the new owners, I couldn't manage my employees the way I wanted
to." Russ was hired when the Warm Springs plant was still
on paper, and he worked with the company's board (two
tribal members and three long-time garment-industry executives) on the initial structure of the enterprise.

"We almost went in on a joint venture with a guy from
Utah," said Russ. "He had his own manufacturing and mer-
chandising company and was looking for some additional
financing. The way he wanted it, we would get paid nine-
sixty an hour to produce his goods, but we had to equip the
factory, provide thread, pay for his freight and shipping
cartons, and pay him a consulting fee *plus* a share of the
profits. I remember my last trip to Utah, tossing and turning
all night. I finally told the tribes I thought they shouldn't go
through with it.

"We decided to go as a straight contractor instead. We're

what you call a CMT shop—cut, make, and thread. We cut the fabric and thread it together to make the garments. We don't furnish any raw materials; we don't do any patterns; we don't do any designing. We're selling our labor now at twelve dollars an hour, and all that stuff we would have had to pay the other guy for is added to our price."

WSAI's customers include Hind Performance—a huge outfit in St. Luis Obispo, California, with a million garments in production at all times—and JM Associates, which owns Duffel and Insport brands. "Most of our customers are marketeers," said Russ. "Take Nike or Patagonia. With all their business, they have no factories, not a one."

Warm Springs Apparel is now in its third year of operation. In its first fifteen months the enterprise grossed $207,000; last year it grossed $434,000. This year they're looking at $675,000. "We're making a total of some four thousand garments a week," said Russ. "If anything, we want to slow our rate of growth so that we can maintain our quality levels." The plant now has thirty-six employees. Russ thinks the peak level will be forty-five workers and $1-million gross. With luck, WSAI could achieve that in four or five years and net the tribe an annual $150,000, which would pay back the tribes' initial $300,000 investment in another five years.

Russ admitted that the timing for a garment factory start-up could not have been better. The economy was strong; "Made in the USA" was popular (although "Made by Native Americans" had yet to catch on), and lower dollar rates were repatriating offshore labor. But Russ gave WSAI workers the credit for the plant's success. "This group of people has come farther faster than any group I've been exposed to," he said.

Warm Springs Apparel is the only business enterprise on Warm Springs's eighty-acre industrial park (although the tribes' motor pool and fire-control center are located there). Before it became a sewing factory, the building housed a subassembly plant where tribal members built high-tech widgets for Tektronix, one of Oregon's largest employers. Like Packard Electric's contract with the Mississippi band of Choctaws, the Tektronix deal was driven by the company's need for minority contractors. The Tektronix arrangement lasted some twenty years and once employed as many as twenty-five people, until Tektronix got bought out and broken up. After a short second life as a maker of balsa-wood airplanes for Boeing, the factory languished as a meeting hall for Alcoholics Anonymous.

Even today, in the flush of success, the space is pretty matter-of-fact—four corrugated walls surrounding a herd of sewing machines. Russ walked me through the plant while the machines hummed their white noise and a loud radio played "Come Together" and "Walk Like an Egyptian." Almost all of the workers appeared to be tribal members, and almost all of them were women.

The garments worked their way forward from the back of the building, where two cutting specialists stapled a sheet of tracing paper on top of several layers of jet-black fabric. The paper was marked with computer-generated patterns, and the cutters followed the patterns with portable band saws rigged with continuous razor blades. The cutters wore chain-mail gauntlets to protect the tendon between their thumbs and forefingers, which were spread to hold the patterns in place. "Years ago you'd see plenty of cutters without thumbs," remarked Russ. "That saw will still cut through that mesh, but the sound it makes gives an operator plenty of warning."

The cut fabric is forwarded to the sewers, who each produce separate stages of the finished product. The sewing machines themselves are highly specialized. Most produce only one kind of stitch but at a rate of eight thousand a minute, whereas the best home machine might do six hundred. We passed by one woman sewing underbriefs into bike shorts. Russ told me that workers are paid on piece rate, which means they are really working as their own entrepreneurs. "In practice, we guarantee them three-seventy-five an hour for their first ninety days here, and then we shoot for everybody to be producing enough garments that they're making six dollars an hour.

"When we first started we had no experience to draw on, so we had to make our own. I interviewed six tribal members for two management positions. I asked each of them a simple question: 'Do you believe in profit?' The only one who answered yes was Bernyce Courtney, so I hired her, along with a woman I'd worked with at Jantzen named Dorothy Pedersen."

Russ's description of his subsequent hiring efforts mildly contradicts the tribal party line of noninterference in day-to-day business operations. "We were forced to hire through the tribes' personnel department for the first couple of months," he recalled. Like all major tribal enterprises, WSAI was established by tribal referendum. "Since the tribal vote to set up this place was carried by only a small margin," said Russ, "the personnel department wasn't entirely cooperative. People at higher levels of Warm Springs government understand this necessary separation of 'church and state,' but when you get deeper down into the levels of hierarchy, you begin to turn up the kind of people you find in any organization who like the status quo. I was warned about this from top tribal guys, but I don't know if I really listened to them."

Minor political skirmishes aside, the real challenge at Warm Springs, according to Russ, is that "people here had had really very little opportunity to gain a work ethic, so it wasn't there. Some outsiders interpret this as bone laziness, but I think that's bullshit." Russ's approach to the problem was not patience but the imposition of a very tight work structure. The strategy was costly: only one of the original five workers is still in place. "We have turned over piles of people, and I think most of it's due to alcohol. Even if my workers aren't alcoholic themselves, they have to deal with some member of their family who is, and they forsake work to care for them."

I asked Russ what sorts of benefits his tribal employees had seen beyond their paychecks. "Well there's Donald Bagley. He started off as a kind of apprentice to a mechanic we'd hired on a contract basis to handle and maintain the equipment. We sent Donny off to a technical school. Now he's back, and it's down to the point where the original mechanic is in only once every two weeks. But you'll want to talk to Bernyce Courtney, our co-plant manager. She of all people has been changed the most by this experience."

I met Bernyce in a small room at the front of the plant, where WSAI employees take their lunch- and coffee breaks. A sizable punch clock dominating the small space was encircled by valentines that workers had pasted to the wall. Bernyce pointed to a white hooded sweatshirt covered with signatures in Magic Marker, hanging alongside the valentines. "That's the very first piece we produced. We bought five thousand yards of fabric; made hooded sweatshirts out of it for practice. We ended up selling them all—even made a little on them."

Young and pretty in her shaggy hair, acid-washed pullover, and faded jeans, Bernyce looked less like a factory manager than an artist. She has a graphic arts degree, in fact, acquired at the Institute of American Indian Arts in Santa Fe. "The institute was an incredible experience," she told me. "You'd see a magnificent painting in the school or in a Santa Fe museum, and then you'd go into a bar and see the artist lying on the floor, dead drunk."

Between studies and rambling, Bernyce spent a total of nine years away from Warm Springs. "When I got back here I tried to make a living designing and making clothes, but I

got so poor that I took a job in the Kah-Nee-Ta gift shop.
After a while I was made the manager of the gift shop in
Kah-Nee-Ta Village, down by the pool." Warm Springs administrators must have had their eyes on Bernyce, because a
year before the sewing plant was ready—before even Russ
had been hired—she was invited to join several government
staffers on a tour of Indian sewing plants in Utah. "It all
looked really neat," said Bernyce. "The girls out there were
doing all this complicated stuff—pipes and ruffles and
skirts. They made it look easy. I had no idea how much work
it was.

"I came in as a trainee manager under Dorothy Pedersen,
and I'm still learning things from her. She has incredible skill
and incredible patience. If she hadn't hung in there, I don't
know if I could have. I mean she was white and I was Indian,
and I thought, 'I'd better hang in here as long as she does.'
Our first big order was for a batch of car covers, the kind you
pull over your car when you leave it on the street. Then we
made kites, then crib bumpers. Finally, we got an order from
Nike, then from JMA, which has been our best long-term
customer.

"The tribal members we hired did high quality work right
off the bat, and my feeling is that it has to do with the fact
that they are Indians. I mean, my mother used to be able to
look at a pattern once and turn around and make the dress.
The natural skill was already there. All we had to do was
teach them the machines, and they did great work. The
problem was efficiency. Our workers wanted every piece to
be perfect to the $n$th degree. Now there's perfect, and there's
manufacturing, and we had to learn to give and take."

Bernyce concurred with Russ that her workers also had
to learn workaday habits. "We'd train these people, invest all
this money in them, and they'd just take off like it was
nothing. If they came in fifteen minutes late every day and I
got on their case, they'd say, 'I don't have to take this crap,'

and leave. We'd just be getting going, and then two or three
people would quit. Dorothy and I would be sewing, inspect-
ing, and bagging until ten o'clock at night. As managers I
guess we took our responsibilities very seriously."

I asked Bernyce if it was hard to manage people who
were older than she. "At first it was. I was brought up to
respect my elders, but I've discovered that some of these
elders don't know as much as I do. I'll always respect them
for their life experience, and I might speak to them on a
different level than I would to someone fresh out of high
school. But basically we're all here for the same thing. We've
got work to do."

Bernyce has a harder time confronting workers on con-
flicts between their work and family or tribal commitments.
"Indian funerals here take three days, five days sometimes,
and if you're a sixty-fourth cousin, you show up, whether the
factory has a deadline or not. I'm not saying give up our
traditions. We're actually exploring trade-off time for
workers, so they can spend time at important gatherings. I
know they're willing to do that, even though Russ says in
other plants he's worked in it would never happen.

"This past Christmas, it all started coming together. We
had a big pre-Christmas deadline, and we'd been threaten-
ing for a week to make everybody work on Saturday and
during their holiday week if we didn't make it. Well, everybody got all of their work done, and Dorothy and I were
sitting back like big bosses, watching them work and take
all their own responsibility. It was just great. We all left
early."

Bernyce worried that the plant, though successful, wasn't
serving a major intended purpose, which was to employ
people in real need—indigent single parents. "For most of
our workers, these are second incomes," she said. Bernyce
explained that Warm Springs had fewer day-care slots than it
had single parents; that shortage, and the tribes' generous

unemployment benefits, removed most of WSAI's allure for them. "So they don't come here, even though this operation was really set up for them."

I asked Bernyce if she was in WSAI for the long haul. "Sure. Until my car is paid off," she laughed. "Actually, I have a little dream that someday we'll design and market something of our own. It may take years, but if we make it, I'll be right back where I started—designing and selling clothes."

On a drive east out of Warm Springs Canyon to the town of Madras, I experimented with Warm Springs radio again and raised Ken "Kenman" Miller, a tribal member with a radio voice like a late-night jazz DJ. "It's eleven minutes away from seven here on the Talking Drum, and the following is a public service announcement from ninety-one point nine FM, KWSO. Hey hey, listen up everyone! Don't you know that February is National Children's Dental Health Month? Let's campaign against baby-bottle tooth decay. For details call the Warm Springs IHS dental clinic."

Like KWSI, its commercial counterpart, KWSO is an FM station that broadcasts from Eagle Butte, above Kah-Nee-Ta. Both stations were founded in 1986 as tribal enterprises and now have twenty-six employees. In radio parlance, KWSI mixes adult contemporary, oldies (songs from the 1970s and early '80s), and supergold (from the '60s and '70s) and holds the biggest market share across several age cohorts in Crook and Jefferson counties. As an educational station, its non-profit KWSO counterpart broadcasts a lot of Native American and educational programming, plus live coverage of local sports events. KWSI station manager Nat Shaw claims that response from advertisers and listeners has been beyond "optimistic expectations." But sales are still lagging, and the station has yet to break even.

The consensus at Warm Springs is that a stable government, respected and supported by its constituency, is the secret to economic success in Indian Country. As one tribal leader said, "Wherever you find a sound tribal government blessed with capable leaders, you're going to find that a tribe is going to make a lot of progress. When you go to a tribe where members are always fighting among each other, you can't get things moving."

Considering their separate and in some cases mutually hostile histories, it is surprising that the Confederated Tribes don't fight among themselves more often. A century of shared resources and intermarriage has clouded old identities, but three separate cultures, languages, and territories still exist at Warm Springs. Although the Wascos and the Warm Springs were both Columbia River tribes, their Native languages are mutually unintelligible.

The Wascos now comprise the largest reservation population. Their river forebears were traders, who dealt more easily with Europeans than their neighbors. Interestingly, the seat of Warm Springs government in the Agency district is considered Wasco territory. (Although it may be entirely coincidental, the majority of people in tribal and business management are Wascos.) The Warm Springs tribe is habitually associated with the Simnasho district, some twenty-five miles north. Warm Springs members are said to be the strongest "traditionals" on the reservation, and there is some evidence that this had been the pre-European case as well. Wascos now looking to reclaim some Native culture sometimes turn to Warm Springs for guidance.

The Paiutes' home district is in the southern part of the reservation, called Seekseequa. Descendants of the desert nomads of the Great Basin, their Native culture is as different from the Columbia River people's as, say, English culture is from Italian culture. On top of that, the Paiutes were traditional raiders of Warm Springs and Wascos, and this habit continued for generations after they settled on the Warm Springs reservation. The Warm Springs and Wascos returned these favors by scouting for the United States, as the cavalry prepared to run the Paiutes down.

Such anthropolitics are still dying a slow death. According to Bob Macy, "I can remember within the last ten years an old woman at a council meeting—in front of a whole mixed audience of Paiutes, Wascos, and Warm Springs— saying she thought we should move the Paiutes off reservation. She had been a victim of a Paiute raid as a girl. She and her mother had been out cutting cattails in a swamp; she made it home but her mother was killed."

A current apportionment petition circulating in the Agency district owes something to ancient tribal differences. The eleven members who make up the Warm Springs Tribal Council include three elected representatives from the Agency district, plus the Wasco chief; three representatives from the Simnasho district, plus the Warm Springs chief; and two representatives from Seekseequa, plus the Paiute chief. (The representatives are elected to three-year terms; the chiefs are appointed by their respective tribes for life.)

While there are some 1,800 Wasco voters, there are only 170 Paiute voters. Paiute council members can therefore win council seats with only thirty votes, whereas it takes a Wasco three times as many. Living up to their progressive reputation, the dissenting Wascos see this as inadequate representation, the kind no mainstream American community would stand for. But as a tribal member with long experience in Warm Springs government points out, "That may be the way things are done in the rest of America, but here it is an attack on a system that has brought the tribes a long way in a short time."

In general, tribal government has excelled in maintaining

mutual respect among districts and tribes. The governing body is highly attuned to these constituencies and seeks their opinion to a degree that would make mainstream politicians blanch. Warm Springs organizational charts always put the people at the top, with the tribal council directly beneath them and the administrative bureaucracy and business enterprises in various configurations below. A referendum is held for every major tribal initiative, from water and land development to new housing construction, business development, or the adoption of a person into the tribes. The government invites tribal members into its budgetary process through an annual information fair and in 1985 even submitted to a grassroots petition that nullified its budget.

If an outsider doubts the need for such extreme accountability—or the persistence of ancient cultural differences—Warm Springs points north to the Yakima Reservation across the Columbia in Washington State. At 1.3 million acres, Yakima is twice the size of Warm Springs, with annual timber yields of $20 million. But in 1988, unemployment at Yakima topped 61 percent, and four-fifths of those who did work made less than $7,000. With an enrollment of 7,100 members, Yakima is among the twenty largest Indian reservations in America, but the treaty that created it in the same year as Warm Springs was signed by fourteen separate tribes and bands. The friction created by so many groups forced to share a common resource has atomized Yakima society. The Yakima received a federal cash settlement for The Dalles Dam similar to that received by Warm Springs; the money disappeared into per-capita payments because the Yakima government didn't have the clout to retain it for their common good.

Non-Indians have long benefited from Yakima's political divisions. Huge swaths of the reservation have come into white ownership. Yakima boasts a $100-million farm economy, compared with Warm Springs's handful of family farmers. But farm production at Yakima is controlled by white farmers, leaving impoverished Yakimas overdependent on the vagaries of timber income.

Bob Macy left his stint as a forester at the Colville Reservation with an appreciation of the internal damage such infighting can do to tribal business development. Like Yakima, Colville is home to more than a dozen tribes, many of whom were traditional enemies and many of whom maintain strict factions today. "When I was there," said Bob, "they were trying to decide where to build a sawmill. Each tribe group wanted it in their district, and as a result it never got built.

"I remember one day I was out in the woods. I ran into a guy I'd grown up with at Warm Springs who was working as a metal prospector for the Colville. He showed me a core sample he'd taken out of a hillside they'd stripped. There were pure droplets of molybdenum in it. [Molybdenum is a heat-resistant metal used in steel alloys.] At that point he was estimating a tribal mining income of twenty-five million dollars a year for twenty years. But the tribes kept screwing around and screwing around with the mining outfit, and now moly-metal prices are in the basement."

Warm Springs's relative prosperity brings to the reservation a steady stream of other tribal leaders seeking answers to their own economic and social dilemmas. Confederated leaders respond with modest advice. "The only thing we can do is articulate why things have worked here," said one Warm Springs official. If Warm Springs is sometimes reticent about dispensing broad prescriptions for Native American economic development, it is probably because they know they are lucky.

Warm Springs's holdings sprawl over five counties, bounded by the Cascades to the west, the Deschutes River to the east, and the Metolius River to the south. The reservation's northern border has recently been extended to encompass a legal slice of land called the McQuinn Strip, reacquired by the tribes after a century-long dispute. The McQuinn Strip adds over 61,000 acres to the reservation, for a total of more than 600,000 acres, or close to 1,000 square miles. The strip incorporates rich forests on the slopes of the Cascades, adding stumpage income to the tribal coffers. The reservation has twenty-six lakes, ten streams, and three rivers. Tribal wildlife administrators count four thousand deer, fifteen hundred elk, and who knows how many coyotes.

Warm Springs is as rich in natural resources as any community in Indian Country. Unlike some tribes, whose barren topographies conceal lakes of oil and mountains of coal, Warm Springs treasures can be exploited without major environmental disruptions. And unlike so many Indian reservations, which were turned into checkerboards of ownership in the heyday of individual allotments, 99 percent of the Warm Springs Reservation is owned and controlled by the tribes. All of this natural "working capital" prompted a member of another, less successful, tribe to gripe, "It was all laid out for Warm Springs; all they had to do was use it."

Warm Springs leaders readily admit their advantages but hasten to add that preserving those advantages is not so easy at all, considering how closely bound they are to tribal income. That Warm Springs Indians are able to care for their surroundings more effectively than most American communities the tribes attribute to a cultural environmentalism that preceded the mainstream grass-roots movement by millennia. As Ralph Minnick told me during our meeting at WSFPI, "The thing to remember when thinking about Warm Springs's resource income is that the council's point of view has always been conservative by nature. They just keep salting it away. Only in crises have we ever spent what we'd taken in for a given year, and to my knowledge we've never gone into deficit. When the timber market plummeted in 1979, we just screwed government operations down, compressing and compressing to keep from running in the red."

Ralph rummaged around his desk until he found the words he was looking for to define these trial habits in a quotation by Eugene Greene, a former Tribal Council chairman: "We did not inherit this land or its resources from our ancestors, we are only borrowing it from our children's children and their children. Therefore, we are duty-bound and obligated to use it wisely and protect it until they get here, and they will have the same obligation."

This constitutionally mandated long view of things has helped the tribes resist some projects with wildly lucrative potential. The Confederated Tribes own half of Mount Jefferson, only slightly shy of Mount Hood's eleven thousand feet and just as snow-rich. At one point, some council members considered developing a ski area, like the ones on Mount Hood that draw skiers from all over the Northwest. The plan was torpedoed in a tribal referendum.

"We need to be leaned on by people with other perspectives," declared Bob Macy. "The forest creates a wealth of income for the tribe; with my forestry background, I'm naturally inclined to take up my chainsaw. But who's to say I'm right to cut down this Number-one, Grade-A tree for the money that's in it? Is money more important than the fact that the tree was in a place where, in our history, important meetings took place? The best trees I can see around here are the ones that grow by the river, all of them straight and tall. But my colleagues over in Fish and Wildlife and Water Resources remind me that if I go after them I'm going to screw up the water temperature and destroy a fishery. All these trade-offs can occur." Bob told me that tribal foresters planted 1.5 million seedlings in 1987 alone.

Warm Springs has fought some of its conservation battles in larger arenas than its tribal council. "A couple of years ago there was a tremendous battle along the Columbia over fishing rights," said Ralph Minnick. "The Indians were the scapegoats, as usual. We won anyway. Now the states along the river are saying if it wasn't for the Indians fighting as hard as they fought for this resource, we might not have *any* fish today. It's nice to hear that Indians aren't such bad people."

Chinook salmon spawn in Oregon's rivers, and for years they have bolstered the economy of the Pacific Northwest. Industrial pollution and the clear-cutting of timber (which exposes rivers to sunlight and overwarming) have helped reduce the number of salmon caught from 120,000 in 1957 to zero when a blanket ban was imposed in 1979. Since then, the numbers have bounced back considerably, thanks in part to an operation three miles north of Kah-Nee-Ta that bills itself as the "most modern, up-to-date fish hatchery on the West Coast." The hatchery is a project of the U.S. Department of Interior, built by the Bureau of Fish and Wildlife. Its ten employees collect eggs from female Chinook and fertilize them in buckets of water saturated with male sperm. The young are cared for in the hatchery and released into streams as fingerlings. The Warm Springs Hatchery now produces 750,000 spring Chinook salmon and rainbow trout a year.

The most recent and most spectacular case of resource exploitation at Warm Springs is the tribes' new hydroelectric plant—Warm Springs Power Enterprise. The first federally licensed power project granted to any Indian tribe, Warm Springs Power generated 80 million kilowatt hours in 1987, which translated into about $4 million in tribal income.

There are three dams on the Deschutes River, all owned by Portland General Electric and all aligned in a single system. All of the dams fall within Warm Springs territory, because the reservation's boundary is drawn down the middle of the Deschutes. Upstream are the Pelton and Round Butte dams. The third dam, down near Agency, is a re-regulating dam, which ensures that the upper dams don't send water levels careening in violent up- and downswings.

In the 1950s, when the first dam was proposed, wily Warm Springs representatives called the power company's bluff. A dam by definition had to straddle the midstream divide, and that meant the Confederated Tribes could command lease payments, which they did. The first leases on the two upstream dams brought a combined annual income of between $200,000 and $300,000 through the 1960s and early 1970s. In the agreement for the third, the reregulating dam, the tribes reserved the option to install their own powerhouse.

"In the early 1980s we decided to exercise that option," said Ralph Minnick, who in his former life as tribal secretary-treasurer was deeply involved in creating Warm Springs Power. "First we had to surround the capital costs. We were looking at a price tag of thirty million dollars, and Warm Springs could put up a third of that in cash. We could afford it because we had driven a hard bargain when those original Portland General Electric leases were renewed in the 1970s."

The tribes had positioned themselves to negotiate for a lease more in line with the après-oil-embargo price of hydroelectric power. The power company fought Warm Springs tooth and nail but in the end signed a lease in 1984 to pay $6.5 million a year, more than twenty times their original fee and one that would rise with the Consumer Price Index in subsequent years. The company also paid the tribes a whopping $18 million in back rent unpaid during the course of the price dispute. Ralph has a framed Xerox of the $18-million check on the wall beside his desk at WSFPI.

"With some of that as a down payment, the BIA figured they could loan us another five million dollars," said Ralph, "and about that same time the state was floating a big bond for hydro projects in general." Jeff Sanders had boasted that Warm Springs's credit in the Oregon State house was so good it took the legislature only five minutes to approve

Warm Springs's portion of the bill. Ralph Minnick said it took longer than that. "Every time we deal with a new state agency we have to go around and introduce ourselves. 'Yes, we're the Warm Springs Indians. Yes, we're a federal reservation within the state.' Then we let their lawyers sniff around to make sure that they won't get stuck holding some expensive bag. If I was in their shoes I'd be the same way.

"In the meantime we worked on companies who might be interested in buying our power. Pacific Power and Light in Portland agreed to enter into a long-term sales agreement, and with that piece of paper in hand we were able to secure the necessary financing."

With a staff of two, the hydroelectric plant will never amount to much of a Warm Springs employment center. But between its kilowattage and Portland General Electric's lease payments, the Deschutes River has turned into such a cash cow that the Confederated Tribes are already half-weaned from their dependence on timber income to make ends meet. This has been a relief for Bob Macy. "It's good to spread out income, so you're not overdependent on one source. In 1979, stumpage payments to the tribe were eleven million dollars, and we were fat and happy. Then the market collapsed, and our timber income was halved. Hydro income, and the income from those renegotiated leases, has helped us go from being about seventy-five to eighty percent timber dependent to about a fifty-fifty split between timber and river income."

Portland General Electric still operates the dams under an agreement with Warm Springs, despite whatever bad blood generated by the lease dispute might linger on. All three dams are interlinked, and the entire operation is controlled by microwave transmissions from the Round Butte operation. Jim Manion, son of the tribes' community-services manager, Ed Manion, and fellow tribal member Tracy Graybael are training to become Warm Springs Power's permanent two-man work force.

Whereas the Ak-Chin prefer to ignore it, and the Mississippi Choctaws prefer to bully it, Warm Springs has a remarkably close and easy relationship with the federal government, what they call a "working partnership." "We try to stay as close together with BIA as we can," said outgoing Secretary-Treasurer Larry Calica. "We want them accountable, but we also want them with us, not against us. You won't find Warm Springs pointing our finger at the BIA and saying it's all their fault. Our relationship with the federal government has worked so well because BIA serves as adviser, not director. The BIA is a great resource, if you know how to use 'em. And we *use* 'em."

According to Ralph Minnick, who preceded Larry in the secretary-treasurer's seat, "Our tribal budget has to be approved by BIA, so we get the bureau's area superintendent up from Albuquerque to sit in each year while we're pulling it together. He's intimately aware of our planned expenditures." Other tribes might balk at having so powerful a United States presence so close to their books, but at Warm Springs, the superintendent is just another tenant. The BIA rents all of its local office space within the Confederated Tribes Administration Center. As one tribal leader told me, "We work so close it's often hard to tell who in that building is BIA and who's the tribes."

Not that Warm Springs thinks the feds are perfect. Ralph would like to see the assistant secretary for Indian affairs promoted to a full-cabinet position, and none of the tribal members I talked to liked the laissez-faire initiatives of then Assistant Secretary Ross Swimmer. Said Larry Calica, "We may not agree with Joe Delacruz at Quinault or Roger Jourdain at Red Lake Chippewa [both vehement Native American critics of U.S. government policy], but we sure don't agree with Swimmer [who advocated dismantling the BIA while he was head of it]."

Jeff Sanders likes to say, with a near wink, "We jealously guard our sovereignty, but we don't want to relieve the federal government of its commitments."

Like the Mississippi Choctaws, Warm Springs leaders find themselves serving at times as opinion makers for Indian Country generally. "When a new federal policy for Indian Country is announced," said Jeff, "a lot of tribes look to Warm Springs for their reaction before deciding whether to go along with feds or not." If this is a common occurrence, it may have less to do with Warm Springs's business acumen than with the fact that Ken Smith, the man who has served the Warm Springs government for almost a quarter of a century—and has run it for more than eleven years—served as assistant secretary for Indian affairs during Reagan's first term.

I was eager to meet this refugee from the most powerful position in Indian Country. As the living incarnation of the hopes and fears of Native America, whose actions and decisions touch every American Indian life, however subtly, Ken Smith was open to the most scathing criticism, and received surprisingly little of it. Tim Giago, publisher of America's largest and most respected Indian-owned newspaper, the *Lakota Times*, has strong opinions about assistant secretaries for Indian affairs. In an editorial dismissing Ken's predecessor, Forrest Gerrard, as "totally ineffective," and reviling Ken's successor, Ross Swimmer, as a "doormat . . . a bowing, scraping sycophant," Giago wrote, "I have deep respect for Ken Smith. . . . I can imagine the frustrations he must have felt in dealing with blockheads on a national level."

I met Ken Smith on my last night in Warm Springs. Compact and dapper, with the features and haircut of a news anchorman, he was wearing the only suit I saw in Warm Springs. We sat in deep chairs by Kah-Nee-Ta's titanic fireplace. He answered my questions as carefully as if we were on the air, which I took to be a holdover from his time in

Native America's hottest seat. He tended toward the Latinate expressions of the executive branch, and only a country boy's wheezing laugh betrayed his roots.

Ken told me he was a member of the Wasco tribe and had grown up on a ranch south of Agency. "I was brought up by my grandparents. They preached education to me, and I ran with a group that knew we were going to go on to college. I graduated from the University of Oregon with an accounting degree in 1959. I pretty much knew I'd come back here after I graduated. This was my home, and my grandparents had said it'd be nice if I came back afterwards to help our people."

As a protégé of Vern Jackson, who had received his college diploma only a year before, Ken was hired as a tribal accountant. He cut his teeth on the council's efforts to explain the Comprehensive Plan to the Warm Springs people. Ken even served a council term in 1962, "but I found out real fast that I couldn't do that and a full-time job at the same time."

Vern Jackson died in the late 1960s, and Ken—barely thirty years old—took his place as Warm Springs's chief executive in 1971. He held the position for eleven years straight, overseeing the growth of Kah-Nee-Ta, the transfer to tribal management at WSFPI, and the evolution of Warm Springs into Indian Country's most famous success story. It seemed natural that the Reagan Administration would tap the leader of an Indian community that had outgrown a good portion of its federal dependence.

"I do think Warm Springs's reputation was a big part of it," said Ken. "And then I had affiliations that showed I could deal with different types of people: I served on the Oregon Federal Reserve Board, the department of education, the state tourism organization. I'd been one of those 'outstanding young men' of Oregon one year. But I think they were also looking for someone who'd managed a big organization

for a long time. The BIA has some fifteen thousand employees, and that's a handful.

"I had a call from Jim Watt one day in January 1981 asking
if I'd be interested. I said I might be. He invited me to
Reagan's inauguration, and afterwards he asked me questions, and I asked him questions. A week later, he called back
and said, 'I'd like to submit your name to the president.' I
mulled it over for a little bit, and I talked to some of the tribal
people, who thought it would be a good opportunity for me.
I guess I finally took it because I thought I could learn
something, and because I thought the tribe would be proud
to have one of its own members in that job. I also thought I
couldn't bad-mouth the bureau if I didn't try to do something about it. I'd probably kick myself if I hadn't taken this
opportunity to do something for all Indian tribes."

Ken and his second wife, a non-Indian, moved to D.C. in
1981, and Ken took the position of assistant secretary for
Indian affairs in the Department of the Interior. I asked him
what it was like working under James Watt. "Fine," he said.
"I got along with Jim real well, and I had a lot of respect for
him. I think Jim Watt supported Indian affairs as well as any
secretary. It was an era of cutbacks, and Indian affairs got cut
back less than any other department in Interior. He was real,
real sharp, and he was a good manager, a good team builder.
He would give us pep talks, saying, 'You're going to get
criticism from Congress; sometimes you're going to wonder
why you're here.' But he had a way with words that would
make you perk up a little bit."

More than dealing with other branches of government or
even BIA's tribal constituents, Ken found motivating BIA
employees his biggest challenge. "I think I had a better
understanding than most of what the real needs were, but it
was difficult sometimes being between the constituency and
the people I had to work with." I asked him if while in
Washington he ever got an earful about federal policy from

his Warm Springs friends. "Sure, sure. Everybody criticizes the assistant secretary. I worked for the president, after all. But I also had a lot of support from Warm Springs; they always stuck up for me in public."

Zane Jackson, chairman of the Warm Springs Tribal Council, remembers Ken's federal stint as a pretty heady experience for the troops back home. "It isn't often you have the ear of a government official at the subcabinet level," Zane told me, "and Ken and I are second cousins. When Ken was in Washington, we here were quick to respond to things we didn't think were right."

"It was a great experience," said Ken. "But it was a sacrifice. I'd taken a major reduction in salary when I left here, and D.C. was a lot more expensive. I was burnt out after four years."

What did he think the federal government ought to be doing for Indian Country now?

"I feel very strongly that Indian people will succeed because of Indians themselves, tribes themselves. It won't be because the federal government back in D.C. is trying to do things for them. The feds can assist by supporting tribal governments, by developing the basic capabilities of tribes to help themselves. My philosophy is that you have to have strong tribal government before you can really deal effectively with some of these other problems. It's no different than working with a third-world country. With undeveloped tribal governments, you can pour millions down the drain. You have to build that foundation, then they'll have the tools to start making their own decisions, doing their own thing, making their own opportunities.

"I'm tired of fighting Washington, D.C., for more money. I really feel that the way we're going to succeed here is what *we* do. Not what Washington does. We only have to make sure that they fulfill their responsibilities. If we're going to progress as people, improve ourselves, then that's *our* re-

sponsibility. But I also understand that it takes time. I think
Ross Swimmer [Ken's successor] felt the same way I did, only
he thought everything should happen immediately. In Indian Country you can only go as fast as the pace of each
tribe, and some move faster than others."

Ken returned to Warm Springs as a consultant, lobbying
for the Confederated Tribes in Washington and helping to
fine-tune their management structures in preparation for a
new phase of economic development. He had been rehired
as the tribes' CEO days before I talked to him, and in deference to his leadership, the council upped his title from
"secretary-treasurer" to "CEO/general manager."

Ken's time away from Warm Springs had increased his
respect for his hometown. "Warm Springs learned a long,
long time ago how to separate politics from the day-to-day
management of its business affairs. Our real foundation was
sound government, but we learned that business delegation
was key. When a new council is elected at Warm Springs, it
doesn't automatically fire all the top managers. You'll find in
other tribes, a new government comes in and they start all
over from scratch."

Finally, because he had spent so much of his life dealing
with them, I asked Ken what he thought were non-Indians'
most persistent and frustrating misconceptions about his
people. "I think there's misunderstandings on the part of
both Indians and non-Indians," he replied. "A lack of knowledge; a lack of education. The non-Indians don't really understand what happens here, but sometimes the Indians
here don't understand the other side. The more exposure
both sides have the better. That's why I think having Warm
Springs students enter the public school system is good. The
more those kids are together, on teams, in classrooms, the
sooner we tear that brick wall down.

"As you get older, your priorities become simpler, and that
helps melt distinctions. What matters? Your health, for one

thing. We should give our members healthy bodies and minds. If we give them those basics and then start creating job opportunities to make them self-reliant producers, I think you'll end up with a very strong Warm Springs population."

In addition to his general oversight of all tribal businesses, Ken presides over Warm Springs's largest enterprise of all—the tribal government. Six hundred of Warm Springs's twelve hundred jobs are in government administration, almost twice as many as in WSFPI, Warm Springs's biggest business. Compared with most American bureaucracies, Warm Springs's public sector is an infant. "We've only been in the self-government business for what, fifty years?" Ralph Minnick told me, "and then we weren't really active 'til we started economic development twenty years ago." Yet, in many ways Warm Springs delivers government services more efficiently and effectively than most.

"One of our advantages is that we coordinate our services," said Ed Manion, Kah-Nee-Ta's founding manager and now the tribes' community-services director. "On the outside, governmental agencies are redundant and often compete with each other. Here we've had cooperation and continuity," which is mandatory, considering the breadth of services Warm Springs government provides. The tribes' housing office, for example, provides dwellings for half of all tribal members.

"Twenty-five years ago, sixty, seventy percent of the housing on this reservation was substandard," declared Jeff Sanders. "Now you'd be hard pressed to find any." In 1966, the tribes established a credit office to help finance individual ownership of these houses with low-interest loans.

The tribes also offer extensive adult-education programs. "If I want to get skills in automotive," said Jeff, "even at fifty years old, I can apply to the government for money to do so."

Despite all of these efforts and the tribes' relative prosperity, the intractable problems of Warm Springs boil down to a single, brute measurement: the average life expectancy within the Confederated Tribes is thirty-eight years. I asked every tribal official I met to verify that figure, and every one of them did. "Put it this way," said Ralph Minnick, "ninety percent of our people my parents' age, who would now be between fifty-five and sixty-five, are dead." The tribes recently completed a reservation-wide analysis, which revealed that 100 percent of the deaths under age thirty-three were related to substance abuse. "That's one of our scary statistics," said Ralph. "Now we're saying we can change."

Unlike many mainstream public officials, Warm Springs administrators freely admit their shortcomings. The tribes issue a glossy annual report, which looks like those circulated by corporations to stockholders. The difference is that Warm Springs reports don't obscure bad news in euphemisms. A section on the tribes' health department in the 1983 report read, "1983 was a year of facing the facts. . . . The Tribes have not done a good job of [substance abuse] treatment in-house."

"I really admire the tribes for taking ownership for this problem," said Ralph. "Maybe it's easier for us. Our drinkers tend to be more visible. In a non-Indian town like Madras, say, they're in the closet, harder to get at."

The tribal council had run in 1988 by mandating drug testing for all employees in tribal government and businesses. Ken Smith had offered to be tested first of all. Such government initiatives have followed grass-roots efforts. "When I was chief of police," said Jeff, "AA was a joke. Now there are eight meetings a week on the reservation and Alateen and Adult Children of Alcoholics too." The tribes are currently modeling a pilot program on alcohol rehabilitation in conjunction with the Indian Health Service.

This progressive governance in social services has failed, however, to budge two stubborn Warm Springs statistics: one out of three tribal members able to work do not, and more than half the jobs generated by Warm Springs government and business are held by non-Indians. Tribal leaders are beginning to think this is because too many solutions to social problems are driven by tribal government and not enough by individual initiative. "Let's take a family of four," said community-services director Ed Manion. "Say they rent a house or they're paying a five-percent loan on one worth about forty thousand dollars. That's three hundred bucks a month. They pay no state tax, and of course there's no property tax. They have free sewer and water delivery, free garbage pick-up. They get one hundred dollars each in tribal per-capita payments, which would be four hundred dollars in this case. If one family member was previously employed, they qualify for unemployment: that's another three or four hundred, for a while. There're food stamps, the WIC programs [surplus food for children and pregnant women], and low energy assistance to help pay for power and heating.

"Now some members would say that's the way it should be. However, I think there's a silent majority here that want to see people take responsibility for themselves and not to have us reaching in and rescuing them every step of the way. The tribal members are so forgiving and so helpful to one another, they don't like to see people hurt or down. But we need some tough love here, allowing people to hurt a little bit."

Ralph Minnick tried to instill these values when he was the tribes' chief executive. "I was raised by my grand-parents," Ralph said. "We lived in an old army barracks, we had kerosene lamps, we had to pack water, we bathed in a sweathouse, we had wood heat. We weren't rich, and yet we survived. We lived within our means. We have to reinforce these values. That's what I was trying to bring to the tribal organization and how it dealt with its constituents."

Tribal education policies offer another example of misguided goodwill. The tribes put a premium on education, but the current high school dropout rate is over 50 percent. "Sometimes motivating the young ones gets frustrating," sighed Ralph Minnick. "I've got nieces and nephews who head for the back door as soon as they see me coming."

Again, part of the problem is based in tribal policy. A third of the tribes' per-capita payments to minors are held in trust to their eighteenth birthday. The accumulated sum is rolled over into a money-market account, which can be applied to that young person's education or handed over in cash. Torn between college and money, most Warm Springs teenagers choose the latter. Some tribal officials think finding other means to finance higher education or waiting to dissolve the trusts until members hit the age of twenty-five or thirty would be more appropriate. "But it's one of those things that's been going on so long," said one council member, "that it will be awfully hard to change."

According to Ken Smith, Warm Springs is waking up to the fact that in attaining self-determination its government has also inherited the regressive role of the federal government on Indian reservations. "Like anybody who was poor and came into some money, sometimes you spend too much," said Ken Smith. "I don't blame the tribes a bit. We've been blessed with resources, and we turned them into fine services for our people. But maybe we provided too many services, doing everything for everybody, making our own people dependent upon us. As long as we're in that position, we're no different than the Bureau of Indian Affairs.

"We don't want to be that kind of government. We want to provide *basic* services. Beyond that, members have to become self-sufficient. We're trying to wean people from the old way, but it's hard." Particularly, it is hard to wean Warm Springs government of its own propensity to expand. "We started with the idea of helping everybody," said Ken. "They needed help. Like most budding communities, we started by building our government, so most of our first generation of jobs were government jobs. People coming back to the tribe after high school or college came into government positions because we were the only place in town with lots of skilled positions."

The Warm Springs 1987 Annual Report echoed the hopes of tribal leadership for their new role: "Tribal Government will play a supportive role—not a dominant one which erodes individual responsibility, initiative and self-sufficiency. Our children will grow up with a sense of pride and purpose because they will be capable, needed and useful."

Larry Calica had been dealing with government attitude adjustments since he inherited the secretary-treasurer's position from Ralph Minnick in 1984 and before he handed it over to Ken Smith in 1989. Larry's mother is a Wasco, born in Agency; his father is from the Philippines. Neither had more than a fourth-grade education. Larry went to Oregon State to study forestry and graduated in 1969 with a social sciences degree. He took graduate courses in social rehabilitation at the University of Oregon and directed a student support program for Native Americans while he was there.

I had seen snapshots of Larry depicting a short, smiling man-child with his hair held in two thin braids. By the time I entered his large office, the braids had disappeared and his hair was short. But his slow, hushed speech in the sparely appointed, twilit room, gave our conversation the air of a meditation. Larry dwelt on large issues and time frames, working hard to find the deeper structural issues underlying the tribes' day-to-day concerns. Larry would soon pass his position over to Ken Smith and move to head of strategic planning, the guardian of the Comprehensive Plan.

According to Larry, Ken Smith's first stint as tribal CEO was geared toward getting things done, come hell or high water. "Ken as general manager was very influential; he almost overshadowed the council. When he left, Ralph Minnick said, 'Let's go back to the letter of the constitution,'" which meant reelevating the council to an unquestionably top-dog status. Ralph saw himself as the council's chief of staff, and his position was "demoted" from general manager to secretary-treasurer accordingly. The result was an executive vacuum of sorts, although with Ralph's urging, the tribes took time to look head-on at some long-standing issues that eluded economic solutions.

Larry believed that Ken had picked up some of Ralph's broader view in Washington and that a synthesis of these two perspectives would create the most dynamic Warm Springs leadership to date. Business development would continue to be the primary solution to the tribes' social problems, but Warm Springs would be more discriminating in its development strategy.

"Our natural resources are so plentiful," said Larry, "that our tribal businesses haven't emphasized our human resources enough. Timber and the Hydro are big cash cows, but the sawmill's work force is full and the Hydro only employs two people. To create jobs we have to be more attuned to the marketplace. The tribes will have to learn to adapt to industry rather than to their constituency."

And they will have to work fast. Like the Choctaws, Warm Springs's birth rate is running at about twice national levels. Twenty years ago there were about thirty births a year; Warm Springs members produced 130 babies in 1988. In 1985 almost 50 percent of the population was under twenty years old. "If we don't want a young, unemployed population creating a miniature version of an inner city on this reservation," warned Ken, "we've got to find six hundred jobs over the next ten years. Not everybody wants to work at a resort or at a mill. How will we diversify the job market for those who are coming up?"

"The problems here are the same as elsewhere," said Bob Raimondi, a former faculty member at Central Oregon Community College and now an economic-development specialist for Warm Springs. "We have to diversify the economy to create new jobs, and we'll probably look to see more self-supporting jobs rather than government jobs. Oregon's economy has already proven that small business is the wave of the future; so will it be here."

One of Warm Springs's best living examples of tribal entrepreneurship is Zane Jackson, Vern's surviving brother and chairman of the tribal council. Elected by the council from one of its own number, Zane performs many ceremonial duties but also retains the power of a tie-breaking vote. Zane is Ken Smith's ultimate boss, but he has made few concessions to the conventional image of a chairman of the board. He met me in running shoes and brown canvas slacks. His round head emerged from a velour sport shirt, and his sage, smile-lined countenance begged to be called "tortoiselike," except no turtle wears a Rolex as big as Zane's.

"I was born here," he told me, "six or seven miles from Agency, and I've lived here all my life, except for a stint in the navy in World War Two. The only other place I'd been before the navy was Oklahoma, for a week on a school exchange program. After the war, I went to work for the sawmill, before the tribe owned it.

"When the tribes bought the mill, they asked me if I wanted to go into business as a logger. The tribes loaned me some money, and there was a dealer in Redmond who fronted some equipment. We started with ten employees. I thought I knew a lot about the business, but it was tough going for the first five or six years. From time to time we hid from creditors, but they'd always catch up to me and we'd come to some kind of agreement. When I sold the business in 1980, there were thirty employees. We were logging twenty million board feet, and netting about twelve percent."

Zane would like to see others have a dream like that come true. "We've got well-trained people here who'd like to work, but we have no place for their talents. There's a couple people want to open up a beauty shop. We've had somebody try the laundry/dry-cleaning business. We've got some trained motor mechanics, some trained body-and-fender guys. I'd like to see them use that training. At the same time, the tribe has to recognize that small business is risky. There were eleven hundred businesses started in this state in 1988, and something like nine hundred fifty-nine of them failed."

One Warm Springs path to entrepreneurialism will be a Margaret Thatcher–like privatization of government services. "The tribe has a hundred and fifty buildings to maintain," said Ken Smith, "and we hire janitors onto the government payroll for that work. We shouldn't be in that business. We have a tribal garage; there's no reason why we should be in the garage business. Same with waste management. We run a print shop, and we shouldn't. There was talk here a while ago about the tribal government putting up a supermarket, and we could have found all sorts of ways to screw *that* up. There's got to be somebody out there who'll say, 'I can do that as cheaply as you can, Tribe.'

"I think if we start privatizing these functions, in five, ten years from now you'll find a lot of Indian people in business, a lot of retail outlets on the reservation, and a much healthier community. To help them do it, we have to create an environment in which smaller businesses will thrive." Ken's already at work trying to get a bank to locate on the reservation. (Currently tribal members bank at the Warm Springs credit office or down in Madras.)

"Another thing we'll have to do real soon," said Ken, "is build 'Downtown Warm Springs.' First we'll have to decide where it ought to be. Near the school campus? Around Macy's? After we've chosen a site, we'll have to get the infrastructure laid out, put the sewage and water in, maybe get some streets laid out, and say, 'Okay, this is the business district.' "

The Confederated Tribes are known to outsiders by their talismans of mainstream culture—Kah-Nee-Ta, the mill, the power plant. Warm Springs is famous for money, jobs, and clout, but its people value the incorporeal as well as the concrete. "We must pass along not only the tools to manage all the resources, but also the values and beliefs," proclaimed Zane Jackson in the tribes' 1987 annual report. The tribes were left to themselves for longer than many other Native American communities, and the economic triumph of Warm Springs obscures a persistent and distinct, if complicated, culture. "The languages damn near died out," said Jeff, "but they're still spoken here, and we're working with tribal elders to rebuild them." The Warm Springs Culture and Heritage Office has developed preschool curricula and training materials for teachers of Warm Springs and Wasco languages and is working on a similar program for Paiute.

To strangers, Warm Springs cultures are visible only occasionally and usually in the form of mysterious dichotomies. The Warm Springs police force occasionally employs the clairvoyant services of tribal religious leaders. Warm Springs Baptists also attend pre-Christian Washat services, or "worship dances," in the tribal longhouses. There are still feasts to celebrate salmon, roots, and huckleberries. People with day jobs at the sewing plant will dance all night in slow circles to the chanting voices and steady drumbeats of music thousands of years older than ancient Rome. Warm Springs is large enough to encircle such seeming contradictions and strong enough to choose what it needs from the great American marketplace, forsaking the rest for goods beyond the reach of economics.


I decided I could not leave Warm Springs without braving the pool at Kah-Nee-Ta. Driving down from the lodge, I could see steam rising off the springs from half a mile away. The buildings around the pool follow the arrowhead lines of the lodge; the long sides of the open-ended triangle are walkways between the bathhouse, a restaurant, and a snack bar. Both eateries were closed for the season. The temperature was eleven degrees. Under its shroud of suspended frost, the pool appeared empty.

I changed into a suit in the village locker room and pushed through a large metal door into weather so cold it blew me into the enormous, steaming expanse. The clear, odorless water pumped in from the Warm Springs River is so hot that even in tundra conditions it has to be cooled to ninety degrees by jets of tap water.

I was surprised to find three other bathers in the pool, and startled to hear them speaking French. On reflection I assumed they were Canadian, but their accents were suspiciously continental. I crawled twenty lazy laps; my back was protected from the real air temperature by a quilt of steam. As I turned my head to breathe I heard, "Cedric! Regard, ici!" I looked up and saw a family of sculpted bears welded onto the divider between the lap pool and the wading pool. They appeared to be standing on the water; their iron claws clasped iron salmon.

I stood for a moment in the frigid air and saw the skeletons of dormant tepees, waiting to be filled with next summer's tourists. Back in my room, I could watch CNN on cable television or listen to Native American songs on the radio. In

the restaurant I could eat a grilled-cheese sandwich or veni-
son and frybread. On a subfreezing afternoon I was swimming with Parisians in a block-size pool filled with hot water
from the earth's core, at the bottom of a canyon in a wild-
western landscape. And I doubted that anybody at Warm
Springs would find any of those incongruities out of place.

MAINE

CANADA

*St. Croix River*

*Penobscot River*

**INDIAN
TOWNSHIP** ■

**Calais** ●

■ **INDIAN ISLAND
(PENOBSCOT)**

**PLEASANT
POINT** ■

● **Old Town**

**(PASSAMAQUODDY)** ● **Eastport**

**Bangor** ●

**Columbia Falls** ●

● **Augusta**

**Thomaston** ●

**Portland** ●

*ATLANTIC OCEAN*

# 6

## The Passamaquoddies: 1989

I made my last pilgrimage to the Portland offices of Tribal Assets Management around Christmas of 1988. Six months had erased the bad taste of Passamaquoddy Homes Incorporated's failure. The sale of a major asset had flooded the Passamaquoddy coffers with cash, and the tribe was gearing up for an economic boom in 1989.

In October, the Passamaquoddies had sold Dragon Cement to a Spanish consortium called Cementos del Norte for $81.3 million. It was the highest price ever paid per ton of capacity for a cement plant—and almost exactly the same amount as the total 1981 land-claims settlement for both the Passamaquoddies and the Penobscots. The tribe had earned a four-year, $60-million profit on its original $25-million investment. In fact, the tribe did much better than that. Because they had plunked down only $2 million of their own cash for Dragon, the Passamaquoddies' return on equity was about 3,000 percent.

And that was only the beginning. When the Passamaquoddies sold Dragon, they were careful to retain its most valuable asset: a sulfur-dioxide-emissions scrubber so efficient and so cost effective that it could go a long way toward erasing smokestack-industry contributions to acid rain. The tribe had received close to $5 million from the Department of Energy to develop a prototype, for which it held worldwide patents, that could someday earn the tribe perhaps hundreds of millions of dollars.

Tom Tureen and Daniel Zilkha were out of town. Tom was in Hawaii, meeting with a new client, the Bikini Island people. Daniel was in France on vacation. The Passamaquoddies' economic news was delivered with pleasure and some relief by their partner, Rob Gips. I met with Rob down the street from TAM, in a Portland photography studio. He was sitting for his baby daughter while his wife, who manufactured infant outerwear, directed a commercial still shot of her product for the L. L. Bean catalog. His thoughtful answers to my questions were delivered with mildly absurd gravity as he bounced his daughter on a pinstripe-clad knee.

In addition to the Dragon coup, Rob told me of PHI's resurrection as a new enterprise. The tribe had just entered an agreement with a major American auto supplier to make the raw material of trunk liners. The business was going to operate from the former PHI building and would eventually employ thirty to forty people, twice as many as the PHI factory. TAM secured the financing with a $1-million Urban Development Action Grant, one of the largest UDAG grants of 1988. The tribe borrowed an additional $6 million from Fleet Bank and put up the building as collateral, so no additional cash of the tribe's was required. After a nasty fight, the Finns were forced to live up to their PHI contract agreements. Makroscan took back all its equipment and paid the bank for it, which cut down a large portion of outstanding debt.

"The Passamaquoddies' new partner is Gates Formed-Fibre Products [GFFP]," said Rob, "one of the most professional companies we've dealt with." The company is based in

Auburn, Maine, and is a subsidiary of Gates Corporation, one of the largest privately owned corporations in the country. (The company's founder, John Gates, invented the V-belt, which formed the capital base of an industrial empire of batteries, hoses, and other car parts. At one time Gates even owned Lear Jet Corp.)

According to the new arrangement, the tribe controlled the building and the manufacturing equipment. "We won a major battle with the state over whether the equipment we were buying would be subject to sales tax," said Rob. "We got them to accept the unique theory that this was indeed a governmental function, because the tribe had received a UDAG grant for it." Gates would lease the space and equipment for twelve years, run the business, and pay the tribe enough rent to cover the mortgage on the factory and service the equipment.

The tribe won't take a lot of money out of the new enterprise for a while. But eventually the new enterprise will wipe out any remaining debt from PHI, and the Passamaquoddies will own a fifty-thousand-square-foot building free and clear, plus the equipment (which should still be worth what they paid for it). The partnership will also create a lot of good jobs. Most important, perhaps, the risk of operations and debt service is on Gates, not the tribe. It will be nearly impossible for TAM's clients to get burned on this one.

"The manufacturing process is beautiful," said Rob. "No pollution comes from it. In fact, the raw material is recycled plastic, empty soda bottles. The tribe is already buying land surrounding the factory so it can expand later on. We've all put PHI behind us, and I believe our clients are very excited about this new venture."

Rob also said that an industry had finally been established at Indian Township, and that plans were well underway for another. The first was called Indian Township Manufacturing, another arrangement with Gates, this time for a six-person factory to sew borders around one of Gates's car-trunk-mat products. Because the working capital for this venture amounted to a half-dozen heavy-duty sewing machines, it cost the tribe practically nothing, and there were plans to double its work force in six months.

"We expect to close on a second Indian Township deal in early January," said Rob, "with a fellow named George Rybarczyk. George owns a company called Belfast Manufacturing that sews sportswear for some of the country's biggest manufacturers and warm-up jackets for professional sports teams." Rybarczyk had been operating close to capacity at his factory in Belfast and wanted to expand. He needed some capital, so the Passamaquoddies bought half of his business. To do that, TAM arranged a $70,000 loan from a private foundation called the Eastern Maine Development Corporation. "We've created a partnership, in effect, called Creative Apparel Associates, which is doing business as Belfast Manufacturing," said Rob. "George has already opened up an operation in Indian Township. There are fifteen people working there now, half of them Passamaquoddies. And we expect more hires very soon."

In the early summer of 1989, I returned to Maine to see how all of the ventures had fared. I called on Tom Tureen at his home in Parsonsfield, an impeccably restored farmhouse on a hill overlooking miles of wooded view untarnished by other homesteads. Through a sunny afternoon of conversation, Tom appeared more relaxed and reflective than his workaday self, smiling as his son, Rufus, solemnly wetted our paper work with a water pistol.

There was also an undercurrent of mortal relief at the Tureen household. A month earlier, Tom and a young TAM protégé named Donald Perkins had survived a crash landing that totaled Tom's plane. They were on their way to the

Portland airport when the Beechcraft's single engine quit. Tom had managed to glide to the wooded edge of a field before the plane hit the treetops. Perkins had dragged Tom, unconscious and bathed in fuel, away from the wreck. Tom recovered quickly from the accident and was already flying a new plane, with two engines.

TAM's groundbreaking and controversial strategy— starting economic development off the reservation and gradually moving onto it—was finally paying off, in ways their clients could see and feel. Moreover, by using other people's resources to build businesses, the Passamaquoddies had spent only $5 million of their original $40-million settlement—including what was lost in PHI—to do it all. In Tom's view, the Passamaquoddies embodied the latest stage of an economic evolution in which Warm Springs and Ak-Chin represented the "early" stage and the Mississippi band of Choctaw the "middle" stage.

According to Tom, the success of Warm Springs's and Ak-Chin's economies made subsequent success stories possible, because they proved that tribes could harness raw resources. All the same, both economies remained somewhat artificial. The wealth of Warm Springs's resources had endowed the Confederated Tribes with exceptional advantages, and Ak-Chin's water, its primary resource, was shipped in by the feds.

The Choctaws, said Tom, had taken a giant step further, starting with no resource but labor and catching the jobs that headed south in the early 1980s. They were also among the very few tribes who had managed to translate federal programs into real jobs. "With so many unemployed, the type of arrangements they made were pretty irresistible," said Tom. "But they're also the sort we've always been leery of— low-end jobs in non-capital-intensive industries." In these cases, he said, a tribe is always at the mercy of whoever is buying the labor. Their "partners" have no stake in the operations and are free to walk away from the arrangement without notice.

"In the new Eastport operation," said Tom, "Gates is tethered to the Passamaquoddies by eight million dollars worth of equipment. The partner can't just pick up and go to Mexico or Thailand or wherever the cheapest labor is." Tom also thinks that competing along the labor-market's bottom rung creates a limited range of job opportunities. "The Choctaws' wire harness is a classic example," he said. "There's no place to work up to."

Tom contended that the types of opportunities being created in Maine take much longer and are much harder to develop but are potentially much better. While waiting for the future to arrive, Tom acknowledged that TAM and the Passamaquoddies had "broken down" and pursued exactly the same sorts of arrangements as the Choctaws; a case in point is the Gates trunk-liner factory in Indian Township. "But the little Gates deal was really cheap for us," he insisted, and given their big Eastport commitment, Gates wasn't likely to run out on the smaller Indian Township operation.

Tom believes that by thinking business first and jobs second Indian tribes can break the "community development" mentality that was handed down from the federal government in the 1960s and that has been stagnating ever since. The perception that there is no growth to be had on reservations, that "development" simply means transferring to Indians the government jobs held by whites, equals a zero-sum game. "It's inherently unhealthy," said Tom. "One person wins, and another must lose. Growth puts a whole different picture on the thing because it creates an ever-larger number of jobs." In the world according to Tureen, a tribe with one hundred members ought to have ten different enterprises and one thousand jobs. Each tribal member is then free to pick and choose between a variety of good jobs and leadership opportunities.

In time. Tom thinks that in twenty years each Passamaquoddy reservation will have about four businesses employing ten to fifty people, that the ratio of Indian to non-Indian
workers will be 25 percent or less, and that every Indian who
wants a job will have one. The changes will be unsettling,
but the Passamaquoddy community will endure because its
members have a common base of wealth, communally held,
and because they have a permanent land base, held in trust,
where free-market factors can't impinge.

"Go Down East," said Tom, "by all means. The new tribal
industries are terrific. Things are really beginning to move."

I drove the long coastal route to Eastport, passing through
Columbia Falls and Bibby's blueberry empire along the way.
After talking to Tom Tureen, I half expected to see America's
most eastern city transformed into a set out of *Metropolis*. But
Washington County seemed to be maintaining its own
rhythm. It was June 1 and still early springtime.

David MacMahon, the president of Gates Formed-Fibre
Products and a transplant from Yorkshire, England, was
introduced to the Passamaquoddies when he heard Pleasant
Point Governor Melvin Francis give a talk about Dragon at an
annual conference of the Maine Development Foundation.
Melvin mentioned the tribe's constant search for business
partners; David thought there might be a fit. GFFP's clients
include GM, Chrysler, Harley Davidson, Toyota, Nissan,
Yamaha, and Suzuki, and the company is always on the
lookout for minority suppliers to help its customers comply
with the standards of their federal contracts. Like Oxford
Speaker Company marrying the Mississippi Choctaws,
Gates found the combination of Native Americans and
healthy financing irresistible. And a plant in Eastport would
put GFFP much closer to a supply of raw material for its
trunk liners.

So PHI is now Fiber Extrusion Incorporated. As a Gates

subsidiary, the plant has a corporate attitude to go along with its corporate ownership. I had to sign a "Plant Visitation and Security Agreement" before I could step inside the building I had snake-danced in two years earlier. I was met at the plant's back door by Mark Burns, a young, eager GFFP manager who had been given the task of starting up the new operation. We walked through the factory. The PHI equipment was gone and the new equipment was in pieces all over the shop floor, making the space seem more massive than I remembered it.

Mark took me upstairs to the office where I had once talked to PHI's Passamaquoddy managerial assistant, Bill Harnois. He picked up a clear plastic bag filled with polyester resin, which looked like green plastic bullets. Fiber Extrusion is set up to use this waste stream, which arrives from many sources, including recycled soda bottles. The extrusion process renders the polyester pellets into plastic cotton. This polyester fiber is even bailed like cotton before being shipped to Auburn. There, it is blended with a mixture of other fibers, then carded, like any other raw fabric; finally, it is needled to a felt and heated into the molded carpeting that lines car trunks.

The Eastport plant was scheduled to begin production September 1. It would produce 11 million pounds of fiber in its first year, and eventually an annual total of 22.5 million pounds. Twenty-five to forty-five people would eventually be employed. Mark had assembled a local skeleton crew to bring the plant up to operating speed. Most of the work he required was highly skilled, setting up and retooling equipment in unique configurations. Three of Fiber Extrusion's four-man SWAT team—Sabbatis Lewy, Leon Socobasin, and Martin Nicholas—were Passamaquoddies and former PHI employees. As part of its contract with the tribe, Gates gives preference to Passamaquoddy job candidates, all other qualifications being equal. "We interviewed about twenty-five people," said Mark, "and these were the best by a long shot."

On the way up to my Calais motel, I stopped at Pleasant Point and poked my head into the Waponahki Museum and Resource Center. Cozy Nicholas was there. He showed me the new Passamaquoddy reference book he and David Francis had just completed. The University of Maine at Machias had awarded Cozy an honorary doctorate in humane letters for his contributions to Passamaquoddy culture. I congratulated him. "Yeah," he said. "I was down at the legislature after it happened. The speaker of the house announced it to the whole floor and they made me get up and give a speech. I told them, 'When something like this happens to you guys, you turn red. When it happens to me, I turn white.'" Cozy laughed me out the door.

The next morning I rolled back on to Route 1, heading inland and northward for a last visit to Indian Township. The day was perfect, blue and seventy-two degrees. It was the first time I had seen the Township free of rain, fog, or snow, and the first time I had known what a beautiful place it could be.

Roger Ritter, a tribal member who is Indian Township's chief economic planner and coordinator of the new reservation businesses, met me in his office at the tribal administration building. He dressed the part of a middle manager in a button-down shirt and tie. While most of his male colleagues flaunt their luxuriant hair in longer styles, Roger's was short and neat, like his mustache. He had just received his master's in community-economic development from New Hampshire College, and the newly framed diploma hung on the wall behind him.

Roger grew up in a family that defied certain Passamaquoddy stereotypes, including educational ones. Roger's older sisters had gone to college, and when he graduated from high school in the 1960s, Roger was determined to follow them. He wrote to Senator Edmund Muskie and Congresswoman Margaret Chase Smith. The letters traveled through the bureaucracy and back to Commissioner of Indian Affairs Ed Hinckley, who panicked. Here was a Passamaquoddy raring to get ahead, and as usual there wasn't enough money in Ed's budget to cover the cost.

After some frantic research, Ed discovered that if Roger enrolled in the Institute of American Indian Arts in Santa Fe, the institute would pay Roger's tuition. Roger asked Ed what sort of courses he could take there. Ed told him, "Oh, Native crafts, basketmaking." Roger said, "Listen, I come from a long line of basketmakers; I don't need to go to college for that." But he went, and the experience proved to be an enlarging one. Roger spent the next ten years off the reservation. After college, he moved to Connecticut and built jet engines for Pratt & Whitney, then to Bangor as a supervisor at a General Electric steam-turbo plant.

In the mid-1970s John Stevens asked Roger to come back to Indian Township. He has been a tribal administrator since. Having made it on the outside, Roger was impatient when he first came home. "When I was living away," he said, "I started thinking the solutions to all the Passamaquoddies' problems were obvious. But when I got here, I got knocked down a bunch of pegs. There's pride here; the tribe wants change, but at their own pace. And a lot of things *have* changed, or I wouldn't have stayed."

Roger met his father for the first time in 1980, when he was thirty-five years old. Wolfgang Ritter had been a German prisoner in the Indian Township detention camp in World War II. Camp security was apparently as lax for Wolfgang as for American actors in "Hogan's Heroes." Three hundred strapping German youths mingled freely with the Passamaquoddies, and Wolfgang fell for a tribal member named Mary Gabriel, who had three daughters and an estranged husband.

The war ended. Wolfgang went home. After he left, Mary discovered she was pregnant. She tried to write to him after Roger was born, and she later learned he had tried to write to her. American veterans in the post office saw the addresses and threw the letters away. Times, morals, and small-town gossip being what they were, Mary revealed little to Roger about the mystery of his creation.

Wolfgang went about his colorful life in postwar Frankfurt. He married, made a million dollars dubbing American movies into German, drank the money and his marriage away, and eventually rebounded in the travel business. In 1980, when he was in his late sixties, Wolfgang returned to Indian Township on a mission of nostalgia. Roger's older sister read in the Calais newspaper that he was coming to town, and she recognized his name.

Roger and Wolfgang met in one of Plaisted's old tourist cabins (now owned by a Passamaquoddy Indian). They were spitting images of each other, and Wolfgang embraced Roger as his son. They have since made up for considerable lost time. Roger Gabriel changed his name to Roger Ritter. He has been over to see his father three times, twice to Frankfurt and once to France, where Wolfgang is now retired. Wolfgang has two other sons, and they and Roger get along like brothers.

As Roger was telling me his story, his office mate, Joe Socobasin, wandered in. Joe was in his early thirties, with a sharp sense of humor and little about his appearance to distinguish him as a Passamaquoddy to an outsider. He was light-skinned, with silvering blown-dry hair and a patch over one eye that he hopes will someday earn him a stint as the Hathaway Man. (Roger told me that Joe's last name, far from being some exotic Passamaquoddy moniker, was a bastardization of the French "Jacque Sebastian," just as the common Passamaquoddy surname *Tomah* was a bastardization of "Thomas.")

Roger and Joe sit on the board of Creative Apparel Asso

ciates, the tribe's joint venture with Belfast Manufacturing.
They strolled with me down the road for a look at the factory.
On our way out of the administration building, we passed
Governor Bobby Newell. Bobby had swapped the leather
jacket he had on when I first met him for a tie and gray
flannels. He was preoccupied with his secretary and a
mound of paperwork, and vaguely waved us by when we
tried to greet him.

According to the Passamaquoddies I talked to, Bobby
had ripened into an exceptionally effective leader. But a price
had been paid when his earlier open-door style ended. One
of Bobby's administrators, who also happened to be a close
childhood friend of his, told me, "These days, it's easier for
me to reach Jock McKernan [Maine's governor] than it is to
reach Bobby Newell." This same administrator walked by
Bobby's office one day and found the secretary gone and the
door ajar. He crept in and saw Bobby scribbling furiously
away on some deadlined materials.

"What do *you* want," snapped Bobby.

"Nothing. I just want to shoot some shit," said his colleague.

Bobby's face melted into a grin. They locked the office
door and spent two hours doing just that.

As Roger, Joe, and I made our way down to Creative
Apparel, the two explained how the tribe had hooked up
with Belfast Manufacturing to create the Indian Township
plant. Belfast is a cut, make, and thread shop, like Warm
Springs Apparel. Its owner, George Rybarczyk, is an athletic, near-forty-year-old Penn State graduate who bought
Belfast from its aging owners in 1986.

A year after he purchased the moribund operation,
George was turning away more work than his sixty employees could handle. He wanted to expand but had already
exhausted the local labor pool, and the bank's 15-percent
interest rates were just too rich for his blood. Along came

PHI's former president, Larry Horwitz. (George had counseled Larry's wife when she was starting up a women's
clothing company.) Larry told Tom Tureen about George,
and TAM approached him, first to ask if George would
consider opening a Belfast satellite in Indian Township.

George was interested, but the Passamaquoddies wanted
some insurance that the plant would keep running if the
market soured. In the end, the tribe bought 51 percent of the
company (although George still owns his Belfast building
and the tribe owns the entire Indian Township plant). Both
parties trusted each other enough to deal on good faith, and
the new plant was up and operating early in 1989, though
nothing was signed until April.

The garment factory is located in what used to be the
Passamaquoddy Shop and Go. The grocery signs had disappeared, and in their place was a sign with the company's
name and a painted swallow developed as the company logo
by a tribal member. Roger pointed out to me that the sign
had attracted a nest of swallows, which darted in and out
of the eaves above it. The plant had twenty-four employees,
and the number was expected to rise to almost forty by August. The work crew was about evenly split between Passamaquoddies and non-Indians. Just before the Indian
Township plant opened, a sewing factory in Calais called
Ware Knitting closed down, so the fledgling Passamaquoddy operation had an instant pool of trained employees.

This created a challenge for management: half of the
tribal employees had never worked anywhere in their lives.
"We faced the same problems among tribal employees that
you would find anywhere in this region," said George. "I've
seen plenty of people in Washington County, Indian and
non-Indian, who grew up in families where their parents
and even their grandparents never worked. Some of these
people firmly believe in their worthlessness, until they prove
something different to themselves. What has happened to

these people at Indian Township, and the kind of work they're doing now, is amazing. Four tribal members are already earning bonus rates for their work."

Joe and Roger had a trench-eye view as their fellow tribal members grew into their jobs. The process was far from smooth. Tribal funds underwrote a six-month stipend program for workers in training. In order to shield the novices from the daunting skill of their experienced co-workers, George segregated them in a separate training area. This is standard practice in the sewing business, but to some of the tribal workers it stank of bigotry. After all, they owned the joint. Joe said that at one stage the entire Passamaquoddy crew was taking its lunch break *en masse* in his office to kvetch about their non-Indian bosses and co-workers.

One Passamaquoddy woman was particularly incensed, and Joe remembered trying to referee an argument between her and the plant's manager, a non-Indian refugee from Ware Knitting. In an effort to convince her Passamaquoddy colleague that she was anything but a racist, the manager noted that her own grandmother had been black.

"Don't you compare me to no fucking nigger!" shouted the woman.

"I died," said Joe. "All I wanted to do was get out of there."

There are few American workplaces where an employee's job would survive such an outburst. But Joe, Roger, and other tribal administrators knew from their own experiences how one type of bigotry begot another. They persuaded the Passamaquoddy worker to enter therapy. She was still working at Creative Apparel, and according to Roger she was beginning to distinguish the situation from her anger. "There's lots of confusion between what is Indian and what is plain human," he said. "It's awfully convenient to scream prejudice when a white person isn't going your way."

The scene inside the plant was no different from the one I had seen in Warm Springs: a mess of cloth and sewing machines, mixed with radio music and the occasional shouted instruction or joke. Management had eventually bowed to its tribal employees' wishes, and the barrier between the trainees and old hands had been removed. Creative Apparel's current customer was Starter, the maker of satin warm-up jackets worn by major leaguers and by their fans, who buy them by the thousands in stadiums and hometown outlets. The day's only controversy was that the workers—Red Sox fans to a one—had to sew warm-up jackets for the Chicago White Sox.

The three of us walked back to the tribal parking lot, picked up a car, and drove a mile down Route 1 to a sagging green building that was once the Indian Township community center. The building now houses Indian Township Manufacturing. The tribe financed some equipment and now had a contract with Gates Formed-Fibre Products to "serge" trunk liners (which means stitching borders around units that end up in the trunks of fancy cars). "Serging is really a decorative thing," said Roger. "*My* car doesn't have a serged trunk liner. Does yours?"

Indian Township Manufacturing looked like a real cottage industry—four tables and four sewing machines. But four female employees there serged about eighteen thousand trunk liners a month. There were a total of six employees. Four of them, including the manager, Robert Tomah, were tribal members. Eventually the business would employ ten to twelve people.

Combined with George Rybarczyk's long-term projections for Creative Apparel, the two businesses could create a hundred sewing jobs at Indian Township in a few years. The tribe was already working with TAM to finance a larger Indian Township facility to house both Indian Township Manufacturing and Creative Apparel with the help of an EDA grant.

This left Roger and Joe with an interesting problem. The

twenty or so tribal members who filled the existing manufacturing jobs had nearly exhausted Indian Township's official
labor pool. Joe reminded me that this meant only the list of
*applicants* had been exhausted. He and Joe were working to
encourage others from the Township's three hundred
employment-age residents to apply. "It's slow going," said
Roger, "especially with the men, who have no interest in
sewing."

"Right after the settlement," said Joe, "we fell into the
same trap as non-Indians—that money was everything.
We're learning that we have a long way to go, that dollars
alone won't do it for us."

Wayne Newell had left his post in tribal administration to
become assistant principal of the Indian Township School.
The school is a large, modern structure dominating Peter
Dana Point, a beautiful spit of forest on Lewey's Lake, where
Township residents who don't inhabit the Strip reside. I
arrived there on a Friday afternoon. The principal, a nun,
had left for the weekend, and Wayne was working in her
office to get away from the mess in his own. A student had
made the principal a halo out of cotton balls, and the halo
was hanging from the ceiling on a fishline, suspended a foot
above Wayne's head.

His new job included teaching as well as administrative
duties, which suited Wayne fine. In addition to his Harvard
master's degree, Wayne has the natural qualifications and
inclinations of a teacher. He was happy to be back at it again.

Wayne was pleased with Dragon's financial coup and
excited about the commercialization of the new sulfur-
dioxide-scrubber technology. (He also saw the scrubber as
environmental expiation for the tribe's treating its wild blueberries with chemical herbicide.) Once-removed from the
larger Passamaquoddy economic picture, though, Wayne

seemed much more interested in the smaller measures of achievement among individual tribal members. He told me that when the tribe recently opened a construction job to blind bids, the winner and runner-up had both been Passamaquoddy contractors (and PHI alumni), which pleased him immensely. So did the news that Bibby Nicholas had hired a young tribal member named Daryl Newell as an assistant manager of Northeastern Blueberry.

"My biggest concern has always been human development," said Wayne. He had just completed a semester of teaching sixth, seventh, and eighth graders about substance abuse. "We lost four teenagers to suicide this past year," he said, "all of them alcohol related." Fortunately, the community could afford to address the problems head on. Wayne told me Bobby Newell had instituted an alcohol-treatment policy that paid tribal employees and unemployed tribal members all expenses associated with addiction recovery, including rent and car payments while they were in de-tox. "Three guys I know who were real hard-core alkies," said Wayne, "including one who landed in jail for hitting a cop with a baseball bat, have all been sober for three years and are training to become alcohol counselors."

Commenting on the high rate of Passamaquoddy substance abuse, Wayne observed that Native Americans in general seem to accelerate negative trends in overall society. "I believe it's part of the two-culture syndrome," he said. "When people don't know who they are or where they belong, there's nothing to keep them from going off the deep end. I know a tribal member, a recovering alcoholic, who told me, 'I'm fifty-four and I'm just learning how to be an Indian.' If our business development doesn't have a strong grip on these deeper and larger issues, then we're only a bunch of poor people who got rich. We want to get *better*."

Like Cozy Nicholas, Wayne saw the Passamaquoddy language as a tool for reestablishing cultural foundations.

Wayne was the first to introduce bilingual education to Indian Township. Now he was busy resurrecting the program after it fell apart under his successor. "I would like to see my grandchildren know our language and our values," he said. "But building it up again is hard. When I first came here, Passamaquoddy was my students' first language. Now a lot of them speak English first."

Wayne believed the answer lay less in a literal revival of old rituals than in the application of a specifically Passamaquoddy "stamp" to improving material circumstances. "There are many sides to the struggle we have been going through to be strong, independent; and economic development is certainly one of them. But we need to find our own pace, not related to dollars or balance sheets but to things that make you click inside. These are things *we* are responsible for. It's not something that Tom Tureen or Tribal Assets or all the money in the world can help us with.

"We can never really go back," he said softly, "nor should we." Then he broke into a schoolboy's grin. "But hell, you get me out on my boat heading up the Musquash Stream, I become a totally different person. Sometimes I don't want to come back."

The fog had rolled in across the lake. Wayne was late for dinner. His house is on the Point, a short way from the school. I watched his broad back as he walked, head down, along a path into the woods.

# 7

## The Means and Ends
## of Sovereignty

The four tribes discussed in this book by no means exhaust successful examples of economic development in Indian Country.

For twenty years, the Cherokee Nation of Oklahoma has owned an electronics plant that manufactures equipment for the Department of Defense. The enterprise now grosses some $24 million. The tribe also has a greenhouse business with forty-three satellite stores in regional shopping malls. Tribal income has shifted its 90-percent dependence on federal monies to a 60-percent dependence on business revenue. Wilma Mankiller, principal chief of the Cherokees, is working on a $100-million bond issue to finance a hydroelectric plant on the Arkansas River.

The eastern band of Cherokees in North Carolina own Carolina Mirror, the largest mirror manufacturer in America. The tribe also owns a charter-bus company and captures a large portion of the lucrative tourist traffic heading into the Great Smoky Mountain Park. The Devils Lake Sioux on North Dakota's Fort Totten Reservation have maintained a long-standing joint venture with the Brunswick Corporation, employing 350 people to make camouflage netting and other military supplies.

The Mescalero Apache, in addition to a brisk business in timber off their half-million-acre New Mexico reservation, own cattle ranches, a ski resort, and a 230-room luxury retreat near twelve-thousand-foot Sierra Blanca called the Inn of the Mountain Gods.

The White Mountain Apache of Arizona own the state's largest ski resort.

The Pima Indians in Gila River, Arizona, lease space to more than thirty companies on their string of industrial parks, south of Phoenix. They also own a racetrack.

In Washington State, the Swinomish Indians are building an eight-hundred-slip marina, a restaurant, and a $15-million hotel on Padilla Bay.

The Hualapai of Peach Springs, Arizona, fly and bus tourists to their breathtaking home on the lip of the Grand Canyon. The Hualapai charge hunters to shoot desert big-horn sheep on their reservation: $18,000 for each sheep bagged. (Marketed in Reno, these permits are sold out through the early 1990s.)

None of these tribes (except the Oklahoma Cherokees) are particularly large, nor are any of the four described in this book. Next to the Navajo Nation, with its 140,000 reservation inhabitants, the Mississippi Choctaws with 5,000 members, or the Ak-Chin with 500 members, seem insignificant. In fact, however, these smaller tribes are most representative. Only twenty American Indian reservations count more than 4,000 Native residents; the vast majority hold less than 1,000. Besides, the megareservations—like Navajo—are enormously complex societies. Navajo business covers everything from General Dynamics missile contracts, to Coca-Cola bottling plants, to shiitake mushroom farms for Japanese gourmands. Yet half the Navajo population is out of work; the average individual Navajo's income is $2,400; and there are still plenty of Navajo homes without electricity or plumbing. This bizarre spectrum of eighteenth-to-twentieth-century economies deserves at least one book of its own.

Is tribal business the panacea for the multitude of problems facing Native America? No more than business can solve all of *any* society's problems. Can tribal business help most tribes secure a degree of self-sufficiency? Probably. To spend any time among the Passamaquoddies, Mississippi Choctaws, Ak-Chin, or Warm Springs is to believe that the private sector indeed offers Native America a better way out of poverty and powerlessness than does the public sector.

The miserable lowest common denominators of contemporary American Indian life, and the garish stories that accompany them in the mass media, have led many non-Indian Americans to ascribe to Natives an innate incapacity. The roster above and the triumphs that comprise the body of this book should banish such a notion. Many in Indian Country would agree, however, that America's Indian policy has thrust an institutional incapacity upon them in the form of federal "aid." According to one federal official, "American Indian policy reflects the national guilt complex of Americans regarding the Indians. We try to solve the Indian problem by making Indians increasingly dependent on federal funds and services." The result, according to Tim Giago—an Oglala Sioux and publisher of the *Lakota Times*—is "failed policy after failed policy initiated and implemented by remote control from the dungeons of social thought in Washington, D.C."

On this point, even the federal government seems to agree. "Many failures have been generated by federal policy," said Ross Swimmer, assistant secretary for Indian affairs and head of the BIA during the second Reagan administration. As a single example of federal incompetence in Indian money matters, a recent congressional investigation estimated that the BIA has failed to collect $1 billion in oil and gas royalties owed to tribes.

"My general recommendation is that tribes should start talking to private capital markets. If they have a good idea, with a good manager and a good market—if they've done their homework—they can find private capital. As an economy of any kind develops it will begin to eliminate a lot of social failures."

These are the words of a political appointee in the "trickledown" administration. But as a lawyer, sometime bank executive, and former principal chief of the Cherokee Nation, Mr. Swimmer has seen Native America's problems from a number of pertinent viewpoints, and his estimation of federal solutions—even under his own leadership—was bleak.

Three billion dollars a year fuel some twenty programs in various federal departments devoted to Native Americans. A billion dollars is absorbed by the Bureau of Indian Affairs alone: the Great Father—more precisely, the Big Daddy—of Indian Country. Born in the War Department during the age of Indian subjugation and now a branch of the Department of the Interior, the BIA employs some fifteen thousand civil servants to manage the relationship between Native America and the United States.

As federal agencies will, the BIA ingests a great deal of its budget—as much as a third of it—before any money leaks out to any reservation. According to Arizona Senator John McCain, a member of the Select Committee on Indian Affairs, only twelve cents of every federal dollar reaches a Native American. And because federal and tribal jobs account for almost half of Native American incomes, there is little incentive for bureaucrats to change the status quo.

The bureau grows and grows, poking tendrils into every aspect of Indian life. As Phillip Martin, chief of the Mississippi band of Choctaws, once wrote, "Nothing, or next to nothing, happens on an Indian reservation without it being a result of, a reaction to, an attempt to get around, or a violation of an action or policy of the federal government." The oldest joke among American Indians is that when they die they must pass through the bureau before they are allowed to enter heaven.

Congress may be about to apply a machete to the thicket of federal Indian agencies. Noting that the "time for tinkering is over," the December 1989 report of a special Senate committee established to investigate corruption and mismanagement in Indian affairs recommended a "New Indian Federalism." The committee's proposals included abandoning paternalistic federal controls and transferring all Indian appropriations—on an individual and voluntary basis—to tribal governments. "All federal resources, functions and programs, fully funded, as well as the physical assets and land of BIA, IHS [Indian Health Service] and the other federal agencies, must be transferred *in toto* to the tribes entering new agreements." In the words of committee member Senator Dennis DeConcini, "The billions now wasted on self-perpetuating federal bureaucracies will belong to the tribes themselves, to determine their own destiny."

We shall see. Although the report's admissions of federal shortcomings please Indian leaders in this book, who have all enjoyed great success in managing their own affairs, many Native Americans are wary. They have heard similar promises before, and some are concerned that a "New Indian Federalism" will mark a return to the disasters of the "termination era."

Regardless of the outcome of this latest wave of legislative concern, national Indian policy will never do what individual tribes can do for themselves on their own terms and in their own time. Tribal businesses may be difficult, frustrating, risky, even at times destabilizing, but they *are* tribal—locally generated and particular to the needs, resources, and vision of each tribe. "The best solutions to our problems are within our own communities," said Cherokee Chief Wilma Mankiller.

Communities like the ones in this book, which secure a foothold in a real economy, have greater potential for true sovereignty now than at any time since their encounter with European immigrants. When they succeed economically, tribes repossess some of their original power and become sovereign in reality, not only by decree or legal definition. American Indian reservations will never be entirely independent of their trust relationship with the federal government; many Native American resources are so precious and so fragile that they will always require the protection of the nation's most powerful authority. But by reestablishing the livelihoods and the pride of their people, tribes can increase their leverage to the point at which they call the shots in their federal relationships and employ federal resources to their own best advantage.

The presumption of this book, then, is one shared by most of the Indians I met: material gain is a good thing for Native America. There are Indian and non-Indian experts who think otherwise, who believe the introduction of competition, company hierarchies, and nine-to-five mentalities will erode Native culture. An honest assessment of that concern presupposes a thorough and intimate knowledge of each tribe's culture—a point at which a non-Indian writer falls immediately into the depths of ignorance. There are entire worlds of Indian existence outside the purview of economic development that the author wouldn't presume to assess.

As long as any culture is defined in static terms, however, economic progress will surely seem a threat. The mind of mainstream America bears its Native citizens back ceaselessly into the past. Whereas many feel that economic progress is fine for every other ethnic group (thinking the quicker the better) too many of us non-Indians prefer our Natives as living museum pieces, in the saddle or the dugout, living out some storybook version of "natural" subsistence. In this view, economic progress is corrupted into a fall from aboriginal grace.

Native American culture has persisted through centuries

of economic hardship. After half a millennium under foreign domination, most Native Americans still speak their own language, and more than a hundred Native tongues are still alive. Why should a life less cruel pose a greater threat to these unvanquished identities? As a Navajo tribal chairman has said, "Traditional Navajo values do not include poverty."

Perhaps fears of lost cultural identity are based on the experience of American society in general. In the main, American economic development is centrifugal. Living far from their own anthropologies, both in space and time, non-Indian Americans "progress" by whirling out from "back home" to join the flux of an undifferentiated, atomized society. Our unrootedness is a chronic, pervasive, and legitimate obsession. The pattern in Indian Country, though, is centripetal. As its economy develops, a tribe's far-flung members, even those born a generation away from the reservation, are drawn in toward home.

As one scholar neatly expressed it, "Indians borrowed white modes of behavior, belief, and organization, [but] they did not necessarily come to admire whites or identify with them." The Indians I met defined economic success as gaining the leverage to live on their own terms. They have no plans to melt into America's pot.

It may offend non-Indians to discover that Indians employ the American marketplace toward other than mainstream goals. It bothered Ronald Reagan, who told (of all audiences) a group of Soviet students, "Maybe we made a mistake. Maybe we should not have humored [Native Americans] in wanting to stay in that kind of primitive life-style. Maybe we should have said, 'No, come join us.' " The communities I saw were far from primitive—and just as far from dreaming that American's dream.

At the same time, economically successful tribes have made a practical peace with the society surrounding them and are comfortable hiring non-Indian expertise. Like many

whites—and not a few Indians—I came to this project with
the notion that the only "true" measure of economic development was a head count of Indians occupying managerial
positions in tribal business. But as Tom Tureen, the Passamaquoddies' (white) investment banker, told me, "Why should
Indian businesses play ball with their arms tied behind their
backs? You wouldn't expect a Fortune Five Hundred company to operate without outside legal and financial counsel.
The Indians have enough problems without being forced to
go into business blindfolded." The tribes in this book have
succeeded in part because they hire the best technical and
managerial help they can find or afford. Their leaders are
keenly interested in creating jobs for their constituents but
have no interest in setting up their people for failure just to
satisfy a half-baked conception of "doing it themselves."

In the end, material progress will certainly alter the patterns of day-to-day tribal existence. But as Mark Trahant, a
reporter for the *Arizona Republic* and a Shoshone-Bannock
Indian, reminded me, "Cultures evolve, or they die out."

Tom Tureen seconded Trahant's motion: "You don't have
to be Jewish to love Levy's," he said, "and you don't have to
be a hunter-gatherer to be Indian." Both believe that Indian
communities with growing economies will be much stronger
tomorrow, ethnically as well as materially, and that economic
development may well be the key to ethnic survival.


Certain social problems of Indian Country may be imper-
vious to whatever benefits tribal business has to offer. Alcohol abuse runs like background noise through each chapter
of this book, as it does in almost every Native American
community. By some estimates, alcohol accounts for one out
of every four Indian fatalities. In his beautiful, wrenching
book about fetal alcohol syndrome, *The Broken Cord*, Michael
Dorris paints a terrifying picture of an entire generation of

the Native population, victims of their mothers' alcohol abuse, who are abusing alcohol and bearing children with *physiological* emotional and intellectual handicaps that render them highly susceptible to alcohol abuse themselves. According to Dorris, the cycle is unbroken and widening, perhaps exponentially, claiming a larger and larger percentage of Native America.

Alcoholism is a disease of denial; people and communities submerged in alcoholism cannot admit that the problem exists. The four communities in this book seem to have arrived at a point where their accomplishments have given them the confidence to admit the extent and gravity of local alcohol abuse. Officials in each tribe told me that the growing economies of their communities gave them the means to address the problem head on, through medical treatment, support groups, education, and awareness campaigns. While they were all hopeful of success, they cautioned that it was too early to know whether the community response would be widespread or long lasting.

Many Indian communities will take years, perhaps generations, to reach this point. Societies so long degraded by imposed circumstances are delicate, and no tribe's problems will be solved by a single business success. Flashy Indian enterprises are standard fare in the business press, which reports each showy start-up as the panacea for that tribe's every ill. Business reporters have neither the space nor the inclination to mention that in the fragile political economy of many tribes a single election can bring down an entire tribal bureaucracy, and with it, last year's cover story.

Concerns about instability apply also to certain types of enterprise. Tribes that rely on gambling as a primary revenue source are cases in point. Some one hundred tribes bring in $400 million a year in gaming revenue, mostly high-stakes bingo. There have been a few hugely successful examples of Indian gaming, but there are also huge problems with the trade. Bingo creates few jobs, so tribes must invest their bingo profits wisely if they intend to address employment problems. The Seminoles in Florida, who control ten thousand seats in four bingo parlors and net some $10 million annually, have done just this. By investing bingo money in other enterprises, they have created an almost totally self-sufficient economy—except that the industry may be legislated out of existence. Federal agencies, officially fearful of organized crime (and under pressure from state governments with nongambling ordinances and abiding jealousy of untaxable tribal profits) have already subjected all Indian gaming to state or federal control. This could be the first step to the industry's extinction.

Many tribes who have tried and failed to build internal economies will rightly blame their federal trustees. "It seems to me," said Assistant Secretary Swimmer, "that we have burdened the tribes with such a large cost of doing business, it's just about prohibitive for the private sector to get going on a reservation. If it's going to happen, we're going to have to eliminate barriers." Those barriers include eight hundred pages of federal regulations governing American Indian affairs. A business lease in the Navajo Nation requires no fewer than forty-seven separate permits and licenses.

Even without such obstructions, economic development will be difficult for tribes with few resources. Free markets can be cruel to communities like the Rosebud Sioux and their farm economy. A few years ago things were looking up in Sioux country because the Dakota agricultural markets were strong, but then the agricultural markets collapsed. Nor will tribes be able to create businesses in economic vacuums; they will always be subject to the vagaries of the local economy. A tribe a hundred miles from nowhere has to find customers and markets.

There are also justifiable concerns about "windfall" economic opportunities sometimes imposed on Native communities without long-term commitments and sometimes with unwanted long-term effects. The *New York Times* recently carried a front-page story about English Bay, an isolated village of 170 Aleut natives who held no "jobs" to speak of but obtained an ample subsistence in salmon and other seafood off their coastal home. The Exxon oil spill changed all of that, wiping out at least one season's fish harvest. Exxon offered food and jobs to English Bay as compensation. The result was the serious disruption of the community. Hourly wages of up to $16.70 inundated the unprepared citizens in cash, which was spent on liquor and television sets. A number of English Bay youths, lured by the possibilities of further wealth, talked of leaving town for Anchorage and other cities to the south. The events of a single year threatened to destroy a community that was centuries old.

The lesson to be learned from English Bay is that economic development must occur on a community's own terms. Economic sovereignty is the freedom to say no to jobs that don't fit a tribe's specific needs, the freedom gained through strong internal priorities and internal resources.

But it is *possible* for tribes to overcome these obstacles. The Passamaquoddies, Mississippi Choctaw, Ak-Chin, and Warm Springs tribes have proved it already. Many others are about to prove it to themselves. "The most important thing that has come out of all of this," said John Stevens, the father of the Maine land claims, "is hope. Now we have a future, not just a past."

# Acknowledgments

I must first thank my American Indian sources, who are the subjects of this book. Having anticipated much suspicion and little cooperation from people who have suffered almost as much at the hands of non-Indian journalists as they have from non-Indian government officials, I encountered instead much hospitality, candor, and help.

Though I am indebted to every person who appears in the previous pages, I mention by name—for time and effort beyond any reasonable expectation—Wayne Newell, Cozy Nicholas, and Roger Ritter of the Passamaquoddy tribe; Chief Phillip Martin of the Mississippi band of Choctaws; Leona Kakar, executive director of the Ak-Chin Community council; Bob Macy, Ralph Minnick, Ken Smith, and Jeff Sanders of the Confederated Tribes of Warm Springs. This book's ambition is to represent faithfully their knowledge and views. Any mistakes of fact or inference are mine.

For information about early Ak-Chin history and water issues, I am indebted to Thomas R. McGuire of the University of Arizona for his 1987 paper prepared for the First Casa Grande Valley History Conference, entitled *The Ak-Chin Project, 1914: Illusions of Choice in the Indian Irrigation Service.*

My thanks to non-Indian sources in Maine go out to Rob Gips, Ed Hinckley, Daniel Zilkha, and the incomparable, irascible, indispensable Tom Tureen; in Mississippi, to Arthur Bridge, Lester Dalme, and Bob Furgeson; in Oregon, to Ed Manion.

I am grateful to Dr. Ronald A. Wells of the Phelps-Stokes Fund, for taking me under his organization's wing as a Scholar of the Phelps-Stokes Institute for African, African-American, and American Indian Affairs.

Thanks also to Chuck Creesy, former editor of the *Princeton Alumni Weekly*, for introducing me to the subject; to Joseph Carr for his helpful comments on the introduction and epilogue; to Matt Ralph for his map work; to Richard Preston for his wise encouragement and for bringing Thoreau to my attention; and to Amy Hertz at Henry Holt and Company for copiloting the book to a safe landing.

I would like particularly to thank the late Donald Hutter—an editor of such stuff as authors' dreams are made on—who conceived the project, agreed to reasonable terms, waited patiently for a first draft to emerge, and gently wrestled author and manuscript into reasonable literacy. I am one of countless writers who miss Don terribly.

To my agent, mentor, and comrade-in-arms John Wright, I owe a long-distance debt of loyalty, kindness, and good cheer.

An author's first book lies atop a deep archaeology of gratitude, which in this case goes to Ben Bensen and Wilbur T. Albrecht, for teaching me how to write, and to Jane Lagoudis Pinchin and Anne Walsh, for encouraging me to do so.

Finally, and most heartily, I thank my wife, Kaatje, who convinced me to write this book and then cheerfully put up with three years of business that was anything but usual.

# Index